Collaborative Archaeology at Stewart Indian School

University of Nevada Press | Reno, Nevada 89557 USA
www.unpress.nevada.edu

Cover art courtesy of Nevada State Museum, Stewart Indian School virtual exhibit, Object ID: NSM-630-2
Cover design by Iris Saltus

LIBRARY OF CONGRESS CATALOGING-IN-PUBLICATION DATA

Names: Cowie, Sarah E., editor. | Teeman, Diane L., 1967- editor. | LeBlanc, Christopher C., 1972- editor.
Title: Collaborative archaeology at Stewart Indian School / edited by Sarah E. Cowie, Diane L. Teeman, and Christopher C. LeBlanc.
Other titles: Collaborative Archaeology at Stewart Indian School
Description: Reno ; Las Vegas : University of Nevada Press, [2019] | Identifiers: LCCN 2019013792 (print) | LCCN 2019015541 (ebook) | ISBN 9781948908269 (ebook) | ISBN 9781948908252 (cloth : alk. paper)
Subjects: LCSH: Carson Indian School (Carson City, Nev.) | Community archaeology—Nevada—Carson City. | Indians of North America—Education—Nevada. | Off-reservation boarding schools—Nevada—Carson City—History. | Excavations (Archaeology)—Nevada—Carson City. | Carson City (Nev.)—Antiquities.
Classification: LCC E97.6.C24 (ebook) | LCC E97.6.C24 C65 2019 (print) | DDC 371.829/97079357—dc23
LC record available at https://lccn.loc.gov/2019013792

The paper used in this book meets the requirements of American National Standard for Information Sciences—Permanence of Paper for Printed Library Materials, ANSI/NISO Z39.48-1992 (R2002).

FIRST PRINTING

Manufactured in the United States of America

Collaborative Archaeology at Stewart Indian School

Edited by
Sarah E. Cowie, Diane L. Teeman,
and Christopher C. LeBlanc

UNIVERSITY OF NEVADA PRESS *Reno & Las Vegas*

We give our thanks and respect
to the children of Stewart Indian School.
It is an honor to dedicate this book to you.

In memoriam of Mark Johnson,
a friend and mentor who generously shared
his diverse expertise with us.

All royalties from this volume
will be donated to the Nevada Indian Commission's
efforts to preserve and interpret
Stewart Indian School for future generations.

Contents

Figures

Tables

FOREWORD

Digging into Indian Education

Joe Watkins

In 1897, Emile Durkheim argued that education "is only the image and reflection of society. It imitates and reproduces the latter . . . it does not create it" (Durkheim [1897] 1951, 372–73). In the United States, another philosopher (of sorts) offered "all the Indian there is in the race should be dead. Kill the Indian in him, and save the man." Pratt argued that the purpose of Indian schools should not be tribal schools, but fully integrated with "people of all races" so that everyone would become loyal to the government rather than to their tribe (Pratt [1892] 1973).

Indian boarding schools were established to educate Indian students in the ways of the dominant society, whatever that society might have been. Many were created by religious denominations in areas with extremely high densities of American Indians, but others were created by the federal government, such as the first boarding school created by the Bureau of Indian Affairs in 1860 on the Yakima Indian Reservation in the state of Washington. These schools were part of a plan devised by well-intentioned, eastern reformers with the goal of using education as a tool to "assimilate" Indian tribes into the mainstream of the "American way of life." Indian people would be taught the importance of private property, material wealth, and monogamous nuclear families. The reformers assumed that it was necessary to "civilize" Indian people, make them accept white men's beliefs and value systems.

The first 307 of these schools operated by the Bureau of Indian Affairs were reservation-based day schools. While the initial aim of these schools was to provide the rudiments of academic education—reading, writing, and speaking of the English language, arithmetic, science, history, and the arts—quite often these took a backseat to the more rigorous indoctrination in Christianity and the principles of democratic society. The goal was to erase all vestiges of Indian culture and replace them with American ideals of citizenship. Perhaps, more importantly, Catholic or Protestant American citizens.

By the 1880s, the United States operated sixty schools for 6,200 Indian students, including reservation day schools and reservation boarding schools. Reservation day schools were relatively inexpensive and caused the least opposition from parents. Most reservation boarding schools spent half of the day on academics and half of the day on industrial training. Regimentation was the order of the day and students spent endless hours marching to and from classes, meals, and dormitories. This education system was aimed at producing economically self-sufficient students who possessed the values and beliefs of individualism, mostly the opposite of the basic Indian belief of communal ownership.

But because the day-school method was deemed to be not working, in 1876, the federal government felt that all American Indian children should be removed from their families and confined in boarding schools (Charbonneau-Dahlen et al. 2016, 599) in order to be "taught to be yeoman farmers, to read, and to be proper Christians, with hope that they might one day even be citizens" (Dawson 2012, 81). Often these nonreservation boarding schools first did away with all outward signs of tribal life that the children brought with them: children were given standard uniforms to wear; they received new "white" names; traditional Indian foods were abandoned, and students had to acquire the food rites of white society, including knives, forks, spoons, napkins, and tablecloths. Charbonneau-Dahlen et al. cite this as the reason that "more than six generations of American Indian children have grown up filled with fear and shame and with no recourse but to endure the best they could." It was only in 1978 that the Indian Welfare Act gave Indian parents the right to refuse placement of their children in off-reservation schools.

The most well-known of all the nonreservation boarding schools was the school established in Carlisle, Pennsylvania by Colonel Richard Henry Pratt in 1879. His goal, as indicated in the opening paragraph, was complete assimilation. As headmaster of the Carlisle Indian School for twenty-five years, he was the single most important figure in Indian education during his time. Pratt believed that off-reservation schools established in white communities could accomplish this task best by immersing Indians into the mainstream of American life. By having students live among white families during the summer, he hoped to have Indian youth become part of the white community. Carlisle was the only off-reservation boarding school built in the East; all others were built in the West.

The 1928 Meriam Report documented the inadequacies of the Indian education system and the absence of a "well considered, broad educational program" (Meriam 1928, 9). In 1953, Bureau of Indian Affairs policy directed that Indian students should attend public schools where there was room; in 1978, the Bureau began supporting tribal and individual choice in school selection (McBeth 1983, 123).

Aside from the original intent of the Indian school initiative, contemporary researchers have uncovered many (perhaps) unintended results of the program. Cromer et al. (2018, 102) provide a list of some of the trauma encountered by the cultures exposed to the boarding school system. While Brave Heart and DeBruyn (1998) associate this with historical trauma, Cromer, et al. (2018, 99–100) differentiate the transgenerational transmission of trauma from historical trauma by focusing on the effect of the trauma in relation to the loss of parenting skills by the students who were forcibly removed from their cultures and thrust into the assimilation machines of the boarding schools.

The boarding school experience is paradoxical and not one that can be easily understood. Along with the stories of abuse and fear, of "cultural genocide" and historical trauma, there are others that speak of the strong bonds formed among those who persevered and the emergence of pan-Indianism (see Colmant et al. 2004). McBeth (1983) found that, at least on the Southern Great Plains, "Indian boarding schools were often effective in reaching their short-term goals such as teaching English and instilling the work ethic, but that they failed in their long-term goal of assimilating Indians. Assimilation did not and has not occurred" (120). But Matthew Gregg (2018) looked at the economic impact of boarding school attendance among reservation situations and reports that "reservations who were most affected by boarding schools are less poor, more educated and more linguistically assimilated today" (18) and that "boarding schools succeeded in integrating American Indians into the Euro-American culture" (31).

This is the complex tapestry within which the Stewart Indian School was interwoven. The Stewart Indian School admitted its first class in 1890, and, along with the Fort Bidwell Indian School in California, was one of two operating in the Great Basin (Hendrick 1976). It closed its doors in 1980. School attendees came primarily from the Washoe, Shoshone, and Paiute tribes. While there are histories of Stewart Indian School and its attendees (Jackson 1969; Thompson 2013), the Collaborative Historical Archaeology Field School project uses archaeology as another means of trying to explain the uses of the area. But it goes further by integrating American Indian perspectives in research and the practice of archaeology.

There have been other collaborative approaches to archaeology—Atalay's 2012 *Community-Based Archaeology*; Colwell-Chanthaphonh and Ferguson's 2007 *Collaboration in Archaeological Practice: Engaging Descendant Communities*; Kerber's 2006 *Cross-Cultural Collaboration: Native Peoples and Archaeology in the Northeastern United States*; and Silliman's 2008 *Collaborating at the Trowel's Edge* to name but a few—and each one has provided foundation blocks for those that followed. Yet, such collaborative attempts are not without issues of their own. Anglebeck and Grier (2014, 521) discuss some of the issues that might be encountered when external constraints are somewhat overriding and perhaps threatening to the idea of true collaboration. They focus as well on the necessity to develop long-term relationships that help place participants on a more equal basis rather than relationships that have participants with superior-inferior roles.

McAnany and Rowe (2015) argue that contemporary archaeology is undergoing a paradigm shift as archaeologists work more and more closely with contemporary peoples, and as archaeologists attempt to make their work more relevant by reckoning with "the colonial heritage of the discipline and with the contemporary context within which archaeology is practiced" (2015, 500). Their discussion of the challenges of collaborative archaeology (506–7) contributes to consideration of issues brought forward by Anglebeck and Grier.

In a rather comprehensive review of collaborative archaeologies and descendant communities, Colwell (2016) discusses some of the things that make collaborative archaeology meaningful. He asserts, quite correctly, that "collaboration is not one set of practices. . . . [it] lies on a continuum" (116). He closes by asserting, "As we move into the twenty-first century, investigators understand that collaboration with descendant communities is not a simple solution to the complex problems of direct engagement, shared benefits, and equal voice. Rather, it is a vital means to work through the ethical, political, and social quandaries raised by the admirable goal of transforming archaeology into a science that is driven by an ethical engagement with key publics who are invested in the interpretation and management of the material past" (2016, 119).

As Colwell-Chanthaphonh, et al. note, "When Indigenous peoples express dissatisfaction with archaeology, their list of complaints often relates to the role of archaeologists as gatekeepers" (2010, 230). The Stewart Indian School Collaborative Historical Archaeology Field School is a good example of a collaborative project trying to remove "gatekeepers" by providing a multitude of perspectives. It gives voice not only to the local community but also to the students participating in the project.

In closing, let me turn once again to Pratt: "when we allow him [the Indian] the freedom of association and the developing influences of social contact—then the Indian will quickly demonstrate that he can be truly civilized, and he himself will solve the question of what to do with the Indian" (Pratt [1892] 1973). Contemporary American Indian communities *know* what to do with "the Indian"—give them the tools to tell their own stories, and then listen!

Works Cited

Anglebeck, Bill and Colin Grier. 2014. "From Paradigms to Practices: Pursuing Horizontal and Long-Term Relationships with Indigenous Peoples for Archaeological Heritage Management." *Canadian Journal of Archaeology / Journal Canadien d'Archéologie* 38, no. 2: 519–40.

Atalay, Sonya. 2012. *Community-Based Archaeology: Research with, by, and for Indigenous and Local Communities*. Berkeley: University of California Press.

Brave Heart, Mary Y. H., and Lemyra M. Debruyn. 1998. "The American Indian

Holocaust: Healing Historical Unresolved Grief." *American Indian & Alaska Native Mental Health Research* 8: 60–82.

Charbonneau-Dahlen, Barbara K., John Lowe, and Staci Leon Morris. 2016. "Giving Voice to Historical Trauma through Storytelling: The Impact of Boarding School Experience on American Indians." *Journal of Aggression, Maltreatment, and Trauma* 25, no. 6: 598–617.

Colmant, Stephen, Lahoma Schultz, Rockey Robbins, Peter Ciali, Julie Dorton, and Yvette Rivera-Colmant. 2004. "Constructing Meaning to the Indian Boarding School Experience." *Journal of American Indian Education* 43, no. 3 (2004): 22–40.

Colwell, Chip. 2016. "Collaborative Archaeologies and Descendant Communities." *Annual Review of Anthropology* 45: 113–27.

Colwell-Chanthaphonh, Chip, and T.J. Ferguson, eds. 2007 *Collaboration in Archaeological Practice: Engaging Descendant Communities.* Lanham, MD: AltaMira Press.

Colwell-Chanthaphonh, Chip, T. J. Ferguson, Dorothy Lippert, Randall H. McGuire, George R. Nicholas, Joe E. Watkins, and Larry J. Zimmerman. 2010. "The Premise and Promise of Indigenous Archaeology." *American Antiquity* 75, no. 2: 228–38.

Cromer, Lisa DeMarni, Mary E. Gray, Ludivina Vasquez, and Jennifer J. Freyd. 2018. "The Relationship of Acculturation to Historical Loss Awareness, Institutional Betrayal, and the Intergenerational Transmission of Trauma in the American Indian Experience." *Journal of Cross-Cultural Psychology* 49, no. 1: 99–114.

Dawson, Alexander S. 2012. "Histories and Memories of the Indian Boarding Schools in Mexico, Canada, and the United States." *Latin American Perspectives* 39, no. 5, Rethinking Indigenismo on the American Continent (September): 80–99.

Durkheim, Émile. (1897) 1951. *Suicide, a Study in Sociology.* New York: Free Press.

Gregg, Matthew T. 2018. "The Long-Term Effects of American Indian Boarding Schools." *Journal of Development Economics* 130: 17–32.

Hendrick, Irving G. 1976. "Federal Policy Affecting the Education of Indians in California, 1849–1934." *History of Education Quarterly* 2, no. 16: 163–85.

Jackson, Nicholas. 1969. A History of the Stewart Indian School. Master's thesis, University of Nevada, Reno.

Kerber, Jordan, ed. 2006. *Cross-Cultural Collaboration: Native Peoples and Archaeology in the Northeastern United States.* Lincoln, NE: University of Nebraska Press.

McAnany, Patricia A., and Sarah M. Rowe. 2015. "Re-visiting the Field: Collaborative Archaeology as Paradigm Shift." *Journal of Field Archaeology* 40, no. 5: 499–507.

Meriam, Lewis, Ray A. Brown, Henry Roe Cloud, Edward Everett Dale, Emma Duke, Herbert R. Edwards, Fayette Avery McKenzie, Mary Louise Mark, W. Carson Ryan, Jr., and William J. Spillman. 1928. *The Problem of Indian Administration: Report of a survey made at the request of Honorable Hubert Work, Secretary of the Interior, and submitted to him, February 21, 1928.* Institute for Government

Research. Studies in Administration. Baltimore: The Johns Hopkins Press. https://narf.org/nill/documents/merriam/b_meriam_letter.pdf.

Pratt, Richard Henry. (1892) 1973. "'Kill the Indian, and Save the Man': Capt. Richard H. Pratt on the Education of Native Americans." Reprinted in Richard Henry Pratt, "The Advantages of Mingling Indians with Whites." In *Americanizing the American Indians: Writings by the "Friends of the Indian" 1880–1900*, edited by Francis Paul Prucha, 260–71. Cambridge, MA: Harvard University Press.

Silliman, Stephen, ed. 2008 *Collaborating at the Trowel's Edge: Teaching and Learning Indigenous Archaeology*. Amerind Studies in Archaeology. Tucson, AZ: University of Arizona Press.

Thompson, Bonnie. 2013. *The Student Body: A History of the Stewart Indian School, 1890–1940*. PhD diss., Arizona State University.

CHAPTER 1

A Multivocal Collaboration Story

Sarah E. Cowie, Diane L. Teeman, Christopher C. LeBlanc,
Terri McBride, and Ashley M. Long

The woman who initially reprimanded us began to weep as she told us her story. We were in the midst of a collaborative archaeological field school at the site of Stewart Indian School in Carson City, Nevada, with a great deal of involvement from tribal members from multiple tribes, many of whom had members that passed through Stewart, as this alumna had, during its complicated ninety-year history as an off-reservation boarding school in Nevada. Like many other alumni and community members, she had heard about our widely advertised project and was visiting Stewart, as many alumni do on a semiregular basis, to reconnect with the place and the memories associated with it. She had been shouting at us from a distance as she passed by, saying that we didn't know what we were getting into with excavating this place, that terrible things had happened here, and that we should leave such things alone. This is a common sentiment among many American Indians about archaeology in general, that things left by people in the past are too powerful to tamper with, especially things associated with negative experiences. Most people that talked to us about the project were either supportive or curious, but occasionally someone expressed concern. One tribe's attorney contacted us, concerned that we might excavate graves of children who had died at the school, assuming that digging up graves was archaeologists' primary occupation. On each of these interactions we had the opportunity to learn more about the school and what it meant to alumni, their families, and their tribes, as well as the history of the federal government's attempt to forcibly assimilate Native Americans. We also had the opportunity to do better archaeology through public involvement, train students in a multivocal and collaborative approach to archaeological field methods, and demonstrate that archaeologists are not always grave robbers.

As this alumna was admonishing us, we might have ignored her, and continued our excavations as she passed by. But being a public archaeology project designed to learn from tribal members, instead we tentatively approached her and listened.

Her story was a complicated one, as many stories of this place are. There is so much sorrow and trauma here associated with the practices and repercussions of attempted assimilation. But she also wept as she described her childhood, in which her parents could not care for her, and how she wanted to attend Stewart to be a part of that community. She wept as she explained how important this place was to her; good and bad, it was her home. She said more people should know about Stewart Indian School's significance, and agreed that our collaborative project might help raise awareness of Native peoples' experiences there. She embraced some of us who listened to her story, and then she went on her way, walking to another part of campus with her memories.

Who could not be moved by such an experience? This interaction was typical on this project; it and many others humanized the experience of conducting archaeology here. It shows how place-based learning evokes knowledge and memories that are not so accessible elsewhere. It also exemplifies how valuing human relations can overcome seemingly conflicting worldviews, for example, between science and spirituality, or between federal heritage laws and a personal sense of what is right. Such discussions are critical to building relationships, and providing space for historically suppressed voices to tell their truths. Throughout this volume, our work is guided by a large body of literature on decolonizing methods and Indigenous archaeology, with inspiration from Native archaeologists working in their communities and guidance from foundational scholarship in Indigenous heritage studies (e.g., Atalay 2006, 2012; Colwell 2016; Deloria 1969; Dongoske et al. 2000; Ferguson and Colwell-Chanthaphonh 2006; Gould 2013; Gonzales et al. 2018; Laluk 2017; Martinez and Teeter 2015; Nicholas 2010; Schneider 2018; Silliman 2008; Smith 1999; Smith and Wobst 2005; Thompson 2011; Teeman 2008; Two Bears 2010; Watkins 2000).

We combine many voices in this volume: Native and non-Native;

elder and younger; academic, traditional, scientific, and personal. This created a manuscript that is multivocal and shifting in voice, with varied perspectives that may or may not mesh precisely with one another. We hope readers can appreciate the necessity of presenting different discourses in collaboration with each other and have patience with our approach. The result is that we are able to address a wide variety of topics and put them in conversation with each other.

For example, on the one hand, this volume is a historical and archaeological study of Stewart Indian School and its place in the wake of violent state formation processes and settlement in the Great Basin. As historian Ned Blackhawk (2006, 147, 230, 268, 280) details, the 1800s were characterized by violent circumstances for American Indian communities in this region, who experienced not only physical violence and brutal massacres at the hands of settlers and the military, but also experienced devastating ecological and social transformations that left many Native peoples displaced, enslaved, and starving. Eventually, many Native populations, especially those who had been denied reservations, adapted to wage economies to survive. They often created "liminal" spaces for themselves within and near mining and other settler communities (Blackhawk 2006, 15, 281). Federal and state officials sought to address the "Indian problem" of displaced and impoverished Native peoples whom many considered disdainfully as an eyesore. Influential media figures also called for action, as did Mark Twain, who, in his book *Roughing It*, described Shoshones in Nevada as a "silent, sneaking, treacherous looking race . . . eating what a hog would decline" (as cited in Blackhawk 2006, 276). Off-reservation boarding schools such as Stewart Indian School were instituted in the late 1800s by the federal government in an attempt to forcibly assimilate Native Americans and facilitate the federal confiscation of their traditional homelands. Historian Andrew Woolford (2015) maintains that these boarding schools were more than experiments in social engineering or even cultural genocide. He asserts that the brutal early years of these schools were in fact part of the process of genocide itself, the intentional destruction of a group. Drawing from early anthropologists such as James Frazer and Bronislaw Malinowski, who held that culture was necessary for the survival of a collective, Woolford asserts that schools attempting to erase Native languages and spiritual/cultural practices were seeking to destroy Native cultures, and as such, fit the United Nations' description of genocide (Woolford 2015, 9, 26). In other words, "To remove the tools of culture is to seek to eliminate the group as a group (Woolford 2015, 289; for related research on genocide of Native peoples in California, see Lindsay 2012; Madley 2016). This is not to say that Native children and their families were passive recipients of such brutal treatment. Clearly, Indigenous children and their communities had agency and used it to resist and negotiate boarding school systems, even within severe constraints (Woolford 2015, 44; Lomawaima 1994), and we document similar efforts at Stewart Indian School here.

Thus, this volume is certainly about Stewart Indian School. But on the other hand, it is also about interrogating colonialist policies within heritage preservation law and current archaeological practices that perpetuate the oppression of Native peoples today and dismiss both their history and agency. Here we decolonize our own archaeological methods within Indigenous archaeology and take direction from foundational Indigenous perspectives on heritage management (especially Atalay 2006; Smith 1999; Watkins 2000). We also follow cues from holistic perspectives in traditional ecological knowledge (TEK), a framework that recognizes Native sciences as having collected data on complex human-environmental interactions since time immemorial. TEK has begun to be productively applied in other fields such as biomedical and environmental sciences research (e.g., Finn et al. 2017). We argue that archaeologists also can and should welcome TEK's holistic perspectives connecting past and present, and recognize that how we handle heritage will have an effect on the health and well-being of present and future generations. Archaeologists have some catching up to do, changes to implement, and amends to make. Native peoples of the Great Basin have not forgotten that famous anthropologists caused them harm in the past, which continues to have lasting effects. For example, as Ned Blackhawk (2006, 12, 278–79) observes, famous anthropologists Elman Service and Julian Steward argued that Shoshones were underdeveloped and primitive. Steward went so far as to petition the federal government, arguing that they should deny Shoshones' requests for federal recognition and reservations. In anthropology's neoevolutionary paradigm, family bands such as theirs were assumed to be incapable of self-governance; Steward asserted it would only "baffle them" (as cited in Blackhawk 2006, 279). Today, as it was then, there is a disconnect between what non-Native land managers and archaeologists consider best practices, and what Native communities know from human-environmental data gathered for millennia. In this volume, we hope to troubleshoot that impasse in communication and demonstrate how collaborative research can be more productive than tackling issues from separate corners.

Likewise, and again drawing from TEK frameworks, we assert that archaeology should not be conducted in a theoretical vacuum, informed only by archaeological sciences and standard historical and ethnographic methods. Rather, archaeologists would benefit from acknowledging and respecting Native sciences and spiritualities and how they inform broader understandings of related research. This would be a corrective to current practices that often use Western science to validate or—more often—invalidate Native understandings of their pasts. For example, in this volume we address the concept of *puha*, which among Numic-speaking peoples represents the life force that resides in all things and connects past, present, and future; it constitutes the fabric of the universe (Carroll et al. 2004; see also chapters 7 and 8, this volume). *Puha* is remarkably similar to recent research from quantum mechanics in which physicists have successfully entangled particles whose relationships to each other then cross time-space continuums. This phenomenon is known as a quantum nonlocality, which historian and philosopher of science Elise Crull (2018) describes as:

> the eerie link that appears to exist between entangled particles. If two quantum systems meet and then separate, even across a distance of thousands of lightyears, it becomes impossible to measure the features of one system (such as its position, momentum and polarity) without instantly steering the other into a corresponding state.

The entanglement of particles in this way is similar to many Native peoples' assertions that artifacts left in place by ancestors still contain energies that can have effects on modern peoples' well-being. This isn't to say that Native metaphysical perspectives need to be validated by the field of physics. Rather, we should acknowledge that researchers in quantum mechanics have only recently begun exploring entanglements, whereas many Indigenous peoples have been making similar observations since time immemorial.

Of course, we are not able to delve deeply into TEK or quantum mechanics in this volume. But we hope that raising these broader issues brings awareness of what archaeologists can explore someday as we increasingly emerge from our archaeological echo chambers. With that said, our primary contributions in this volume are twofold. In some chapters we provide a case study of an Indian boarding school that will be helpful to historians and archaeologists working at related sites. This includes a history of Indian boarding schools in Nevada, including Stewart Indian School (chapters 3, 4, and 5), and archaeological methods and data regarding Indigenous archaeology and archaeologies of childhood and institutional life (primarily chapters 6 and 8). Other chapters contribute to our goals of demonstrating that collaborative archaeology is necessary for best practices in heritage management and for working through conflicting goals and discourses. This includes a discussion of current scholarship in collaborative archaeology and decolonizing methods (chapter 2), how collaborative research design led to choosing Stewart Indian School for this project (chapter 3), multivocal interpretations and discussions of best practices in heritage (chapter 7), and concluding thoughts on how conflicting discourses can be mitigated through collaborative work and social capital (chapter 8).

Why We Embarked on This Project: Conflicting Discourses in the Management of Indigenous Heritage

Conflicting discourses around Indigenous heritage arise from a variety of factors and what much can be done to improve miscommunications. Many American Indian and Native Alaskan tribes are recognized by the U.S. government as sovereign nations. Federal and state mandates require agencies to consult with tribes regarding heritage resources on their traditional homelands now administered by the federal government as public lands. In the United States, the federal government holds a trust responsibility to federally recognized tribes. Additionally, some treaty tribes interact with the federal agencies regarding the protection of their reserved rights to their usual and accustomed places. Government agencies are often not required to interact with tribes beyond immediate heritage project needs, and there is usually very little personal, face-to-face interaction. Tribes are often notified of projects in writing, but they have little control over proposed projects.

This project studied what appears to be a longstanding impasse in federal/tribal communications caused at least in part by institutional norms manifested in the day-to-day interactions between federal and tribal interlocutors. To address conflicting discourses surrounding current heritage management practices, the concept of governmentality (a disciplinary power accomplished through legislative and institutional practices) was applied as an evaluative lens. Throughout the process, points of potential conflict were identified, evaluated, and their potential acceptable alternatives evaluated. Our process engaged all parties collaboratively toward potential solutions by addressing the utility of building social capital (i.e., valued relations with others) as described in practice and agency theories that emphasize the embodiment of personal experiences in creating change.

In an effort to address the conflicting heritage discourses, the contributors to this volume participated in a collaborative archaeological project at the Stewart Indian School in Carson City, Nevada, a site currently listed on the National Register of Historic Places (NRHP). The project was designed to examine the utility of face-to-face discussions among Native and non-Native participants to address different conceptions of heritage preservation and develop a model for improved heritage practices. The project traced the challenges of incorporating the diverse stakeholders' voices (i.e., multivocality) and conflicting discourses at all stages of the project, from its very inception, to the interface with government agencies and legislation, to the production of knowledge through publication.

History of Relationships between Federal Government Agencies, Tribes, and Heritage Management

Colonialist practices of the past several hundred years continue to be a part of today's heritage discourses. In the 1960s Indigenous groups all over the world voiced their concerns about heritage management and the treatment of their cultural and ancestral remains. *Custer Died for Your Sins* is a well-known example of such criticism (Deloria 1969). Vine Deloria describes anthropologists as "creatures" that objectify Native Americans for the sake of science and to produce "useless knowledge" that has "contributed substantially to the invisibility of Indian people today" (Deloria 1969, 81). This issue persisted into the following years and by 1971, the American Indian Movement (AIM), as well as other activists, were protesting excavations like those in Welch, Minnesota, and taking over the laboratory at Colorado State University (Watkins 2000, 7), as well as protesting various roadside attractions where artifacts were on display (Atalay 2006, 291). These protests forced archaeologists to acknowledge Indigenous communities' trepidations over archaeological procedures, and although some archaeologists had begun acknowledging Indigenous peoples' concerns, these events forced the issues into the public eye and eventually brought them to the forefront of discussions in archaeology.

Zimmerman (2001) argues that the basis of these discrepancies is the epistemological differences between each party. Archaeologists generally contemplate heritage from a rationalist and empiricist perspective, which leads them to separate time into three parts: past, present, and future. Significance is placed on the past, as it serves as an example of how to approach specific issues in the present and aids in the preparation for the future. This is exemplified by the antilooting campaign slogan of the Society for American Archaeology—"Save the Past for the Future" (Zimmerman 2001, 171). In contrast, many American Indian communities view the past as living in the present, "with the present viewed as the only 'real' temporal realm" (Zimmerman 2001, 172). As a result, discussions emerged between archaeologists and Indigenous peoples concerning ownership of the past (Jemison 1997), control of Native American human remains (Trope and Echo-Hawk 1997; Tsosie 2012), material culture (Atalay 2006), and related issues of Indigenous intellectual property (Anyon et al. 1997; Jackson and Stevens 1997, 138; Nicholas et al. 2010). Concerns over who should write the interpretations of the material remains were also a part of these discussions and have played a dominant role in archaeology (Hinsley Jr. 1997; Atalay 2006, 288–89; Silliman 2010, 148).

Relevant Legislation, Policies, and Recommendations Regarding Tribal Consultation

This section outlines federal policies that govern cultural heritage resources in the United States, as well as publications by Native American organizations that address those policies and the conflicts that arise from their implementation.

Consultation with the tribes whose ancestors and elders created today's cultural heritage resources is a relatively recent phenomenon, mandated in several laws and Executive Orders, such as the American Indian Religious Freedom Act (AIRFA), National Historic Preservation Act (NHPA 1966, Public Law 89-665 and amendments thereto; 16 U.S.C. 470 et seq.), Native American Graves Protection and Repatriation Act (NAGPRA 1990, Public Law 101-601; 25 U.S.C. 3001-3013), National Environmental Policy Act (NEPA 1969), White House Memorandum for the Heads of Executive Departments and Agencies, Executive Order 13007 (1996) on Indian Sacred Sites, and Executive Order 13175 (2000) on Consultation and Coordination with Indian Tribal Governments.

In addition to the selected legislation and executive orders mentioned above, there are numerous other policy documents by individual agencies that outline procedures for consultation and are relevant to this project (e.g., Department of the Army 1998). In particular, new studies have emerged since President Obama's 2009 Memorandum on Tribal Consultation (November 5, 2009), and currently each major federal agency has established guidelines for performing consultation with federally recognized Indian tribes.

There are a number of tribal organizations that regularly address heritage concerns, such as the National Association of Tribal Historic Preservation Officers (NATHPO), National Congress of American Indians (NCAI), regional organizations such as the Affiliated Tribes of Northwest Indians (ATNI), and individual tribal governments. These governments and organizations have produced a number of policy documents that inform this project, as they address the continued problems associated with cultural heritage management practices. It is critical to address Indigenous-authored documents to better understand diverse perspectives that problematize this issue, particularly from outside the standard discourse that surrounds federally governmentalized cultural resource management (CRM). For example, several of these documents offer alternative definitions about what constitutes effective consultation (e.g., NATHPO 2005; White Mountain Apache Tribe 2004).

Challenges of Heritage Consultation in the United States

Section 106 of the NHPA, as amended in 1992, requires federal agencies that fund projects, issue required permits, or manage land where an undertaking is proposed to consult tribes in order to identify "properties of traditional religious and cultural importance to an Indian tribe or Native Hawaiian organization," which then "may be determined to be eligible for inclusion on the National Register" (54 U.S.C. 100101 et seq.). But this requirement only applies to resources within the project area, or at a maximum, traditional sites within the project's viewshed. An additional issue concerns Section 106's narrow definition of "cultural resource," as its scope rarely includes the breadth of cultural concerns tribes hold for landscapes affected by undertakings.

Evaluating traditional sites, areas, and activities that are important to tribes is extremely limited, usually to within the geographically narrow confines of the direct area of potential effect (APE), as mandated by Section 106. Tribal consultants may help identify sites of tribal interest during in-field consultations and interviews, but if the sites fall outside the APE, these traditional sites are not documented and are not usually written about in Section 106 compliance reports, lest the discussion of nearby sites "confuse the issue." Further, some federal managers are anxious about filling compliance reports with information on traditional knowledge of a specific area due to a perception that they would be required to avoid that area in future projects.

Section 106 works well enough when dealing with historic structures and sites, giving clear-cut direction on how to mitigate adverse impacts to those. But traditional sites and use areas don't fit so neatly into the Section 106 box.

Traditional cultural properties (TCPs) are places that are significant to living communities. The identification and evaluation of TCPs is the National Park Service's method of handling nonarchaeological, nonstructural sites that are nonetheless important to maintaining traditional cultural values (United States Department of the Interior 1998). The limitations of this attempt to include what most of us refer to as ethnographic sites, as listings on the National Register of Historic Places, are still being tested since the TCP category of National Register–eligible sites has only existed since the 1992 amendment to the NHPA.

Federal agencies that work through the Section 106 rubric often employ consultation with tribes in a restrictive way. Discussions of cultural landscapes necessarily do not fit into discussions of effects within a project corridor or APE. So agency officials and contractors are left to dissect a landscape and fit its diverse and numerous resources into categories of affected and not-affected sites, or leave mention of a landscape of sites out of compliance reports altogether.

Another consideration is the commonly held American Indian view that archaeological sites are "alive," embodied with energy left by previous occupants (e.g., Carroll et al. 2004; chapter 7). This interpretation makes archaeological sites TCPs. But that's not exactly what the National Park Service had in mind when it developed the TCP category of National Register sites, and agency officials simply cannot handle the prospect of all precontact-period sites as TCPs, logistically (or even philosophically).

But to Indians, "prehistoric" archaeological sites are traditional sites used by their forebears and in some cases have continuous use to the present. There is not necessarily a distinction between "prehistoric ar chaeology" and sites that form the cultural memory of tribal members taught this traditional history since their childhood. Traditional aboriginal history transcends pre- and post-European arrival to North America, so there is no "prehistory" and "history" in that worldview. It should be noted that the conflict and hardship that accompanies contact with Euroamericans is part of Indian history today. Not to belabor the point, but because many tribes view archaeological sites as living areas not to be disrupted, they are often caught in a quandary during consultation for archaeological projects. For some tribes, excavation itself is considered an adverse effect.

In the authors' personal experiences with American Indians who work in the field of archaeology, a tribal distrust of archaeology and archaeologists has been revealed repeatedly. Unfortunately, the field is viewed by most tribal elders as grave robbing. Those perceptions have persisted since the early days of American archaeology (in which grave looting was de rigueur), regardless of required tribal consultation and the best presentations of archaeology.

There is also the problem of taboos against sharing specialized knowledge with nonspecialists, when involved in tribal consultation. Traditional specialists are not allowed to share their acquired knowledge with nonspecialists in their own tribe, so how can they be expected to share this kind of information with federal officials or archaeologists? While a basic understanding of traditional use of a site may lead to "significant" determinations of eligibility, if knowledgeable tribal members are reticent to share, then Section 106 consultation is incomplete. This leads to inadequate understandings of the aboriginal past in and around project areas and unsatisfactory mitigation.

Tribal and Federal Miscommunications over Heritage Management

Conflicts between federal land managers and tribal members are sometimes ideological, couched in conflicting discourses, which makes understanding difficult. For example, one tribal member (cited in Russell and Adams-Russell 2006, 11) explained the disparity in worldviews regarding a sacred mountain on the Coconino National Forest, in saying,

> The Forest Service has tended to divide that mountain. It is like taking a piece of pizza and slicing it up and saying we will only take this much here. It only represents one percent of the mountain. In this case it is the special-use (Snowbowl) permit. If you look at the spiritual side of what they are doing it is tantamount to slicing up (our culture). The tribes consider that mountain to be a living entity. . . . When the tribes consider that a living entity and they go and desecrate the mountain like that with reclaimed water, it is like cutting a piece of your mother off. Cutting a toe off and it is as if they say "oh that is only one percent of the body."

In response to continued outcry from Native American governments and tribal members, some federal agencies persist in seeking solutions that will allow tribes more voice in the CRM discourse. For example, the Army sometimes accommodates tribal ceremonial activities on Army installations (e.g., sweatlodge ceremonies on Fort Sill, and ceremonial activities at the Leon River Medicine Wheel on Fort Hood) but these are exceptions to the norm. Some agencies have been increasingly progressive in reaching out to tribes, above and beyond what is required by federal mandates. For example,

> The Department of Defense policy supports tribal self-governance and government-to-government relations between the federal government and tribes. These principles recognize the importance of increasing understanding and addressing tribal concerns, past, present, and future. These concerns should be addressed prior to reaching decisions on matters that may have the potential to significantly affect tribal resources, tribal rights, or Indian lands. (DoD 2011)

Many tribes have expressed appreciation for sentiments such as these, as tribes have long struggled to have their concerns heard (NATHPO 2005; NCAI 2008). However, they also express dissatisfaction over the very fact that the federal government still controls what happens to heritage resources through federal legislation, in spite of concerns voiced by tribes (NCAI 2009). For example, in commenting on the DoD (2010) Plan of Action, the Navajo Nation Washington Office (2010) asserted that "The federal government is well aware of the issues we face. Now is the time to advocate for resources and policies that will ultimately improve quality of life for the Navajo people." This suggests the presence of two separate discourses. The governmentalized discourse is one in which government agencies and non-Native archaeologists operate on principles of federal management of heritage (e.g., listening sessions and data collection). In contrast, the second discourse is one in which tribes emphasize tribal sovereignty, preservation, and quality of life for tribal peoples. For example, according to testimony from Chairman Reno Franklin from NATHPO, tribes have been preserving and protecting their cultures successfully for thousands of years, but the last 150 years under the control of the federal government have been some of the most devastating for tribal peoples (NATHPO 2011).

In spite of federal governmental efforts to listen more carefully to tribal concerns, tribes feel they have little agency once they do voice concerns; communication seems perfunctory and controversial projects proceed without reflecting the concerns voiced by the tribes during listening sessions (e.g., Coeur D'Alene Tribe 2010; NCAI 2009). The federal government can meet all procedural requirements, yet tribes can feel their voices have little impact on projects. The concerns many tribes hold is that their tribal knowledge is not seriously acknowledged or incorporated into the process and outcome in meaningful ways. In another example, the Agua Caliente Band of Cahuilla Indians (2010) stated in comments regarding the DoD Plan of Action:

> Consultation is a cornerstone for a productive, respectful and authentic government to government relationship between tribes and the federal government. Indeed, the history of federal-tribal relations demonstrates conclusively that when the United States has implemented policies, however well-meaning, without proper engagement, without asking the tribes themselves what they want, the result has generally been failed policies, all too often with tragic consequences. Thus, we agree with the general idea that meaningful consultation has great virtues and is a necessary precondition to the development of sound Indian policy.... Of course, the key word is "meaningful." Where federal agencies have already decided a policy direction and "go through the motions" of consulting with tribes, that is meaningless. Consultation has to occur at a time where important choices are still available.

Thus, tribal/federal consultation as currently practiced is not sufficient or satisfactory to many tribal peoples, and tribes and federal employees seem to be engaging in separate discourses. As a result, many tribes distrust the consultation process and land managers themselves, and this leads to an inefficient consultation process, damaged public relations, and occasionally, costly lawsuits over disputed projects (e.g., Welch 1997; Williams 1993). Many tribes still feel that there are fundamental misunderstandings in federally governmentalized discourse of consultation. It is a very different discourse from tribal conversations about heritage preservation and tribal sovereignty.

There are a number of productive approaches currently being undertaken in academia and among various federal agencies in the area of tribal consultation. The intent of these approaches is often good and they frequently address the need for collaborative, multivocal approaches. However, as discussed above, they are often being derailed by the continued lack of attention to very fundamental issues such as who ultimately controls what happens to these resources, and how resource control is regulated by federal legislation founded on non-Native discourse.

Anthropologists have recently called for the discipline's increased involvement with conflict resolution, indicating the utility of ethnographic methodologies to promote cross-cultural and interdisciplinary dialogue surrounding contentious issues (e.g., Davidheiser and Treitler 2007). Archaeology is also poised to help living societies reconnect to ancestral landscapes for increased well-being and as a means of "therapy" (Schaepe et al. 2017). Likewise, the editors of this volume see collaborative projects at sites like Stewart Indian School as having tremendous potential for addressing historical and intergenerational trauma in tribal communities as future collaborators may deem appropriate and useful. Much can be accomplished through effective communication that establishes active dialogue, more so than dictating static policy or asking tribes to simply ignore modern repercussions from the past. Likewise, social theory from outside the discipline can shed light on the very nature of the problem, as well as potential solutions (see chapter 2).

Of course, effective communication cannot happen if people are not willing to make time for it. For example, we attempted to involve regional Army land managers in this project. While some Department of Defense (DoD) heritage specialists in our professional networks were interested, we were not able to find administrative DoD personnel who were willing to participate in the project, due to either disinterest or overcommitment to other duties. We return in the concluding chapter to the implications of this choice.

Goals for the Stewart Indian School Project

Goals and objectives for the project were to study the interplay of tribal agency, social capital, and governmentalized archaeological discourse, and then outline a strategy for humanizing the process of respectful consultation among tribes, archaeologists, and the federal government. The project was funded by a three-year grant from the Army Research Office's Young Investigator's Program (Sarah Cowie, principle investigator) with the University of Nevada, Reno (UNR), in partnership with The Nevada Indian Commission, the Washoe Tribal Historic Preservation Office (THPO), and numerous other Native and non-Native heritage specialists, volunteers, students, staff, and community members, many of whom are contributing authors to this volume.

Together we observed and researched areas where conflict arises, why there is still an impasse in conflicting discourses, and how governmentalization both helps and hinders processes of consultation. In chronicling this project's archaeological practice and collaboration with tribal heritage specialists, this volume suggests some opportunities for building social capital and collaborating with tribes. From this work we found that it is possible to shift discourse around consultation to improve satisfaction of outcomes for all parties, at least in this particular case study.

This project involved a qualitative study of the impasse in federal/tribal discourses regarding heritage consultation. A network of partners collaboratively developed a model for improved consultation procedures. This volume, one of the results of the overall project, addresses the repercussions of federal government discourse surrounding Indigenous heritage and the utility of social capital for improving communication. The non-Native archaeologists who initiated the project organized a series of heritage discussions with tribal members who served as tribal consultants or partners in a collaborative, involved exchange of ideas. Tribal members participated as professional heritage specialists, staff, policymakers, and university academics, as well as undergraduate students that participated in the collaborative archaeological field school. In this case, fieldwork served as a foundation for discussing the improvement of tribal/federal heritage management issues. This strategy is informed by practice theory; phenomenology; and the linkages between place, memory, and multivocality that are valued by many tribal peoples (e.g., Basso 1996; Colwell-Chanthaphonh and Ferguson 2006; Cowie et al. 2009), as well as recent pedagogical shifts in teaching collaborative archaeology (e.g., Silliman 2008).

Personnel working on this project worked collaboratively as equal contributors, rather than as subjects in data gathering. Each participant contributed his/her own knowledge about the topic. The UNR Office of Human Research Protection determined that this project did not constitute research on human subjects and was therefore exempt from human subjects review.

The proposed model for this project hinged on the idea that tribal/federal relationships could be improved by establishing relationships before the consultation process formally began; networks would then already be in place before potentially contentious issues arose. Federal agencies would make a minimal investment through heritage outreach activities first, not waiting until there is a problem to consult with tribes. The goal is for open dialog to continue productively when contentious heritage issues eventually arise.

Outreach activities during this project included collaborative work with several tribes and tribal heritage staff in Nevada and Oregon to deconstruct the current consultation process and to assess the ramifications of federally governmentalized discourse. In addition, this study models a heritage project that integrates both federal and Native discourses, in the form of a good faith offer of services to tribes for the mutual, long-term benefit of federal agencies as well as tribes. Services might include facilitating tribal visits to their traditional homelands on federally managed lands, and offering archaeological training and services to tribal entities. This project included funding for tribal undergraduate students to participate in the archaeological field school, and a number of Native consultants were hired for their expertise on various portions of the project. Other tribal members who work in heritage careers also participated in fieldwork as well, creating a productive exchange of ideas for Native and non-Native peoples and building social capital.

This three-year project began in the summer of 2012. Project participants reviewed the large body of literature regarding heritage consultation in both federal and Indigenous discourses. The literature was analyzed within the context of governmentality and agency theories. In the second year of the project personnel networked with tribal heritage specialists who were interested in participating and began a collaborative assessment of tribal needs regarding heritage concerns.

Then, together with tribes, an archaeological site was selected to be the focus of the archaeological field school. It is important to note that only sites deemed suitable by participant tribal organizations were considered during this process. Potential sites considered were either already in need of mitigation due to imminent threat of development or sites that a tribal organization determined would benefit their heritage needs. Specific areas of the Stewart Indian School were selected because the Nevada Indian Commission, the Stewart Advisory Committee, and the Washoe THPO determined that an archaeological field school had the potential to benefit several of their upcoming heritage needs. In addition, it was desirable to many tribal members that we choose a site that would benefit multiple tribes by educating the American public about the traumatic effects of forced assimilation faced by many American Indians. Project collaborators then began contributing to the field school planning, which was conducted in summer 2013. Project personnel worked with tribal consultants in a collaborative, involved exchange of ideas, which occurred both on-site and at off-site locations. Tribal consultants led heritage discussions at the field school and contributed to the professionalization of both Native and non-Native students. After the fieldwork was completed, lab work and artifact processing continued through the fall and spring semesters in consultation with tribal members. The project finished with writing results and requesting essays from participants, and eventually circulating drafts of this volume to all participants for comment and revisions.

We hope the final result here provides not only a community-based case study of an important site, but also some insights into broader heritage issues. Ultimately, this project's goal focused on outlining a strategy for humanizing the process of respectful consultation among tribes, archaeologists, and the federal government. This is accomplished by applying theories of multivocality, governmentalization, agency, and social capital to a qualitative analysis of the impasse in federal/tribal discourses around consultation. In doing so, we offer some potential solutions to address the impasse to help the federal government more fully meet federal trust responsibility obligations, and to encourage archaeologists in public, state, and academic sectors to decolonize methods and recognize tribal members as productive colleagues who share concerns for heritage.

Works Cited

Agua Caliente Band of Cahuilla Indians. 2010. Comments from Chairman Richard M. Milanovich, Agua Caliente Band of Cahuilla Indians on the DoD Plan of Action. http://www.denix.osd.mil/na/upload/Agua-Caliente-Band-of-the-Cahuilla-Indians-of-the-Agua-Caliente-Indian-Reservation-California.pdf, accessed December 19, 2011.

Anyon, Roger, T. J. Ferguson, Loretta Jackson, Lillie Lane, and Philip Vicenti. 1997. "Native American Oral Tradition and Archaeology: Issues of Structure, Relevance, and Respect." In *Native Americans and Archaeologists: Stepping Stones to Common Ground*, edited by Nina Swidler, Kurt E. Dongoske, Roger Anyon, and Alan S. Downer, 77–87. Walnut Creek, CA: AltaMira Press.

Atalay, Sonya. 2006. "Indigenous Archaeology as Decolonizing Practice." *The American Indian Quarterly* 30, nos. 3 and 4: 280–310.

———. 2012. *Community-Based Archaeology: Research with, by and for Indigenous and Local Communities.* Berkeley: University of California Press.

Basso, Keith H. 1996. *Wisdom Sits in Places.* Albuquerque: University of New Mexico Press.

Blackhawk, Ned. 2006. *Violence Over the Land: Indians and Empires in the Early American West.* Cambridge: Harvard University Press.

Carroll, Alex K., M. Nieves Zedeño, and Richard W. Stoffle. 2004. "Landscapes of the Ghost Dance: A Cartography of Numic Ritual." *Journal of Archaeological Method and Theory* 11, no. 2: 127–56.

Coeur D'Alene Tribe. 2010. "Comments from Chief J. Allen, Coeur D'Alene Tribe of the Coeur D'Alene Reservation, Idaho on the DoD Plan of Action." Coeur D'Alene, Idaho.

Colwell, Chip. 2016. "Collaborative Archaeologies and Descendant Communities." *Annual Review of Anthropology* 45:113–27.

Colwell-Chanthaphonh, Chip, and T. J. Ferguson. 2010. "Memory Pieces and Footprints: Multivocality and the Meaning of Ancient Times and Ancestral Places among the Zuni and Hopi." *American Anthropologist* 108, no. 2: 148–62.

Cowie, Sarah E., Christopher C. LeBlanc, Mary M. Farrell, and Nicholas C. Laluk. 2009. "Multivocality in the Forest: A New Approach to Tribal Relations on the Coronado National Forest, Arizona." *Arizona Anthropologist* 19 (Winter): 1–16.

Crull, Elise. 2018. "You Thought Quantum Mechanics Was Weird: Check Out Entangled Time." *Aeon.* Last modified February 2, 2018. https://aeon.co/ideas/you-thought-quantum-mechanics-was-weird-check-out-entangled-time.

Dano Johnson, Christine. 2015. "Not Just Objects: Alaska Native Material Culture at the McClung Museum of Natural History and Culture." *Pursuit: The Journal of Undergraduate Research at the University of Tennessee* 6, no. 1, art. 11: 1–12.

Davidheiser, Mark, and Inga E. Treitler. 2007. "An Analytic Introduction and a Call for Interdisciplinary Engagement." *Anthropology News* 48, no. 6: 12–13.

Deloria, Vine, Jr. 1969. "Anthropologists and Other Friends." In *Custer Died for Your Sins: An Indian Manifesto*, 78–100. Norman: University of Oklahoma Press.

Department of the Army. 1998. Pamphlet 200–4 Environmental Quality. Cultural Resources Management. Headquarters Department of the Army, Washington, DC.

DoD (Department of Defense). 2010. Department of Defense Plan of Action to Implement the Policies and Directives of Executive Order 13175, Consultation and Coordination with Indian Tribal Governments January 2010. Submitted to the Office of Management and Budget February 2010. Washington, DC: Department of Defense.

———. 2011. Department of Defense Instruction 4710.02: DoD Interactions with Federally Recognized Tribes. DENIX-Native American Affairs, Policies, Laws, and Regulations. Organizations. Washington, DC: Department of Defense.

Dongoske, Kurt E., Mark Aldenderfer, and Karen Doehner. 2000. *Working Together: Native Americans and Archaeologists*. Washington, DC: Society for American Archaeology.

Ferguson, T. J., and Chip Colwell-Chanthaphonh. 2006. *History Is in the Land: Multivocal Traditions in Arizona's San Pedro Valley*. Tucson, AZ: University of Arizona Press.

Finn, Symma, Mose Herne, and Dorothy Castille. 2017. "The Value of Traditional Ecological Knowledge for the Environmental Health Sciences and Biomedical Research." *Environmental Health Perspectives* 25, no. 8. Published August 29, 2017. DOI: https://doi.org/10.1289/EHP858.

Hinsley, Curtis M., Jr. 2000. "Digging for Identity: Reflections on the Cultural Backdrop of Collecting." In *Repatriation Reader: Who Owns American Indian Remains?*, edited by Devon A. Mihesuah. Lincoln, NE: University of Nebraska Press.

Gonzalez, Sara L., Ian Kretzler, and Briece Edwards. 2018. "Imagining Indigenous and Archaeological Futures: Building Capacity with the Confederated Tribes of Grand Ronde." *Archaeologies: Journal of the World Archaeological Congress* 14, no. 1: 85–114.

Gould, Rae. 2013. "Cultural Practice and Authenticity: The Search for Real Indians in New England in the 'Historical' Period." In *The Death of "Prehistory,"* edited by Peter Schmidt and Stephen Mrozowski. Oxford: Oxford University Press.

Jackson, Loretta, and Robert Hank Stevens. 1997. "Hualapai Tradition, Religion, and the Role of Cultural Resource Management." In *Native Americans and Archaeologists: Stepping Stones to Common Ground*, edited by Nina Swidler, Kurt E. Dongoske, Roger Anyon, and Alan S. Downer, 135–42. Walnut Creek, CA: AltaMira Press.

Jemison, G. Peter. 1997. "Who Owns the Past?" In *Native Americans and Archaeologists: Stepping Stones to Common Ground*, edited by Nina Swidler, Kurt E. Dongoske, Roger Anyon, and Alan S. Downer, 57–63. Walnut Creek, CA: Alta Mira Press.

Laluk, Nicholas, C. 2017. "The Indivisibility of Land and Mind: Indigenous

Knowledge and Collaborative Archaeology within Apache Contexts." *Journal of Social Archaeology* 17, no. 1: 92–122.

Lindsay, Brendan C. 2012. *Murder State: California's Native American Genocide, 1846–1873*. Lincoln, NE: University of Nebraska Press.

Lomawaima, K. Tsianna. 1994. *They Called It Prairie Light: The Story of Chilocco Indian School*. Lincoln, NE: University of Nebraska Press.

Madley, Benjamin. 2016. *An American Genocide: The United States and the California Indian Catastrophe, 1846–1873*. New Haven, CT: Yale University Press.

Martinez, Desireé R., and Wendy G. Teeter. 2015. "Ho'eexokre 'eyookuuka'ro 'We're working with each other': The Pimu Catalina Island Project." *Society for American Archaeology Record* 15, no. 1: 25–28.

NATHPO (National Association of Tribal Historic Preservation Officers). 2005. *Tribal Consultation: Best Practices in Historic Preservation*. Washington, DC: National Association of Tribal Historic Preservation Officers.

———. 2011. Testimony of Reno Keoni Franklin (Kashia Pomo), Chairman, National Association of Tribal historic preservation officers. Hearing on Issues Affecting Management of Archaeological, Cultural, and Historic Resources at Mesa Verde National Park and Other Units of the National Park System. U.S. Senate Subcommittee on National Parks. Dated November 5, 2011. http://www.nathpo.org/PDF/NATHPO-SucbmteNatParks2011.pdf.

NCAI (National Congress of American Indians). 2008. Testimony of the National Congress of American Indians Before the House Natural Resources Committee on HR 5608, "Consultation and Coordination with Indian Tribal Government Acts." Washington, DC: NCAI.

———. 2009. Letter from NCAI Urging Agency Action. Washington, DC: NCAI.

Navajo Nation Washington Office. 2010. Comments from Sharon Clahchischillage, Executive Director, Navajo Nation Washington Office, on the DoD Plan of Action. Washington, DC: Navajo Nation Washington Office.

Nicholas, George, ed. 2010. *Being and Becoming Indigenous Archaeologists*. Walnut Creek, CA: Left Coast Press.

Nicholas, George, Catherine Bell, Rosemary Coombe, John R. Welch, Brian Noble, Jane Anderson, Kelly Bannister, and Joe Watkins. 2010. "Intellectual Property Issues in Heritage Management, Part 2: Legal Dimensions, Ethical Considerations, and Collaborative Research Practices." *Heritage Management* 3, no. 1 (Spring): 117–47.

Russell, John C., and Peggy A. Adams-Russell. 2006. *Values, Attitudes and Beliefs toward National Forest System Lands: Arizona Tribal Peoples*. Placerville, CA: Adams-Russell Consulting.

Schaepe, David M., Bill Angelbeck, David Snook, and John R. Welch. 2017. "Archaeology as Therapy: Connecting Belongings, Knowledge, Time, Place, and Well-Being (with Comments and Reply)." *Current Anthropology* 58, no. 4: 502–33.

Schneider, Tsim D. 2018. "'Suffering hunger and a thousand labors in the mountains . . .': The Archaeology of Indigenous Resistance, Runaways, and Refuge in Spanish Alta

California." In *Franciscans and American Indians in Pan-Borderlands Perspective: Adaptation, Negotiation, and Resistance*, edited by Jeffrey M. Burns and Timothy J. Johnson, 265–80. Oceanside, CA: Academy of American Franciscan History.

Silliman, Stephen W., ed. 2008. *Collaborating at the Trowel's Edge: Teaching and Learning in Indigenous Archaeology*. Tucson, AZ: University of Arizona Press.

———. 2010. "Writing New Archaeological Narratives: Indigenous North America." In *Handbook of Postcolonial Archaeology*, edited by Jane Lydon and Uzma Z. Rizvi, 145–63. World Archaeological Congress Research handbooks in Archaeology, Vol. 3. Edited by George Nicholas and Julie Hollowell. Walnut Creek, CA: Left Coast Press.

Smith, Claire, and H. Martin Wobst, eds. 2005. *Indigenous Archaeologies: Decolonising Theory and Practice (One World Archaeology)*. London and New York: Routledge.

Smith, Linda Tuhiwai. 1999. *Decolonizing Methodologies: Research and Indigenous Peoples*. London: Zed Books Ltd.

Teeman, Diane L. 2016. "Cultural Resource Management and the Protection of Valued Tribal Spaces: A View from the Western United States." In *Handbook of Landscape Archaeology*, edited by Bruno David and Julian Thomas, 626–32. New York: Routledge.

Thompson, Kerry F. 2011. "The Navajo Nation, Diné Archaeologists, Diné Archaeology, and Diné Communities." *Archaeologies: Journal of the World Archaeological Congress* 7, no. 3: 502–17.

Tsosie, Rebecca. 2012. "NAGPRA and the Problem of 'Culturally Unidentifiable' Remains: The Argument for a Human Rights Framework. *Arizona State Law Journal* 44, no. 2: 809.

Two Bears, Davina. 2010. "Navajo Archaeologist Is Not an Oxymoron." In *Indigenous Archaeologies: A Reader in Decolonization*, edited by Margaret Bruchac, Siobhan Hart, and H. Martin Wobst, 196–98. Walnut Creek, CA: Left Coast Press.

Watkins, Joe E. 2000. *Indigenous Archaeology: American Indian Values and Scientific Practice*. Walnut Creek, CA: AltaMira Press.

Welch, John R. 1997. White Eyes' Lies and the Battle for Dzil Nchaa Si'an. *American Indian Quarterly* 21, no. 1: 75–109.

White Mountain Apache Tribe. 2004. Cultural Heritage Resources Best Management Practices. Version 9.13.2004. Whiteriver, AZ: White Mountain Apache Tribe Heritage Program, Historic Preservation Office.

Williams, Robert A. 1993. "Large Binocular Telescopes, Red Squirrel Piñatas, and Apache Sacred Mountains: Decolonizing Environmental Law in a Multicultural World." *West Virginia Law Review* 96: 1134–64.

Woolford, Andrew. 2015. *The Benevolent Experiment: Indigenous Boarding Schools, Genocide, and Redress in Canada and the United States*. Lincoln, NE: University of Nebraska Press.

Zimmerman, Larry J. 2001. "Usurping Native American Voice." In *The Future of the Past: Archaeologists, Native Americans, and Repatriation*, edited by Tamara L. Bray, 169–84. London: Garland Publishing, Inc.

CHAPTER 2

Theoretical Approaches to Collaborative Archaeology

Diane L. Teeman, Sarah E. Cowie, Christopher C. LeBlanc, and Ashley M. Long

The need for collaborative archaeology largely arose from efforts to address the difficult relationships that exist between researchers and Indigenous peoples. For decades, archaeology has been dominated by a discourse characterized by inequality and colonialist ideology. A primary goal of collaborative archaeology is to correct the inequality that exists between Indigenous groups and archaeologists by transcending standard consultation requirements and reaching a truly cooperative relationship that begins at the onset of research projects (Lightfoot 2008). Collaborative archaeology is "an inclusive practice that includes people of different backgrounds, cultures, and perspectives who share a common interest (as stakeholders) in the archaeology of a particular place" (Lightfoot 2008, 214). For these reasons, and many more, archaeologists have shown increasing interest in making archaeology a more inclusive field that incorporates multiple perspectives into the interpretation of the past.

Collaborative archaeology endeavors to include Indigenous perspectives throughout the entire research process, beginning at the basic levels of research design, continuing throughout fieldwork, and into the writing and publication processes (Lassiter 2005). The basis of Indigenous archaeology also follows many of the same principles as collaborative archaeology, which may be why the term Indigenous archaeology has sometimes been used synonymously with the former (Nicholas 2008b), although Indigenous archaeology (or "Indigenous archaeologies," considering the diversity with which Indigenous archaeology is practiced) has been developing in numerous directions over the course of the last two decades. Research partnerships founded on doctrines such as these have proved to profoundly transform theory and method in archaeology.

This chapter outlines theoretical approaches to collaborative archaeology and discusses how it interfaces with related theories on governmentality, social capital, and multivocality, as well as knowledge production, ethics, and Indigenous philosophies.

Theoretical Foundations

Collaborative archaeology arose from the need for a more community-based and reflexive archaeology, and various theoretical frameworks inform collaborative archaeology. This subfield follows fundamental elements of archaeological theory such as those associated with culture-historical, processual, and postprocessual approaches. It was greatly influenced by theoretical perspectives that emerged during the late twentieth century (Atalay 2006; Nicholas 2008b), and has become increasingly important in pedagogical considerations in higher education (Silliman 2008).

The late twentieth century saw a shift in archaeological theory from an empirical, problem-oriented paradigm, to a more reflexive, agency-oriented, postprocessual archaeology (Nicholas 2008a, 1665). Significant debates brought about by postprocessual thought include issues surrounding self-reflexivity, multivocality, ethical issues, and inclusion of multiple perspectives. Postprocessualism created a reflexive environment that allowed for the recognition of archaeology as a field that is greatly affected by the social and political setting of the time (Atalay 2006, 291). As this idea was further developed, archaeologists began to view issues concerning the past as a product of the time. They started to understand the influence of cultural context upon knowledge production. The emergence of Indigenous protests raised awareness in public and academic spheres about the unfair treatment of Native Americans in archaeology, while the development of postprocessualism as a theoretical perspective in the discipline was occurring simultaneously. The concurrent appearance of these two factors brought colonial attributes of archaeology to the foreground (Atalay

2006, 291), and subsequently decolonization theory was developed as a way to address the colonialist ideology and the inequality apparent in archaeology (Nicholas 2008a, 1665).

Similarly, the decolonization of theory, practice, and terminology is at the heart of any Indigenous approach to research. Decolonization sets out to transform the relationship between researcher and Indigenous community by shifting the relationship from one that is centrally focused and founded in Western conceptions of knowledge, to one that is collaborative and multivocal and brings into consideration various epistemologies (Smith 1999). Decolonization necessitates non-Indigenous archaeologists to educate themselves on contemporary Indigenous issues and to show respect and sensitivity to the needs of the community, while actively promoting Indigenous projects and research interests (Wobst 2010, 78). Essentially, it is a process that alters the power dynamics within research with Indigenous communities—shifting the power from the archaeologist to the community. To successfully decolonize archaeology requires a firmly collaborative approach to research (Bruchac 2014, 2069). We return to decolonization theory in more detail later in the chapter.

Along with decolonization, issues surrounding the contemporary representation of Indigenous groups and the obstacles to Indigenous groups imposed by centuries of oppression are central to Indigenous approaches in science. Two of the most important concepts that are seen repeatedly in literature on Indigenous research are that of identity and representation. These two issues are often seen in relation to each other as Indigenous communities continue to define their identities and maintain control over how those identities are represented to the public.

Since the beginning of European colonization, many Native communities have suffered the perceptions of Western researchers. Indigenous peoples were assigned the station of Other and were represented as insignificant and unable to be civilized (Smith 1999, 25). This notion is epitomized in the story of the Moundbuilders. Early researchers found it impossible to believe that Native Americans were capable of building the extravagant mound complexes found throughout the country. Often the mounds were explained as evidence of aliens or other supernatural powers. As a result, Indigenous groups were essentially dehumanized since they were seen as incapable of participating in any sort of civilized behavior (Watkins 2004, 62). For Euro-Americans, this justified enactment of policies that sought to eradicate Native cultures and to assimilate their people (i.e., Indian boarding schools) (Smith 1999, 26). Eventually, archaeological investigations at the mound sites showed that Native groups did actually create them (Meltzer 1983). Other marginalized groups, such as women, have dealt with similar issues as they have historically been denied certain rights and represented as subordinate beings.

Jayati Lal (1996) discusses the politics of identity and the Other as she experienced it through her research, which was framed in a feminist perspective. Feminist and Indigenous academics have sought to eradicate this issue of the Other by delineating a perspective specific to the marginalized group—the feminist standpoint and the Indigenous voice (Johnson and Murton 2007; Lal 1996). The feminist standpoint can be interpreted as representing any subordinated group and the Native voice represents the unique and Indigenous identity of the community.

Identity, as many social scientists view it, is known as "a reflexive construct or experiential modality through which one knows oneself and claims recognition" (Leve 2011, 513). Indigenous peoples around the globe have been working to revitalize traditional Native identities by laying claim to foundational elements such as their lands, histories, and cosmologies (Alfred and Corntassel 2005). Of particular importance is the spiritual relationship with nature that most Indigenous cultures hold. Gregory Cajete (2000) describes this relationship with the natural world as "ensoulment" since the earth is known as a living soul. Indigenous developments are typically founded on this spiritual relationship with the landscape and result in Indigenous approaches to research that are founded on an ecological mindset that emphasizes a spiritual relationship with the landscape (Cajete 2000, 187).

Issues of identity are also important to decolonization efforts since the designation and manipulation of social identities was integral to colonial rule (Leve 2011). In fields such as anthropology and geography, where investigations concerning the histories, epistemologies, material cultures, traditional cultural properties, and land rites of Indigenous communities are frequent, the acknowledgment and consideration of the perspective informed by Native identity is essential for the growth of the disciplines (Atalay 2006; Johnson and Murton 2007). Cross-disciplinary approaches to Indigenous research have many similarities, but there are several distinct features for each field.

Governmentality, Social Capital, and Multivocality

Given the last several hundred years of conflict between the federal government and tribal organizations, and given the ideological conflict surrounding current handling of heritage resources, it is tempting to reduce the current problem to two-sided debate, in which one group appears to dominate another. However, reducing the debate to a binary opposition is not productive, because it does not adequately frame the origins of the discourses surrounding the debate. It will be more illuminating to explore these issues and potential solutions using a different set of theoretical approaches.

For example, the very nature of power and truth is a relevant debate. While Marxists focused on agency and intentionally exerted power, postmodern theorists like Michel Foucault explored less intentional forms of power that are pervasive throughout society and may go unnoticed. He critiqued notions of absolute truth, suggesting that discourses accompanying different institutions might produce different kinds of knowledge (Foucault 1980a). Instead, there have been different kinds of knowledge accompanying different institutions, and there has "probably been an ideology of education, and ideology of the monarchy, an ideology of parliamentary democracy etc." (Foucault 1980b, 102). So whether something is true or false is perhaps less illuminating than how exactly that particular knowledge or discourse was produced, by whom it was produced, and the effects of power that accompany it.

Thus, this volume explores how knowledge about effective consultation is perhaps an ideological production of federal legislation, which generates an imbalance in power relations between the state and its subjects (in this case, tribes). This is likely accomplished through a process that Foucault describes as governmentality, a disciplinary power accomplished through governmental policies, laws, instruments, and apparatuses of economic and legislative management (Foucault 2007). This concept has only recently been applied to critiques of cultural resource management (CRM) and heritage legislation in the United

States (e.g., the Native American Graves Protection and Repatriation Act [NAGRPA]), but there is tremendous potential for using this concept to deconstruct conflicting discourses around heritage (Palus et al. 2006; Smith 2000, 2001, 2004; Smith and Campbell 1998).

In this volume, we use the concept of governmentality to mean, not just power through federal government, but also related codes, policies, institutions, and practices within state organizations (e.g., State Historic Preservation Offices [SHPOs], the Nevada Indian Commission), tribal organizations (tribal councils, THPOs), academic institutions, professional archaeological organizations (see below), and the like. However, we see the federal heritage legislation and federal agencies as the most influential apparatus that controls most of the formalized heritage discourses in the United States today.

There is potential to bridge this impasse in communication by creating a model of policy that recognizes human agency in the process of heritage consultation and the subsequent power relations emerging in different contexts. Individuals negotiate different forms of power within a social field, described as "a social arena within which struggles or maneuvers take place over specific resources or stakes and access to them" (Jenkins 1992, 84). Within those interactions, people strategize how to accrue several forms of capital, including "economic capital, social capital (various kinds of valued relations with significant others), cultural capital (primarily legitimate knowledge of one kind or another) and symbolic capital (prestige and social honor)" (Jenkins 1992, 95).

Most important to this study is social capital, which can be gained by having meaningful social relationships with people within and outside of one's own social networks. According to sociologist Daniel Brisson (2009, 168), some social capital promotes bonding within the community, while bridging capital crosses into extracommunity relationships. Some forms of capital are formally developed through organizations, while others are informal. This is similar to the different types of social capital available in accessible, open versus less accessible, closed networks. Furthermore, some kinds of social capital are useful for "getting by," and others can be used for "getting ahead" (Brisson 2009, 168; see also Briggs 1998). This project examines (relatively closed) social networks and discourses that are a part of heritage consultation, and construct a model for heritage consultation that creates opportunities for social capital that can be used for more effective communication.

There is also great variability in how communication operates and how narratives are constructed by various stakeholders. Key to understanding this is the concept of multivocality, which generally indicates parallel discourses or different narrative understandings. It is related to Derrida's (1978) concept of decentering in open systems of communication, which allows participants to explore a number of parallel discursive paths (Cowie et al. 2009, 5–6). Multivocality has become an important part of archaeological practice, particularly with an increased use of reflexive methods and acknowledgment of alternative histories (Barkan and Bush 2002; Dongoske et al. 2000; Dowdall and Parrish 2003, 100; Hodder 1999, 160; Shackel and Chambers 2004; Shanks and Tilley 1987, 245; Watkins 2000, 2002). Multivocality is particularly relevant for CRM and federally mandated archaeology where the past is debated and projects can be controversial (e.g., McDavid 2002; Zimmerman 1995). Archaeologists and Native stakeholders increasingly recognize the need to decolonize archaeological practice through collaborative research. Often, participants in multivocal, collaborative projects find important linkages between places, memories of places, and the stories and wisdom that these places embody; studying these linkages humanizes the past and present people on the landscape (see Basso 1996; Ferguson and Colwell-Chanthaphonh 2006). Likewise, the ultimate goal of this project is to humanize the consultation process by recognizing the importance of tribal agency and social capital within federally governmentalized discourse.

Cross-Cultural Perspectives: Ontological, Epistemological, and Ethical Issues

This section intends to provide a philosophical perspective on the question: Why are archaeological practices so highly controversial for some Indigenous communities? The discipline needs to reevaluate past and current practices to broaden the knowledge that is generated by archaeological endeavors. Because Western culture dominates mainstream society in many of the colonized regions of the world, it is the ontological and epistemological beliefs of Western culture that usually prevail over the knowledge bases of the colonized. Looking at the issue of conflict from a philosophical approach should provide a leveled playing field so to speak by identifying how and why such conflicts have developed and continue to exist, without discussing, at least initially, the specific aspects of any particular problem previously or currently existing between cultural groups.

The primary discussion here relates to the first of two central hypotheses that are primary factors affecting most, if not all, relationships among stakeholders. Specifically, that much of the conflict that waxes and wanes in varying degrees between archaeological and Indigenous communities is rooted in differences in worldviews between the cultural groups. It is argued here that the conflict begins with ontological and epistemological differences, and continues with debate over whose knowledge system is correct and right. Because of the existing sociopolitical power differential between mainstream American culture and the Indigenous communities involved in these debates, the result of many debates has been the silencing of the Indigenous communities, with mainstream archaeological methodology and practice prevailing.

The goal is to level the playing field by discussing, in a purely philosophical sense, how the ontological and epistemological assertion of all human cultures is rooted in human perception, and therefore fallible and incomplete. A further goal is to argue that although humanity may never have a truly complete picture of what exists beyond our ability to perceive, we can achieve a much broader picture of what can be known through inclusive discussion between all observers.

Archaeological theory and practice need inclusivity of Indigenous communities' perspectives to achieve a more complete picture of the past. Indigenous communities have major concerns about past and current archaeological practice, and they have a relatively limited voice in the archaeological realm. There is a clear need for increased communication and collaboration between archaeologists and Indigenous communities about how archaeology can become more inclusive of cross-cultural ethical concerns and standards, and more ethically sound as a national and international mode of knowledge creation.

In Western philosophy, ontology concerns "what exists," epistemology concerns "how we know it," knowledge concerns "what is known," and ethics concern "what is right and just." Although the terms for such concepts vary cross-culturally, the concepts themselves appear to be universal across all known human cultures. However, different cultures have differing beliefs related to each topic, and those beliefs can and do have major effects on the relationships cultures have with one another.

Western philosophy is foundational to Western knowledge, and thus a foundation of all disciplines within North American universities. Within Western philosophy, ontology is a theory of being, used to describe the intelligible and visible world, including such things as forms, concepts, objects, and images (Palmer 1988, 64). It would seem at first glance that it would be easy to agree upon what exists as an object or image, in form and concept, but this is not the case. A long history of debate within Western philosophy continues as to what is really real, and whether the really real exists, if knowledge of it is attainable by humans, and if so how.

Plato asserted that an objective reality exists beyond the reaches of human perception, and that in order to attain knowledge of it, humans needed to identify what was knowledge based on human perception, in order to move beyond such knowledge to the really real. Since at least the time of Plato, a search for what is real and how we can access knowledge of it has been underway in Western society. A sweeping change in Western philosophical thought occurred during the Enlightenment. During the Enlightenment, or Age of Reason, Western philosophers began to widely question the existence of God as the creator of what exists. The effort to identify a full-proof reasoned argument proving God's existence, and therefore the existence of all else, was undertaken by numerous philosophers, including René Descartes and John Locke. Such efforts resulted in the inability of Descartes to show God exists irrefutably, and Locke concluding that the existence of God could not be proven. Without the ability to show there was a God who had created the really real, the role individual perception had in the accumulation of knowledge lingered as an unanswered question. Despite the myriad of unanswered philosophical questions raised during the Enlightenment, faith in the emerging practices of Western science and scientific objectivity prevailed. It was not until the early twentieth century that the question of the really real was again taken up in major fashion by Western philosophers.

As anthropological studies of the last centuries have affirmed, perceptions of reality cross-culturally differ greatly. From this, it can be assumed that culture plays a large role in determining how reality is defined, and therefore problems can and do arise when the lines differentiating forms, objects, concepts, and images are not alike cross-culturally. In addition to issues of what exists, there is also a difference cross-culturally in how knowledge of what exists is derived. The Western philosophical term for how we know what we know is epistemology.

In Western philosophy, epistemology concerns a theory of knowledge and is categorized in the following way: conjecture and belief fall within opinion, while knowledge is derived from understanding and pure reason (Palmer 1988, 64). Epistemological questions go hand-in-hand with ontological debate, but in Western culture the development of Western science and the scientific method became the litmus test for all knowledge creation. However, the reality of anthropological study has shown again and again that knowledge creation, and what is considered to be knowledge, varies between cultures.

Ethics and morality each play major roles in this philosophical soup. The existence of and adherence to cultural beliefs is dependent upon the belief of the practitioners of the culture that there is a moral imperative to behave in specific ways. In order for the practice of colonization to be justified, the colonizing culture must be able to justify their actions. When trying to show that the culture one belongs to is moral, yet needing to rationalize how and why it is morally okay to take primary resources from others, and perhaps even to use others for one's cultures own gain, it is crucial to rationalize why one's own culture is superior and therefore morally right in controlling or otherwise taking from or destroying other cultures.

Taking a position on what exists, whether we can know it, and who is capable of knowing it is critical to finding an inclusive ethical approach to and for the discipline of archaeology. The search for an ethics of archaeological collaboration proceeds on the assumption that there is no way to know whether anything beyond perception exists in any other way beyond the way we experience it. That our ability to experience things continues to increase as a result of technology, that all experience leading to knowledge is subjective, and that whatever good humankind hopes to achieve must be a good for humanity, and does not allow undue harm as a means to an end; even if good is that end. With those prerequisite understandings of the standpoint from which we proceed, we can now consider what a more inclusive approach to archaeology might look like.

Inclusion of Indigenous Ontological, Epistemological, and Ethical Viewpoints

It is important to note that the problem of the silencing of Indigenous voices is not specific to archaeology, or anthropology for that matter. The inclusion of Indigenous voices in all aspects of archaeology, and especially within the discussion of ontological, epistemological, and ethical cross-cultural difference, is a focus of this archaeological project. In the last decades, others have worked to bring to light the problems associated with a lack of inclusion of Indigenous voices in academia and federal discourses. Instances of the move for greater inclusion of the voice of the Other within academia writ large are emerging. For instance, there have been ongoing efforts to included Indigenous perspectives in educational pedagogical models. Of this transition from what is to what could be, Maenette Kape'ahiokalani Padeken Ah Nee-Benham and Joanne Elizabeth Cooper (2000) published an edited volume that chronicles the discussions and work of Indigenous peoples from around the world. This work group concluded within their first discussions of transition toward a more inclusive educational system that Natives don't have a "legitimate voice in the arena of pedagogy, so what is true for our people is not included in the larger picture" (Wetere-Bryant 2000, 26). At the conclusion of these early discussions, the group concluded that for education:

> This highly charged discussion clearly identified the need for Native leaders to define an epistemology that will emerge from Native ways of thinking in regard to time, space, relationships (as bound to nature), and orality as central to learning and knowing. In addition, a Native framework such as this must counter dominant educational models that have subjugated the Native as an outsider. (Ah Nee-Benham and Cooper 2000, 28)

The group discussions presented by Ah Nee-Benham and Cooper highlight the fact that Indigenous peoples continue to be forced to participate in ways of knowing the world that are often very foreign from their own cultures' perspectives.

Of Western academic research practices and theories in general, Linda Tuhiwai Smith argues that a combination of factors continue to control the degree to which Indigenous knowledge systems are incorporated into mainstream education. She highlights Foucault's assertion that Western civilization is a conglomeration of cultural histories and knowledge traditions that have evolved together in such a way that provides a process for developing new knowledge, as well as perpetuating and/or affirming old knowledge beliefs within that system (Tuhiwai Smith 2002, 44). Because of this system's ability to draw from a knowledge archive to explain new things, it does not need input from other knowledge systems in order to explain previously unencountered situations. Furthermore, Tuhiwai Smith (2002, 39) asserts that Western research has traditionally been a method of objectification and dehumanization of Indigenous peoples and therefore without decolonization, a very problematic endeavor. Tuhiwai Smith (2002, 129) points out that access to participation in Western research, as a researcher, is achieved through the Western research university. She (2002, 129) states:

> Research is a distinguishing characteristic of universities. Universities are committed to the creation of knowledge through research, reflection, scholarship, and academic freedom. It is a role, historians of the university have argued, which has been hard won over centuries of development. The curriculum of a university shapes the way knowledge is reproduced as a curriculum for schools and society. Intellectuals provide leadership for society in relation to knowledge. For indigenous peoples universities are regarded as rather elite institutions which reproduce themselves through various systems of privileged. Even those universities which are state-funded are considered major bastions of Western elitism. It is not surprising, then, that many indigenous students find little space for indigenous perspectives in most academic disciplines and most research approaches.

Following Tuhiwai Smith's discussion, there are multiple reasons why the current academic system is unaccommodating to moves toward greater inclusion of Indigenous perspectives in academic research.

One of the reasons this lack of inclusion is so particularly distressing within anthropology is that the proponents and practitioners of anthropology, until fairly recently, have held it as being the objective process for identifying and discussing humankind and its cultures. The primary problem with this assertion is that the story of humankind and its cultures has been predominantly told by people representing a very narrow sociocultural position, who although for the most part sincere in their efforts, cannot begin to conceive of the totality of positions that need to be considered without the input of the cultural groups who hold those varying positions.

Perhaps one of the problems is that non-Indigenous peoples participating in dialogue focused on the inclusion of Indigenous voices must understand that they do not hold all of the keys to having effective discussion. Diane L. Teeman, lead author of this chapter who is an archaeologist and an enrolled tribal member, has personally had the frustrating experience of trying to introduce a perspective that falls outside of commonly accepted anthropological norms, only to find her words fall to the floor in silence. The fact that no one engaged in discussion of those ideas at the time seemed offensive, but perhaps it was more often the case that no one had the experience of seriously engaging in discussion of ideas that were outside of the discipline's norm, and therefore did not know how to respond.

The idea that Knowledge with a capital "K" can be achieved by any individual and/or culture is philosophically problematic (Descartes [1641] 1996; Locke [1689] 1961; Kant [1770] 1977; Hume [1748] 1961; Russell [1912] 1997; Dewey [1925] 1988; Gettier [1963] 1988; Foucault 1976). A major area of philosophical dialogue concerns itself with the debate over whether knowledge is independent of the "knower," or is the "knower" responsible for the creation of "knowledge"? Certainly, the enormity of this philosophical problem is easily observed when tracing the evolution of knowledge of a specific culture through time, or when performing cross-cultural comparisons of contemporaneous cultures.

So, how do we improve the situation? Zimmerman (2000, 302) argues that archaeology must change to be inclusive of Native American epistemologies. Likewise, Smith (1999, 39) argues that all academic theory must be "decolonized":

> One of the problems . . . is that the methodologies and methods of research, the theories that inform them, the questions which they generate and the writing styles they employ, all become significant acts which need to be considered carefully and critically before being applied. In other words they need to be decolonized. Decolonization, however, does not mean and has not meant a total rejection of all theory or research or Western knowledge. Rather, it is about centering our concerns and world views and then coming to know and understand theory and research from our own perspectives and for our own purposes.

Mihesuah (1998, 1) discusses the importance of including Native scholars' voices in academic research, arguing that much of what is advertised and accepted as Native American history continues to be Native American history as interpreted by non-Natives.

Anthropology has created a narrative of Indigenous peoples' identities for the modern world (Gero and Root 1990, 19). Archaeology continues to create a narrative of Indigenous peoples' histories. For various reasons, Indigenous voices have been silenced and/or largely silent in archaeological dialogue, leaving many archaeological narratives absent of worldviews other than those of the majority culture. We argue that it is essential for archaeology to be inclusive of Indigenous epistemologies, because knowledge, and therefore reality, is derived from cultures' epistemological systems, and without Indigenous knowledge, Western anthropologists and anthropology will continue to represent only the reality and narratives of the dominant society from which it emerged.

From these discussions among Indigenous scholars, it is easy to see that tensions remain in the questions of Indigenous representation in academia generally, and archaeology specifically. Mainstream archaeology is a mechanism of the Western epistemological system, but how can we increase the relevance of archaeology for Indigenous peoples? White Deer (1997, 43) states:

> Most importantly, a new paradigm needs to be developed, one that includes a sense of both the sacred and the secular. Increasingly, the use of Native American traditional practices in conjunction with traditional scientific approaches is widening the scope of the work as presently conceived, and it appears that a form of holistic archaeology is beginning to emerge.

If we are successful in increasing representation of both Indigenous peoples and Indigenous theories and methods in archaeology, we will greatly increase the robustness of the knowledge claims that archaeologists make, improve the reputation of archaeologists among Indigenous peoples, and increase the ability of archaeologists to build strong working relationships with Indigenous communities. Echo Hawk (1997, 101) calls this move toward greater inclusiveness "the end of conquest archaeology."

Perhaps some "traditional" archaeologists find it easy to dismiss Indigenous epistemological claims and will dismiss claims that inclusion of Indigenous voices is essential to the survival of anthropology. Philosophically, however, there is no known way of proving that any culture's knowledge system is any more advanced, modern, or valid, than that of any other. All cultures have anthropology, the study of humans, but because academic anthropology is derived from Western culture, the epistemological system working within it is largely Western European. The problem inherent to the current hegemonic situation brings to mind the parable of "The Blind Men and the Elephant," where each man feels a different part of the elephant and therefore has a different perspective on it.

> Then they began to quarrel, shouting, "Yes it is!" "No, it is not!" "An elephant is not that!" "Yes, it's like that!" and so on, till they came to blows over the matter. . . . For, quarreling, each to his view they cling. Such folk see only one side of a thing." (Udana 68–69)

Relativists may argue that the elephant doesn't exist, or that the elephant transforms its shape through time, or that a herd of elephants exist causing each culture to have knowledge of their own unique pachyderm. But if any of these things are true, then all viewpoints are relevant to the "big picture" of archaeological discourse. If you are an absolutist, you must admit that observing every part and angle of the elephant will only assist in finding and verifying "the Truth." Either way, moving toward greater representation of Indigenous peoples' epistemologies is beneficial to the pursuit of a capital "K" Knowledge.

If it is possible to agree that no one culture—despite how "advanced" their own way of knowing the world is claimed to be—is capable of attaining absolute knowledge, then it can be concluded that the most exhaustive effort to attain complete knowledge must be inclusive of as many perspectives as are available.

Given this assertion, it stands to reason that we must work to come to some level of cross-cultural understanding and agreement that it is in the best interest of all humanity to provide an opportunity for all cultures to be heard on issues of the creation of knowledge. If we can agree to this, it then becomes important to broaden the scope of considerations when determining what is moral and ethical in any given circumstance. Nowhere is this more true than when looking at how one culture will treat another culture, or how it will be agreed upon that knowledge of one culture will be developed by another culture.

Ethical Approaches and Collaboration in Archaeology

The subject of ethics is as multifaceted within archaeology as it is in any other discipline. But, most discussions focusing on ethics within archaeology have traditionally focused on how archaeologists will perform their research; consideration of preserving the archaeological record, as well as responsibility to other archaeologists and anthropologists. Widespread in-depth discussion within archaeology focusing upon ethical consideration of, and responsibility to, Indigenous communities is one that continues to grow as people become aware of issues that were previously rarely considered (see Atalay 2012; Colwell-Chanthaphonh and Ferguson 2008)

In the following section, we first discuss the similarities and differences of the current (as of 2018) codes of ethics in use by professional North American archaeological associations and those of the World Archaeological Congress. Following, we provide discussion of the debate that continues to rage among North American archaeologists in terms of where our allegiances as professional archaeologists should lay, and to whom and what we should feel an ethical responsibility. From our reflections of the experiences of professional archaeologists working in North America today, it is our intention to prepare readers who may also be training for careers in archaeology for what they might also experience at one or more points in the course of their careers. We close with discussion of the broader factors that have affected the development and current composition of codes of ethics, as well as provide discussion of the potential ramifications of failing to be more proactive with regard to ensuring archaeologists continue the dialogue of what "ought" be our ethical responsibilities to not only the "archaeological record," but also the descendants of the people who created the material record of the past.

Professional Archaeological Associations' Codes of Ethics

There are numerous professional archaeological and anthropological associations active in North America and each has a specific code of ethics. These organizations include the Society of American Archaeologists (SAA), American Anthropological Association (AAA), and the Register of Professional Archaeologists (RPA). Additionally, a growing worldwide archaeological organization, the World Archaeological Congress (WAC), is gaining popularity among North American archaeologists.

Joining these organizations is not compulsory, and they are relatively cost prohibitive for those not holding permanent employment. Additionally, although these organizations have ethics guidelines, there is no well-developed way to ensure that members adhere to the group's standards.

An additional issue relates to the mission statements of national and international archaeological organizations. In order to present one's research to other professionals at a gathering sponsored by an individual society or organization, one must become a member. As part of membership, individuals must attest that they agree with the mission statement of the particular organization. This alone can create an ethical dilemma for some. For instance, numerous personal conversations with Indigenous archaeologists who have joined the SAA suggest that although the majority of Indigenous archaeologists feel the Indigenous communities are at least as important, if not more so, than the "archaeological record," they are required to assert their support of the SAA's mission statement, which prioritizes the "archaeological record" as the most important consideration. One way that individuals within the SAA are mediating their ethical differences from within the organization is participation in and/or support of the SAA's Ethics Bowl. The Ethics Bowl has been held annually since 2004, and brings together graduate students, invited professorial judges, and conference participants to debate the particulars of specific cases.

There is no requirement that makes individuals practicing archaeology join the professional organizations discussed above. Because of this, there is no way to force individuals to adhere to specific ethical principles. Furthermore, a wide diversity of ethical concerns exists among and between Indigenous communities, so it would be difficult if not impossible to find a set of guiding ethical principles that encompassed all of those concerns.

Conclusion: Including Indigenous Philosophies

Little discussion of Indigenous North American philosophies is available from the perspectives of those cultures, but Western philosophers and/or researchers who have used Western philosophical terms and categories to describe Indigenous North American cultures have commonly described such cultures' philosophical approach to the world as empirical and/or pragmatic. One of the difficulties in researching the topic of Indigenous philosophies is the fact that unlike Western society, Indigenous philosophical perspectives are intertwined with other aspects of those specific cultures practices. The philosophy of a culture is actualized in performance, and not set aside as abstract discussion of philosophical thought.

Thus, it is important to consider Indigenous philosophies during the actual practice of collaborative archaeology, particularly by involving Indigenous peoples in all stages of work.

Works Cited

Ah Nee-Benham, Maenette Kape'ahiokalani Padeken, and Joanne Elizabeth Cooper, eds. 2000. *Indigenous Educational Models for Contemporary Practice: In Our Mother's Voice*. New York: Routledge.

Alfred, Taiaiake, and Jeff Corntassel. 2005. "Being Indigenous: Resurgences against Contemporary Colonialism." *Government and Opposition* 40, no. 4: 597–614.

Atalay, Sonya. 2006. "Indigenous Archaeology as Decolonizing Practice." *The American Indian Quarterly* 30, nos. 3 and 4: 280–310.

———. 2012. *Community-Based Archaeology: Research with, by and for Indigenous and Local Communities*. Berkeley: University of California Press.

Barkan, Elazar, and Ronald Bush, eds. 2002. *Claiming the Stones/Naming the Bones: Cultural Property and the Negotiation of National and Ethnic Identity*. Los Angeles: Getty Research Institute.

Basso, Keith H. 1996. *Wisdom Sits in Places*. Albuquerque: University of New Mexico Press.

Briggs, X. D. 1998. "Brown Kids in White Suburbs: Housing Mobility and the Many Faces of Social Capital." *Housing Policy Debate* 9, no. 1: 177–221.

Brisson, Daniel. 2009. "Testing the Relationship of Formal Bonding, Informal Bonding, and Formal Bridging Social Capital on Key Outcomes for Families in Low-Income Neighborhoods." *Journal of Sociology and Social Welfare* 36, no. 1: 167–83.

Bruchac, Margaret M. 2014. "Decolonization in Archaeological Theory." In *Encyclopedia of Global Archaeology*, edited by Claire Smith, 2069–77. New York: Springer.

Cajete, Gregory. 2000. *Native Science: Natural Laws of Interdependence*. Sante Fe, NM: Clear Light.

Colwell-Chanthaphonh, Chip, and T. J. Ferguson, eds. 2008. *Collaboration in Archaeological Practice: Engaging Descendant Communities*. Walnut Creek, CA: AltaMira Press.

Cowie, Sarah E., Christopher C. LeBlanc, Mary M. Farrell, and Nicholas C. Laluk. 2009. "Multivocality in the Forest: A New Approach to Tribal Relations on the Coronado National Forest, Arizona." *Arizona Anthropologist* 19: 1–16.

Derrida, Jacques. 1978. "Structure, Sign, and Play in the Discourse of the Human Sciences." In *Writing and Difference*, translated by Alan Bass, 278–93. Chicago: University of Chicago Press.

Descartes, René. (1641) 1996. *Meditations on First Philosophy*. Translated by John Cottingham. New York: Penguin Books.

Dewey, John. (1925) 1988. *Experience and Nature*. Edited by Jo Ann Boydston. Carbondale, IL: Southern Illinois University Press.

Dongoske, Kurt E., Mark Aldenderfer, and Karen Doehner. 2000. *Working Together: Native Americans and Archaeologists*. Washington, DC: Society for American Archaeology.

Dowdall, Katherine M., and Otis O. Parrish. 2003. "A Meaningful Disturbance of the Earth." *Journal of Social Archaeology* 3, no. 1: 99–133.

Echo-Hawk, Roger. 1997. “Forging a New Ancient History for Native History for Native America.” In *Native Americans and Archaeologists: Stepping Stones to Common Ground*, edited by Nina Swidler, Kurt E. Dongoske, Roger Anyon, and Alan S. Downer, 88–102. Walnut Creek, CA: AltaMira Press.

Ferguson, T. J., and Chip Colwell-Chanthaphonh. 2006. *History Is in the Land: Multivocal Traditions in Arizona's San Pedro Valley*. Tucson, AZ: University of Arizona Press.

Foucault, Michel. 1976. *The Archaeology of Knowledge*. New York: Harper and Row.

———. 1980a. “Truth and Power.” In *Power/Knowledge: Selected Interviews and Other Writings 1972–1977*, edited by Colin Gordon, 109–33. New York: Pantheon Books.

———. 1980b. “Two Lectures.” In *Power/Knowledge: Selected Interviews and Other Writings 1972–1977*. Edited by Colin Gordon, 78–108. New York: Pantheon Books.

———. 2007. *Security, Territory, Population: Lectures at the College de France, 1977–1978*, edited by Michel Senellart. New York: Palgrave Macmillan.

Gero, Joan, and Delores Root. 1990. “Public Presentations and Private Concerns: Archaeology and the Pages of the *National Geographic*.” In *The Politics of the Past*, edited by Peter Gathercole and David Lowenthal, 19–37. Boston: Unwin Hyman.

Gettier, Edmund. (1963) 1988. *Philosophical Analysis: A Defense by Example*. Edited by David F. Austin. Dordrecht, Netherlands: Kluwer Academic Publishers.

Hodder, Ian. 1999. *The Archaeological Process: An Introduction*. Oxford: Blackwell.

Hume, David. (1748) 1961. “An Enquiry Concerning Human Understanding.” In *The Empiricists*, 307–430. New York: Anchor Books.

Johnson, Jay T., and Brian Murton. 2007. “Re/placing Native Science: Indigenous Voices in Contemporary Constructions of Nature.” *Geographical Research* 45, no. 2: 121–29.

Kant, Immanuel. (1770) 1977. “Prologomena to Any Future Metaphysics.” In *Classics of Western Philosophy*, edited by Steven Cahn, 849–924. Indianapolis, IN: Hackett Publishing Co.

Lal, Jayati. 1996. “Situating Locations: The Politics of Self, Identity, and ‘Other’ in Living and Writing the Text.” In *Feminist Dilemmas in Fieldwork*, edited by Diane L. Wolf, 185–210. Boulder, CO: Westview Press, Inc.

Lassiter, Luke Eric. 2005. *The Chicago Guide to Collaborative Ethnography*. Chicago: The University of Chicago Press.

Leve, Lauren. 2011. “Identity.” *Current Anthropology* 52, no. 4: 513–35.

Lightfoot, Kent G. 2008. “Collaborative Research Programs: Implications for the Practice of North American Archaeology.” In *Collaborating at the Trowel's Edge: Teaching and Learning in Indigenous Archaeology*, edited by Stephen W. Silliman, 211–27. Tuscon, AZ: University of Arizona Press.

Locke, John. (1689) 1961. “Essay Concerning Human Understanding,” abridged by Richard Taylor. In *The Empiricists*, 7–134. New York: Anchor Books.

McDavid, Carol. 2002. “Archaeologies That Hurt; Descendants That Matter: A

Pragmatic Approach to Collaboration in the Public Interpretation of African-American Archaeology." *World Archaeology* 34, no. 2: 303–14.

Meltzer, David J. 1983. "The Antiquity of Man and the Development of American Archaeology." In *Advances in Archaeological Method and Theory*, Vol. 6, edited by Michael B. Schiffer, 1–51. New York: Academic Press.

Mihesuah, Devon A. 1998. *Natives and Academics: Researching and Writing about American Indians.* Lincoln, NE: University of Nebraska Press.

Nicholas, George P. 2008a. "Native Peoples and Archaeology." *Encyclopedia of Archaeology* 3: 1660–1669.

———. 2008b. "Melding Science and Community Values: Indigenous Archaeology Programs and the Negotiation of Cultural Differences." In *Collaborating at the Trowel's Edge: Teaching and Learning in Indigenous Archaeology*, edited by Stephen W. Silliman, 228–248. Tucson, AZ: University of Arizona Press.

Palmer, Donald. 1988. *Looking at Philosophy: The Unbearable Heaviness of Philosophy Made Lighter.* Mountain View, CA: Mayfield Publishing Company.

Palus, Matthew M., Mark P. Leone, and Matthew D. Cochran. 2006. "Critical Archaeology: Politics Past and Present." In *Historical Archaeology*, edited by Martin Hall and Stephen W. Silliman, 84–104. Malden, MA: Blackwell Publishing.

Russell, Bertrand. (1912) 1997. *The Problems of Philosophy.* New York: Oxford University Press.

Shackel, Paul A., and Erve J. Chambers. 2004. *Places in Mind: Public Archaeology as Applied Anthropology.* New York: Routledge.

Shanks, Michael, and Christopher Tilley. 1987. *Reconstructing Archaeology: Theory and Practice.* Cambridge: Cambridge University Press.

Silliman, Stephen W., ed. 2008. *Collaborating at the Trowel's Edge: Teaching and Learning in Indigenous Archaeology.* Tucson, AZ: University of Arizona Press.

Smith, Laurajane. 2000. "'Doing Archaeology': Cultural Heritage Management and Its Role in Identifying the Link between Archaeological Practice and Theory." *International Journal of Heritage Studies* 6, no. 4: 309–16.

———. 2001. "Archaeology and the Governance of Material Culture: A Case Study from Southeastern Australia." *Norwegian Archaeological Review* 34, no. 2: 97–105.

———. 2004. *Archaeological Theory and the Politics of Cultural Heritage.* London: Routledge.

Smith, Laurajane, and Gary Campbell. 1998. "Governing Material Culture." In *Governing Australia: Studies in Contemporary Rationalities of Government*, edited by Mitchell Dean and Barry Hindess, 173–91. Cambridge: Cambridge University Press.

Smith, Linda Tuhiwai. 1999. *Decolonizing Methodologies: Research and Indigenous Peoples.* London: Zed Books Ltd.

Watkins, Joe E. 2000. *Indigenous Archaeology: American Indian Values and Scientific Practice.* Walnut Creek, CA: Altamira Press.

———. 2002. "Writing Unwritten History: An Archaeologist and American Indian Walks the Tightrope of a Double Life." *Archaeology Magazine* 52, no. 6: 36–42.

———. 2004. "Becoming American or Becoming Indian?: NAGPRA, Kennewick and Cultural Affiliation." *Journal of Social Archaeology* 4, no. 1: 60–80.

White Deer, G. 1997. "Return of the Sacred: Spirituality and the Scientific Imperative." In *Native Americans and Archaeologists: Stepping Stones to Common Ground*, edited by Nina Swidler, Kurt E. Dongoske, Roger Anyon, and Alan S. Downer, 37–43. Walnut Creek, CA: AltaMira Press.

Wobst, H. Martin 2010. "Power to the (Indigenous) Past and Present! Or: The Theory and Method Behind Archaeology Theory and Method." In *Indigenous Archaeologies: A Reader on Decolonization*, edited by Margaret M. Bruchac, Siobhan Hart, and H. Martin Wobst, 76–78. Walnut Creek, CA: Left Coast Press.

Zimmerman, Larry J. 1995. "We Do Not Need Your Past: Archaeological Chronology and 'Indian Time' on the Plains." In *Beyond Subsistence: Plains Archaeology and the Post-Processual Critique*, edited by Philip Duke and Michael C. Wilson, 28–45. Tuscaloosa, AL: University of Alabama Press.

CHAPTER 3

Consensus in Research Design, and Studying Institutions, Education, and Childhood

Ashley M. Long, Sarah E. Cowie,
and Christopher C. LeBlanc

This chapter outlines how this project came about, how the site was chosen, and how we attempted to incorporate elements of collaborative and Indigenous archaeologies to better understand conflicting discourses in heritage research and preservation. Here we also discuss previous research at Stewart Indian School and broader comparative studies relevant to Indian boarding schools, the archaeology of institutional life, and the archaeology of childhood.

Why Conduct Archaeology at Stewart Indian School?

Archaeologists at University of Nevada, Reno (UNR) did not plan on excavating this site at the beginning of this project, and in fact had not even begun to consider possible locations. The project began with a three-year grant from the Army Research Office intended to outline a strategy for humanizing the process of respectful heritage consultation between tribes and the federal government. The grant, awarded to a non-Native archaeologist at UNR, meant that substantial input from tribal members was necessary before the project even began or the site chosen. Project archaeologists reached out to professional and personal contacts in the regional tribes to ask how an archaeological project might benefit some needs and interests of the communities and who might be interested in collaborating. Eventually, a collaborative approach led us to a consensus that Stewart Indian School brought many threads together as an incredibly important place for past, present, and future generations.

Following numerous discussions and meetings with the Washoe THPO, the Nevada Indian Commission (NIC), and eventually its Stewart Advisory Committee (SAC), the location of the project at Stewart Indian School was unanimously approved by participants in 2013. Each of these organizations became formal partners on the project, alongside UNR researchers and students. One important component of the project was an archaeological field school, created to conduct responsible archaeology that is sensitive to the wishes of Native peoples; this was offered as a six-credit college course through UNR.

The Collaborative Historical Archaeology Field School at Stewart Indian School was conducted in partnership with these organizations, as well as several other Native stakeholders. Native stakeholders were primarily interested in finding the location of the original school building, a wooden two-story building that had been demolished and replaced with stone buildings, as well as the location of a pool that was filled in after it began flooding the administrative office. Stakeholders were also interested in artifacts that could eventually be displayed in a Stewart Indian School Cultural Center & Museum, which is planned for the campus. There was also a public archaeology segment of the field school as the stakeholders wished to gain media attention for the school for fundraising efforts and to educate the public about its historical significance. The school is currently listed on the National Register of Historic Places, and many hope it will eventually be recognized as a National Historical Landmark.

Stewart Indian School: Background, Description, and Significance

Today, Stewart Indian School is a beautiful campus with numerous historic buildings in Carson City, Nevada. The site is located at 5500 Snyder Avenue, three miles southeast of Carson City. The Edmonds Sports Complex and the Northern Nevada Correctional Center are both located near the site (figure 3.1). Today the campus, which is comprised of eighty-three buildings, houses various state offices including the NIC. Most of the buildings on campus are made of local stone, although there are some wooden buildings still standing. Many community members, alumni, and tourists visit the site regularly, and each year a powwow on Father's Day weekend draws large crowds who enjoy festivities, food, arts, and cultural events.

Alumni and historians offer complicated stories of the school's history. The Stewart Indian School was built in 1890 under the administration of the Bureau of Indian Affairs (BIA) and local officials. At that time, Indian boarding schools were being erected all over the country as the federal government was attempting to assimilate Native peoples (Jackson 1969; Lomawaima 1994; Thompson 2013; Woolford 2015; see chapters 4 and 5). At that time, many governing officials believed that the only way to adequately assimilate Native peoples was to strip them of their culture. Therefore, Indian boarding schools were built with the purpose of removing the culture, language, and customs of the children and replacing them with Euro-American values and beliefs. The school admitted its first class in 1890 and continued to educate Native children, although with more tolerance for Native practices in later years, until its close in 1980. This boarding school was one of the only Indian boarding schools operating in the Great Basin, the other being Fort Bidwell Indian School in California (Hendrick 1976). As the only one in Nevada, it was attended by several of the larger tribal groups such as the Washoe, Shoshone, and Paiute. Given the diverse Native communities that attended the school, this site can illuminate a variety of issues concerning institutional life at an Indian boarding school in Nevada.

Stewart Indian School was excavated as a historic-period site for this project, although there is also a precontact component. Prior to this project, there had been one archaeological project conducted on a trash dump across from the Stewart Indian School (Hattori 1978). That site was located across Snyder Avenue and was not re-excavated during this project. Most of the artifacts recovered from excavations were historical-period, although there were precontact artifacts found as well.

In the summer of 2013, archaeologists conducted a study using ground-penetrating radar (GPR) in four grids across the site in order to discover subsurface anomalies, which were used to determine the location of several excavation units. A total of thirteen one meter by one meter test units (TUs) were excavated as part of the Collaborative Historical Archaeology Field School in 2013. In addition to learning archaeological fieldwork, students participating in the field school gave tours to the public and gave interviews with the media. The field school was not limited to students and welcomed various volunteers over the course of the project.

As noted above, the Stewart Indian School is currently listed on the National Register of Historic Places. Young Native Americans from many parts of the Western United States attended the Stewart Indian School, and it continues to hold significance for many Indigenous communities today. The majority of the site, and where the field school activities were conducted, is owned and managed by the State of Nevada. Several adjacent properties are owned and managed by the Washoe Tribe of Nevada & California. Figure 3.1 shows the contemporary Stewart Facility and adjacent property ownership.

Previous Historical and Archaeological Research

The Stewart Indian School has been the subject of several other research projects, including historical accounts of life at the school, and an archaeological investigation of a dump associated with the campus.

Nicholas Jackson (1969) authored a master's thesis that provides a general history of the Stewart Indian School from 1887 until 1963. The author touches on the different tribes whose children attended the school and the types of conflicts that occurred. He also discusses the fluctuating curriculum, which changed repeatedly due to disagreements with tribes and alterations made by the federal government.

In 1978, Gene Hattori conducted an archaeological excavation of a trash dump at the Stewart Indian School. The project was completed as part of an agreement between the Carson City Department of Public Works and the Nevada State Museum. The dumpsite was located across from the Stewart campus, and around 20,400 artifacts were retrieved from the excavations. Hattori (1978, 17) found that the site was divided chronologically into two separate areas, one area with dates between 1890 and 1905 and another between 1920 and 1940. Within these two areas he found a variety of artifacts, including lithics and a wide range of historic artifacts: school items, clothing items, items for personal hygiene, glass bottles, food and drink cans, and a variety of ceramics (Hattori 1978, 21–29). Many of the artifacts found, like toothbrushes

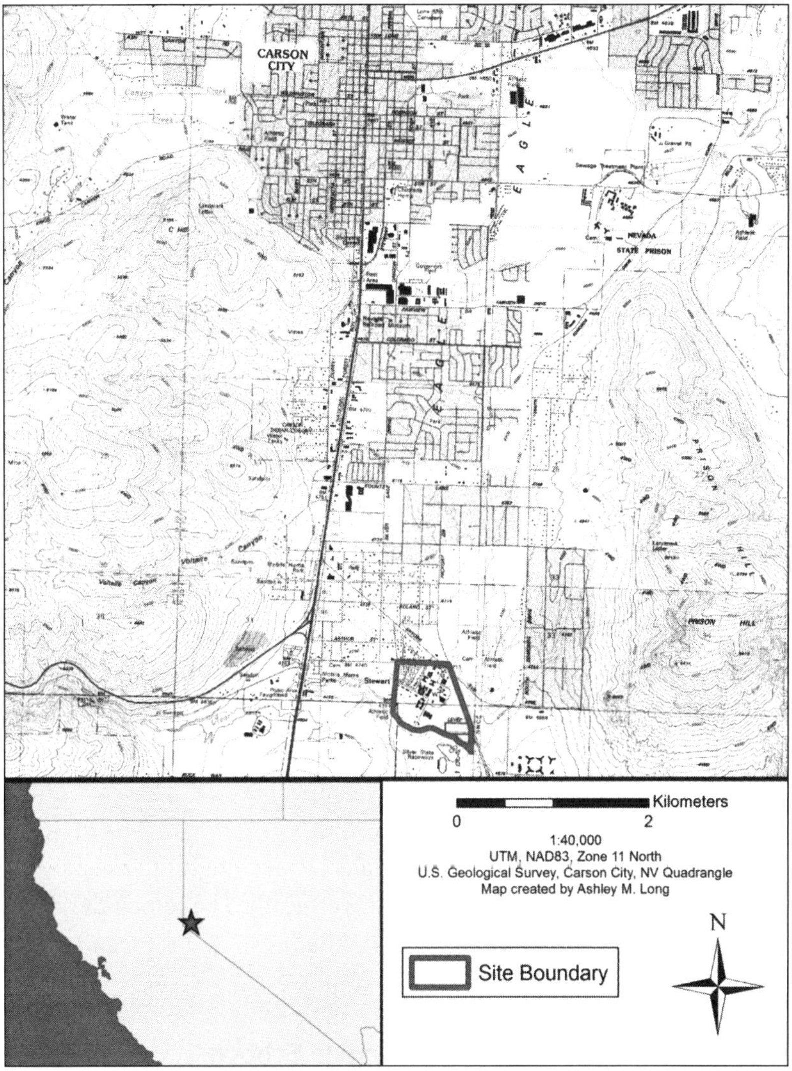

FIGURE 3.1. Project area.

and combs, had been inscribed or personalized by the students with their Christian names and dates that possibly represent the date of their arrival (Hattori 1978, 24–25). Hattori's analysis of the artifacts will be discussed more in chapter 6.

A variety of academic and planning documents have been produced in more recent decades. The Nevada Legislature (Research Division

1983) authorized a background study entitled "Status and Potential Uses of Stewart Indian School Property," and a National Register nomination synthesizes some of the most important and readily available information. A nomination is being prepared for National Landmark status. Bonnie Thompson (2013) conducted a more recent study about the school in her PhD dissertation. She approached the history from the perspective of the body, and specifically, the students' bodies and how they were transformed through the landscape, education, and extracurricular activities at Stewart Indian School (Thompson 2013; chapter 5). In addition, Jessica Hughston (2017) wrote a master's thesis with attention to how students negotiated space at the school, citing diverse sources such as sight lines, phenomenological experience, food remains, and graffiti. Most recently, a master plan of the Stewart Indian School was completed May 2018 by the State Public Works Division outlining future development of the school campus and buildings.

The results of our collaborative research at Stewart are discussed in greater detail in chapter 8. This chapter provides some background on previous archaeological studies of similar sites, including archaeology of institutional life, archaeology of childhood, and archaeology specifically of Indian boarding schools. We also address methods increasingly employed in archaeology to address Native peoples' concerns about artifact curation. This background reading aided researchers in determining additional questions that would be meaningful to ask of a site such as this, and how to handle artifacts ethically. The remainder of the chapter provides some background on the research design and methods employed at the site.

Archaeology of Indian Schools

The project at Stewart Indian School was an archaeology project conducted with members of local and regional American Indian tribes. Hence, a discussion of the methods and theoretical foundations of collaborative archaeology and Indigenous research is central to understanding this approach, as discussed in the previous chapter. The archaeology itself is difficult to address in a literature review, given how little archaeological research has been published on Indian boarding schools (excavation at the Phoenix Indian School in Arizona is a rare example; Lindauer 1997). This may reflect the sensitive nature of studying places with traumatic histories, and the need to address them slowly, carefully, and in accordance with the wishes of communities; excavation might not always be appropriate. In some cases, noninvasive landscape analyses can be very productive, such as Surface-Evans' (2016) work at the Mount Pleasant Indian Industrial Boarding School in Michigan, and Hughston's (2017) work at Stewart Indian School. In the remainder of this chapter, we provide additional context for this topic by looking broadly at the archaeology of institutional life and the archaeology of childhood.

The Archaeology of Institutional Life

The archaeology of institutional life can shed light on site formation processes, excavation procedures, and typical artifact assemblages recovered from investigations of schoolhouses, among other types of institutions such as hospitals, prisons, asylums, and many others (Baugher 2009). Institutions have long influenced the lives of people from all backgrounds; from classrooms to cell blocks, they have shaped society by implementing standards and boundaries on behavior (Gibb 2009). Catholic missions throughout the Americas were some of the earliest institutions investigated by archaeologists because of the strictly governed daily lives of Native Americans who lived there (Baugher 2009; Cordell 1989; Costello and Hornbeck 1992; Hester 1992). These excavations mostly concentrated on locating primary buildings, foundations, privies, and areas dedicated to worship (Baugher 2009).

Institutions make a particularly unique place to practice archaeology because much of the material culture was shaped by and reflected the goals of the institution. The landscapes, the dress, the architecture, the food, practically everything, were constructed to control the occupants' behaviors. There are many theoretical lenses applied to the study of institutions, including power and resistance, individual agency, and feminist theory. Michel Foucault's (1977) concepts on power and incarceration are crucial to an interpretation of historic prisons, asylums, and, in many cases, schoolhouses. He argues that imposing certain experiences of power onto an incarcerated individual will result in reformation of that person (Foucault 1997, 17). This strategy is essential to many institutions, and is similar to the boarding school assimilation strategies discussed in this volume. The archaeology of institutions such as hospitals, prisons, asylums, almshouses, and military compounds has contributed greatly to archaeological data on power, resistance, ritual, and reform. The study of schoolhouses has drawn less attention in comparison, but the field is still capable of producing important data on the socializing effects of education on individuals and the community as a whole (Dielissen 2008, 20).

The Archaeology of Education

James Gibb and April Beisaw's (2000) compilation of nineteen studies conducted at schoolhouses in the Northeastern United States illustrates the dearth of significant data produced from the earliest attempts at schoolhouse archaeology. Archaeologists were often left with an abundance of architectural debris, few domestic artifacts, and ambiguous stratigraphy, which led to reports lacking in critical research questions and interpretations. For example, excavations at the Welsh Tract School in Newark, Delaware, produced few domestic artifacts, or artifacts that have historically been used by archaeologists for "dating sites and defining activities and activity areas" (Gibb and Beisaw 2000, 124–25), such as clothing, jewelry, tobacco pipes, toys, medicine bottles, and glass and ceramic vessels (Gibb and Beisaw 2000, 115).

Some of the studies reviewed by Gibb and Beisaw (2000) did reveal more developed interpretations of schoolhouses. Artifacts such as stove thimbles and collars found at the Letchworth Park School in New York and the Oella Schoolhouse in Maryland, window shutters and light fixtures found at the Boston African Meeting House in Massachusetts, and remains of chemical toilets found at the Letchworth Park School, can speak to issues surrounding the lighting, heating, furnishing, and sanitation facilities present at these sites. Since these were significant concerns for the children, parents, and administrators of these schools, they can be said to represent the communities' opinions on public education and possibly larger social issues such as public health and sanitation (Gibb and Beisaw 2000, 123).

Gibb and Beisaw (2000) and Rotman (2003) all agree that a lack of domestic artifacts at these sites does not necessarily mean that critical interpretations are not possible. Since schoolhouses do not usually represent living domains, domestic artifacts such as whiteware sherds, bottle glass fragments, tobacco pipes, and buttons must have been brought to the school with a "degree of deliberate intention" (Rotman 2003, 10). Since schoolhouses are considered to be representative of the community they are in, the lack of domestic artifacts may provide significant information (Rotman 2003, 10).

Investigation of an early-twentieth-century African-American school in Morganza, Louisiana, conducted by Dena L. Struchtemeyer, offers critical interpretations of the artifact assemblage. These interpretations are supplemented and supported by archival research, an oral history, and informal interviews (Struchtemeyer 2008, 2, 4). Morganza Elementary was different from the previously mentioned schoolhouses because its purpose was to segregate African-American children and to provide them an education focused on industrial arts rather than the purely academic program of most white public schools. Toys found at the site, such as marbles and toy guns, could represent "gendered play" in that administrators would have deemed what was suitable for boys and girls to play with (Struchtemeyer 2008, 61–68). Objects such as metal slag, car parts, sewing machine parts, and shoes are interpreted as evidence of gendered vocational work at the school as well. Although there were no structures found that may have housed those areas, Struchtemeyer (2008, 57–61) was able to interpret the artifacts by information obtained through archival research.

Institutional archaeology provides the theoretical basis of any archaeological study on residential schools or boarding schools. In addition, the study of children and their specific material culture aids in the interpretation of historic boarding schools.

The Archaeology of Childhood

Children have only recently become a significant topic of theoretical and methodological consideration within archaeology. Grete Lillehammer's (1989) article, "The Child Is Born: The Child's World in an Archaeological Perspective," was one of the first studies that explicitly focused on children. This is largely due to children being depicted as invisible or simply difficult to identify in the archaeological record

(Baxter 2008). Since then, many archaeologists have realized that this is not the case. Children can actually be found in the archaeological record in several different ways. The fact that children have previously been seen as invisible could be the result of the dominant ideology to which those archaeologists ascribe, an ideology that supports a notion of children being incapable of contributing to social life because they are unable to determine their standing in society without the guidance of adults (Mizoguchi 2000, 142). In this case children are not seen as autonomous agents and are therefore seen as unworthy of archaeological consideration. However, it is important to consider that given the larger social systems to which all adults adhere, they are not entirely autonomous either (Kamp 2006). Furthermore, this gives reason to consider children as possible active agents in shaping their own lives as opposed to being passive objects. The study of childhood then has become a developing study within archaeology and new research is being done to articulate the extent to which children demonstrated agency in the past and how this is identified in the material culture (Baxter 2006b; Smith 2006; Wilkie 2000).

Children became important subjects of interest as archaeologists became more interested in issues of identity, individuals, and agency (Kamp 2006, 116). Anthropologists began to realize that given the nature of culture being learned rather than inherited, research surrounding children and childhood are excellent sources of information on human behavior. This is a rational conclusion given that childhood is a cultural construct and results in the variation of childhood experiences as well as the definitions of childhood within different cultures. Anthropologists have also noted the fact that families, communities, and societies as a whole often prioritize the treatment and care of children. Studies that do not include children can therefore be seen as incomplete interpretations of the past (Baxter 2008, 160–61).

Baxter has distinguished two main barriers that have kept children from being considered subjects of archaeological interest until recently. The first of these barriers is concerned with the Western constructions of childhood that have dominated the ideologies of archaeologists. As opposed to the more traditional way of viewing past cultures as vitally different than those of today, Baxter argues that many archaeologists have made assumptions about children that reflect their own perceptions and experiences of childhood (Baxter 2008, 161). These Western constructions then have implications on archaeologists' attitudes toward children and childhood. First, children become associated with notions of dependence and innocence and childhood is depicted as a time of preparation for adulthood (Kamp 2001). This notion is often accompanied with "the assumption that political, economic, and social control are held exclusively by adults" (Baxter 2008, 61). A second implication of adhering to Western constructs concerns the emphasis of biological development through the human life cycle (Kamp 2001). Biological categories constructed by Western medicine have resulted in a scientific rhetoric of identifiable stages of personhood, such as infant, toddler, child, adolescent, young adult, adult, and elderly. The repeated use of this rhetoric has naturalized the Western understanding of childhood and has extended it into the greater realm of social scientific research as representing a universal childhood in which children do not make significant contributions to social groups (Baxter 2008, 161–62).

The second barrier to the inclusion of children in archaeological interpretations is based on the notion of children as invisible in the archaeological record. Children are seen as having unconventional ways of interacting with material culture and only utilizing specific types of artifacts. According to Baxter (2008), this is exemplified in the treatment of children in earlier archaeological studies where they were considered as explanations for artifacts that were baffling to the archaeologists as well as in studies where children's actions were seen as disturbing the deposits created by adults. The marginalization of children in the archaeological record has been compared to the previous exclusion of women and has likewise been found analogous with the development of gender studies in archaeology. Like women, children have been categorized as inferior in the adult/child dichotomy and therefore exist beside women in a category of the disempowered (Baxter 2008, 162). Archaeology's emphasis on artifact distributions rather than documents places it at the forefront for studying the less powerful who had little access to media such as documentary records. A study of material culture can therefore expose intricacies of a society that may have gone undocumented or in other ways recorded (Kamp

2006, 119). Due to the similarity in the marginalization of women and children, many archaeologists have chosen to look at the archaeology of gender as a framework for research on children (Kamp 2001, 3).

Now that children have entered the realm of archaeological investigation, there are trends emerging within the analysis of material culture that focus on child behavior and behavior that depicts the cultural construction of childhood in any society. Schwartzman (2006) presents a framework for studying children in her article, "Materializing Children: Challenges for the Archaeology of Childhood." This framework addresses six factors concerning childhood: the nature of children as active participants in their social lives, socialization as a negotiable process between adults and children, the significance of children at a global scale, the realization that the Western construct of childhood is just one among many, the importance of reflexivity when analyzing childhood, and the significance of cross-disciplinary studies in revealing the role of children in historic and prehistoric societies (Schwartzman 2006, 125).

According to Baxter (2008), a significant contribution has been the focus on children's participation in craft production in precontact societies; specifically the investigation of stone tool production, ceramic manufacture, and weaving. Learning a craft can take several years, so it is often believed that individuals start training at an early age, which makes craft production a more than reasonable area to look for children (Baxter 2008, 167). Archaeologically, these novice productions can be identified in a variety of ways. Objects that are small in size, crude in form, and crude in the application of designs are often interpreted as materials produced by children (Smith 2006, 67). Others have also argued that a level of standardization is indicative of experienced craftsmanship and so a high level of variation in craft production is often associated with novice and child crafters (Bagwell 2002).

Another way of discovering children in the archaeological record is through the analysis of social spaces used by children, done by investigating distribution patterns of artifacts at archaeological sites. Some earlier studies did incorporate children into the interpretation of artifact distributions, but they were seen as altering the deposits formed by adults rather than representing the purposeful actions of children

(Baxter 2008, 169). Recent publications, however, have argued that children do not use space in such a random fashion. Adams (1995) demonstrated this by discovering "secret spaces" in the backyard of a historic residential site. Although the children were confined to a play space that could easily be seen from inside the house, she found a concentration of artifacts in the small corners of the yard where they would have been unseen from the adults in the house. Similarly, Buchli and Lucas examined the artifact distributions at an abandoned house that had once been occupied by a single mother and her two small children. The authors found that the children's artifacts far outnumbered those that were associated with the mother. In addition, they found that the children's rooms were distinguished by gendered toys in contrast to the common areas, which contained toys associated with both genders (Buchli and Lucas 2000, 134).

The archaeological study of agency and children are both emerging fields within the discipline that are continuously being refined as further research is conducted. Although agency is often defined in disparate ways (Dornan 2002, 304), the general agreement that agency concerns the "active participation of individuals in the process of change" (Smith 2006, 65) is useful in interpreting the behavior of children through the archaeological record. Whereas early archaeological interpretations of children portrayed them as either invisible or simply randomizing factors that disturbed the deposits of adults, recent contributions have considered the agency of children and their roles in shaping the social, economic, and cultural systems in which they lived (Baxter 2006b; Smith 2006; Wilkie 2000). Childhood should be seen as a distinct period of personhood when particular perceptions and knowledge are exclusive to children (Schwartzmann 2006).

As Baxter says, archaeological interpretations that do not include children are considered incomplete since the study of childhood produces viable information for the interpretation of social systems among different cultures. Simply put, childhood is not only about children. The archaeological study of children is concerned with the relationships that children have with the families and communities in which they participate. It is a revolutionary approach to answering some of archaeology's traditionally significant questions and should therefore be incorporated into all areas of archaeological research rather than as a specialized interest within the discipline (Baxter 2008, 171).

Catch-and-Release Archaeology

In light of theoretical approaches emphasizing ethical shifts in methodologies that are more sensitive to Indigenous peoples' values, a discussion of catch-and-release archaeology is warranted here. The archaeological field school at the Stewart Indian School project employed this method to a limited extent with a small number of flaked artifacts (see chapter 6). Catch-and-release archaeology refers to an approach that emphasizes low-impact field methods such as in-field recording and the reburial of artifacts. While these projects are not necessarily always collaborative projects, the premise of catch-and-release is related to collaborative archaeology. Catch-and-release is primarily focused on reducing curation costs and the expenses surrounding extensive laboratory analysis. However, collaborative archaeology and catch-and-release archaeology are both ways in which archaeologists can show respect when investigating sites (Lightfoot et al. 2013). Creating a standard for such practices throughout the discipline would transform the practice of archaeology into one that is more collaborative, multivocal, and holistic. The incorporation of various perspectives, especially Native American perspectives, can contribute to a more thorough and accurate interpretations of the past (Smith 1999). Implementing catch-and-release field methods is one way that archaeologists can begin to incorporate the concerns of Indigenous communities into research.

The collection and curation of artifacts has long been an essential requirement for recording, dating, and interpreting sites, as well as ensuring future archaeologists access to reputable data sets (Heilen and Altschul 2013, 121). However, archaeologists around the world sometimes turn to in-field artifact analysis, also known as "catch-and-release" archaeology (Modzeleweski and Gonzalez 2006, 24). This transition emerged during the 1980s as several SHPOs began to discourage collection on survey projects as more sophisticated technology began to emerge, the costs of curation grew, and the increasing occurrence of decolonization practices pressured the shift toward a more low-impact archaeology (Gonzalez et al. 2006; Lightfoot et al. 2013; Todd and Burnett 2003).

Generally, catch-and-release refers to in-field artifact analysis, returning artifacts as close to their original provenience as possible after analysis (whether conducted in the field or lab), and in particular cases, the reburial of artifacts after analysis. The methods will inevitably vary across projects, and so other methods such as sourcing lithic materials with a portable X-Ray Flourescence (pXRF) gun (Goren et al. 2011), and the use of silicone putty to take casts of artifacts outside of the lab (Todd and Burnett 2003) are being used to increase the value of data that can be obtained in the field.

During the late twentieth century archaeology saw the emergence of decolonization theory (Atalay 2006), changes in historic preservation policy with the passing of the NHPA (Heilen and Altschul 2013), and an increasing issue with curation costs in the United States (Bawaya 2007). These three factors converged to create new perspectives on the collection of artifacts. Heilen and Altschul (2013, 124) state that these developments resulted in four specific ideas relating to collection: "(1) collection as a cause of site disturbance; (2) artifact identification as being straightforward and adequately carried out by field crews; (3) collection and curation as unnecessary costs; and (4) collection as cause for decreasing availability in storage facilities." As a result, noncollection survey became an instrumental function of many federal and public agencies such as the Bureau of Land Management (BLM) in Nevada, whose policy states that "artifact collection can entail considerable direct and indirect costs both to the operator and to the BLM and should be avoided whenever possible" (BLM 1985, 5). Eventually, noncollection methods were being used in contexts where they were not necessarily required, and so emerged the field of catch-and-release archaeology.

Many elements of standard field methods apply to catch-and-release archaeology as well, such as surface survey, written and photographic records, and in some cases, excavation. It is primarily the in-depth field analysis and noncollection practices that separate standard methods from catch-and-release. Instead of following standard curation practices, artifacts are either reburied in their proveniences, or they are not collected at all (Gonzalez et al. 2006; Todd and Burnett 2003). These are the basics of catch-and-release archaeology, although it may be argued to encompass a range of practices that ultimately result in a low-impact archaeology. By practicing catch-and-release methods, researchers are attempting to evaluate sites to the same degree as they would utilizing standard methods, but with less impact on the site and individual artifacts. Thus the same types of analyses may be conducted in the field by taking advantage of sophisticated technology and creativity.

One common example is the increasing use of portable pXRF to source raw material while conducting fieldwork. This new technology enables researchers to examine the geochemical makeup of raw materials while in the field. Many researchers have conducted comparative analyses of results from pXRF and standard XRF on obsidian sourcing and have found that while there may be differences in the results, they had no effect on the obsidian source assignment (Craig et al. 2007). Researchers have conducted studies on obsidian (Forster and Grave 2012) as well as nonvitreous materials and have found that "broad and detailed classification" is possible for both (Grave et al. 2011, 1674).

Another practice of catch-and-release is the use of Knead-A-Mold silicone putty to take molds of artifacts in the field. Todd and Burnett (2003) utilized this method during the Greybull River Impact Zone (GRIZ) project. Taking molds in the field supplements data on tool attributes such as retouch and use-wear by increasing the amount of data that is retrieved through noncollection methods. More exact measurements can be taken from molds and compared to measurements taken in field and from photographs.

Although various researchers have studied the concept of low-impact field methods, there are still plenty of improvements that are needed. For instance, the development of a fieldwork manual specific to catch-and-release would be valuable. That way, a standard could be created that includes all of the basic variables to record in the field and how to record them given the various techniques. This standard could then be edited as necessary for individual projects. Also, such a manual would allow archaeologists to define specific criteria that can realistically be recorded in the field. A cost-benefit analysis of the time required to do the analysis versus the quality of results would aid in developing these criteria.

With more researchers working to refine the practice, the field can expect to see significant advancements in the applicability of the methods and their effectiveness in obtaining accurate and precise data, while also respecting the wishes of many American Indian communities to leave artifacts on-site. There may also be cases when the scientific community strongly advises removal of artifacts, so ongoing conversations with stakeholders will help develop consensus.

Overall Goals for Archaeology and Preservation Research Design at Stewart Indian School

Goals and objectives of the project were to study the interplay of tribal agency, social capital, and governmentalized archaeological discourse, and then outline a strategy for humanizing the process of respectful consultation among tribes, archaeologists, and the federal government.

In the five-week field school, participants engaged in service learning activities at the Stewart Indian School. Students learned methods of archaeological excavation, as well as noninvasive methods aimed at preservation, such as recording oral histories, conducting archaeological surveys, and interpreting Global Positioning System (GPS) and remote sensing data. Test excavations were limited to very specific areas; methods are detailed below. No activities that would affect any of the current structures or improvements at Stewart Indian School were proposed for the current project.

Based on archival research, personal communications, and field inspection completed by the research partners, several areas were identified that likely possessed subsurface components. Research questions were refined through ongoing discussions with research partners within Native American tribes. General areas of interest included the following:

- Survey, surface inspection, and mapping parts of the facility that have not been extensively documented;
- Locating and documenting foundations and other archaeological resources;
- Using remote sensing (ground penetrating radar) in conjunction with archival research and oral history to locate building foundations and other subsurface archaeological features;
- Finding the exact location of the original school building, which is no longer standing;
- Locating and describing the buried remains of the campus swimming pool, which had also been used as a baptismal, to inform future plans to create a reflecting pool at that location;

- Finding the locations of campsites where families stayed to be near their children, who had been forcibly removed from their families to attend the school (although we were unable to explore this archaeologically at this stage);
- Learning more about Native American children's lifeways at the school during the earliest period of its history;
- Capitalizing on the public's fascination with archaeology to explain the significance of Stewart to the public and to Nevada government entities, with the goals of public education and increased support for preservation. This was largely accomplished through extensive media interviews and site tours.

Locating and excavating subsurface features drove many of the day-to-day activities around which the above goals were accomplished. The following figures were excerpted from the "Cultural Landscape Report for Stewart Indian School: Preservation Approach and Treatment Plan" (Wyss Associates, Inc. 2009) and provide significant information regarding the potential subsurface components at Stewart Indian School.

A map of the original campus plan (figure 3.2) shows locations of

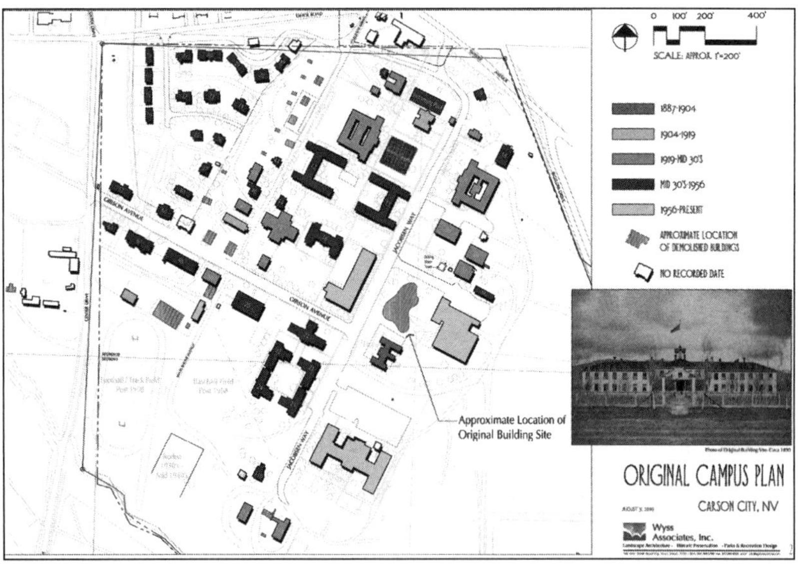

FIGURE 3.2. Original campus plan. Wyss Associates, Inc., 2009.

the demolished buildings, including the approximate location of the original school building. Based on meetings with the NIC and their SAC, locating the original school building was one of their high priorities. The mapped location was used in combination with ground penetrating radar and archaeological testing to determine the exact location of the original school building during this project.

Finally, figure 3.3 shows all existing infrastructure, including utilities. When planning to conduct subsurface testing, it was essential to determine the location of existing utilities. This map helped to guide the planning of excavations in areas with no existing utilities. This map served only as an initial planning guide however, as USA North, a utility locating service, was contacted to mark all utilities prior to any excavations. Also, as mentioned above, ground-penetrating radar was utilized during this project, and was very effective at identifying subsurface utilities that were then avoided in excavations. The methods and results of this work are presented in chapter 6.

Research Themes and Questions

There are several important themes addressed through the collaborative archaeology conducted at the Stewart Indian School. First, the collaborative elements of projects such as this one are important to address since they may require changes to standard archaeological methods and may therefore produce different results. As an element of this collaborative project, it is also important to consider Native perspectives of research and how they differ from and complement other scientific research. This leads to research questions focused on the possible effects of using such methods and how they may or may not benefit communities. These questions include:

- How do collaborative methods affect standard archaeological methods?
- How did collaboration affect the archaeological assemblage and the interpretations extrapolated from it?
- How do collaborative methods in archaeology work with Indigenous communities?
- Does the collaborative archaeology project at Stewart Indian School benefit communities after the project is over?

FIGURE 3.3. Aerial Photographs by date, shows an aerial view of the campus in 1938, 1954, 1974, and 2004. Using aerial photos offered a viewpoint that was used to estimate where additional areas with subsurface components may exist, that are no longer visible from the ground. Also, using aerial photos from various periods allows for sampling that informs on specific occupation and use. Wyss Associates, Inc., 2009.

Second, life at Stewart Indian School can also be examined through a closer look at the issues surrounding institutional life during the nineteenth and twentieth centuries. Artifacts found at the school can certainly speak to the everyday life of students at a boarding school. The main question associated with this theme is:

- How can the archaeology of institutions inform the interpretations of life at Stewart?

Finally, the material culture found at the site also represents the life of children during the turn of the century, which leads to the question:

- How can the archaeology of childhood aid in the interpretations of artifacts collected from Stewart Indian School?

We recognize that there are many questions that could be asked of a project such as this, and these are only some of the ways to investigate the many elements associated with collaborative archaeology and the different experiences people had during their time at the Stewart

Indian School. It is our hope that this provides a part of the story, upon which future researchers and community members can elaborate.

Works Cited

Atalay, Sonya. 2006. "Indigenous Archaeology as Decolonizing Practice." *The American Indian Quarterly* 30, nos. 3 and 4: 280–310.

Baugher, Sherene. 2009. "Historical Overview of the Archaeology of Institutional Life." In *The Archaeology of Institutional Life*, edited by April M. Beisaw and James G. Gibb, 5–13. Tuscaloosa, AL: University of Alabama Press.

Bawaya, Michael. 2007. "Archaeology: Curation in Crisis." *Science Magazine* 317, no. 5841: 1025–26.

Baxter, Jane Eva. 2006b. "Making Space for Children in Archaeological Interpretations." *Archaeological Papers of the American Anthropological Association* 15: 77–88.

———. 2008. "The Archaeology of Childhood." *Annual Review of Anthropology* 37: 159–75.

BLM (Bureau of Land Management). 1985. *Cultural Resources Survey: General Guidelines*, 3rd ed. Reno, NV.

Cordell, Linda S. 1989. "Durango to Durango: An Overview of the Southwest Heartland." In *Columbian Consequences, Vol. 1: Archaeological and Historical Perspectives on the Spanish Borderlands West*, edited by David H. Thomas, 17–41. Washington, DC: Smithsonian Institution Press.

Costello, Julia G., and David Hornbeck. 1992. "Alta California: An Overview." In *Columbian Consequences, Vol. 1: Archaeological and Historical Perspectives on the Spanish Borderlands West*, edited by David H. Thomas, 303–33. Washington, DC: Smithsonian Institution Press.

Craig, Nathan, Robert J. Speakman, Rachel S. Popelka-Filcolff, Michael D. Glascock, J. David Robertson, M. Steven Shackley, and Mark S. Aldenderfer. 2007. "Comparison of XRF and PXRF for Analysis of Archaeological Obsidian from Southern Peru." *Journal of Archaeological Science* 34, no. 12: 2012–14.

Dielissen, Sandra. 2012. "Teaching a School to Talk: Archaeology of the Queen Victoria Jubilee Home for Indian Children." Master's thesis, Simon Fraser University.

Dornan, Jennifer L. 2002. "Agency and Archaeology: Past, Present, and Future Directions." *Journal of Archaeological Method and Theory* 9, no. 4: 303–29.

Forster, Nicola and Peter Grave. 2012. "Non-destructive PXRF analysis of museum curated obsidian from the Near East." *Journal of Archaeological Science* 39: 728–36.

Foucault, Michel. 1977. *Discipline and Punish: The Birth of the Prison*. Translated by Alan Sheridan. New York: Vintage Books.

Gibb, James G. 2009. "Introduction." In *The Archaeology of Institutional Life*, edited by April M. Beisaw and James G. Gibb, 5–13. Tuscaloosa, AL: University of Alabama Press.

Gibb, James G., and April M. Beisaw. 2000. "Learning Cast Up from the Mire: Archaeological Investigations of Schoolhouses in the Northeastern United States." *Northeast Historical Archaeology* 29, no. 1: 107–29.

Gonzalez, Sara L., and Darren Modzelewski, Lee M. Panich, and Tsim D. Schneider. 2006. "Archaeology for the Seventh Generation." *American Indian Quarterly* 30, nos. 3/4: 388–415.

Goren, Yuval, Hans Mommsen, and Jorg Klinger. 2011. "Non-destructive Provenance Study of Cuneiform Tablets Using Portable X-Ray Flourescence (pXRF)." *Journal of Archaeological Science* 38: 684–696.

Grave, Peter, Val Attenbrow, Lin Sutherland, Ross Pogson, Nicola Forster. 2011. Non-destructive pXRF on mafic stone tools. *Journal of Archaeological Science* 39: 1674–86.

Hattori, Eugene M. 1978. The Archaeology of the Stewart Dump Site (26OR121). Report to Carson City Department of Public Works, from the Carson City Department of Public Works and Nevada State Museum, Carson City.

Heilen, Michael, and Jeffrey H. Altschul. 2013. "The Accuracy and Adequacy of In-Field Artifact Analysis: An Experimental Test at Two Archaeological Sites in the Western United States." *Advances in Archaeological Practice: A Journal of the Society for American Archaeology* 1, no. 2 (November): 121–38.

Hendrick, Irving G. 1976. "Federal Policy Affecting the Education of Indians in California, 1849–1934." *History of Education Quarterly* 2, no. 16: 163–85.

Hester, Thomas R. 1992. "Texas and Northeastern Mexico: An Overview." In *Columbian Consequences, Vol. 1: Archaeological and Historical Perspectives on the Spanish Borderlands West*, edited by David H. Thomas, 191–211. Washington, DC: Smithsonian Institution Press.

Hughston, Jessica. 2017. "Negotiating Space and Maintaining Place: Time, Materiality, and Lived Experience at Stewart Indian School." Master's thesis, University of Massachusetts, Boston.

Jackson, Nicholas. 1969. "A History of the Stewart Indian School." Master's thesis, University of Nevada, Reno.

Kamp, Kathryn A. 2001. "Where Have All the Children Gone?: The Archaeology of Childhood." *Journal of Archaeological Method and Theory* 8, no. 1: 1–34.

———. 2006. "Dominant Discourses; Lived Experiences: Studying the Archaeology of Children and Childhood." *Archaeological Papers of the American Anthropological Association* 15: 115–22.

Lightfoot, Kent G., Rob Q. Cuthrell, Chuck J. Striplen, and Mark G. Hylkema. 2013. Rethinking the Study of Landscape Management: Practices among Hunter-Gatherers in North America. *American Antiquity* 78, no. 2: 285–301.

Lillehammer, Grete. 1989. "A Child Is Born: The Child's World in an Archaeological Perspective." *Norwegian Archaeological Review* 22, no. 1: 89–105.

Lindauer, Owen. 1997. "Not For School, But For Life: Lessons from the Historical Archaeology of the Phoenix Indian School." Arizona State University, Office of Cultural Resource Management, Report of Investigations, no. 95, Tempe.

Lomawaima, K. Tsianina. 1994. *They Called It Prairie Light: The Story of Chilocco Indian School.* Lincoln, NE: University of Nebraska Press.

Mizoguchi, Koji. 2000. "The Child as a Node of Past, Present, and Future." In *Children and Material Culture*, edited by Joanna Sofaer Derevenski, 141–50. New York: Routledge.

Modzelewski, Darren, and Sara Gonzalez. 2007. "Creating Trails through Traditions: An Update on the Kashaya Pomo Interpretive Trail, Fort Ross State Historic Park." *Proceedings of the Society for California Archaeology* 20: 23–26.

Rotman, Deborah L. 2003. "Learning and Community: Exploring the Materiality of Rural Education in America." Paper presented at the Annual Meeting of the Society for Historical Archaeology, Providence, Rhode Island.

Schwartzman, Helen B. 2006. "Materializing Children: Challenges for the Archaeology of Childhood." *Archaeological Papers of the American Anthropological Association* 15: 123–31.

Smith, Linda Tuhiwai. 1999. *Decolonizing Methodologies: Research and Indigenous Peoples*. London: Zed Books Ltd.

Smith, Patricia E. 2006. "Children and Ceramic Innovation: A Study in the Archaeology of Children." *Archaeological Papers of the American Anthropological Association* 15: 65–76.

Struchtemeyer, Dena L. 2008. "Separate but Equal?: The Archaeology of an Early Twentieth-Century African American School." Master's thesis, Louisiana State University.

Surface-Evans, Sarah. 2016. "Landscapes of Assimilation and Resistance: A Spatial Analysis of the Mount Pleasant Indian Industrial Boarding School." In *Colonial Institutions: Uses, Subversions, and Material Afterlives*, edited by Laura McAtackney and Russell Palmer. Special issue, *International Journal of Historical Archaeology* 20, no. 3: 574–88.

Thompson, Bonnie. 2013. "The Student Body: A History of the Stewart Indian School, 1890–1940." PhD diss., Arizona State University.

Todd, L. C., and P. C. Burnett. 2003. "Archaeological Catch and Release: Expanding Data Capture for Archaeological Catch and Release: Expanding Data Capture for Non-Collection Survey." Poster Presented at the 61st Plains Anthropological Conference, Fayetteville, AR.

Wilkie, Laurie. 2000. "Not Merely Child's Play: Creating a Historical Archaeology of Children and Childhood." In *Children and Material Culture*, edited by Joanna Sofaer Derevenski, 100–14. New York: Routledge.

Woolford, Andrew. 2015. *The Benevolent Experiment: Indigenous Boarding Schools, Genocide, and Redress in Canada and the United States*. Lincoln, NE: University of Nebraska Press.

Wyss Associates. 2009. "Stewart Indian School Cultural Landscape Report, Volume III of III Preservation Approach and Treatment Plan." Prepared by Wyss Associates, Inc. for State of Nevada Public Works Board, Project Number: 07-S04a.

CHAPTER 4

Indian Education in Nevada (1890–2015): A Legacy of Change

Alex K. Ruuska

"Back in those days they were trying to make Indians white overnight, you know what I mean?"

—Andrew Vidovich

Next to the implementation of federal policies designed to remove Indigenous people from their traditional and aboriginal territories, legislative measures mandating the education of Indian children according to Western tenets of knowledge have resulted in some of the most profound and enduring impacts upon the lives of historic and contemporary American Indians (e.g., Archuleta et al. 2000). Within the state of Nevada, a massive resocializing campaign directed at the youths of each Indigenous community began in 1890 with the opening of the first nonreservation boarding school three miles southeast of the capital in Carson City, Nevada (Margaret Wheat Papers n.d., 83-24/III/4:2/18). Over the next century, Paiutes, Shoshones, Washoes, and Indigenous youths from beyond the borders of Nevada were exposed to educational regimes at the Stewart Indian School, local day schools, and public schools that promised to permanently alter traditional economic and social milieus that had developed over the course of centuries.

Much scholarship already has been dedicated to assessing and critiquing policies directed at reshaping and eliminating Indigenous cultures via compulsory education. The Meriam Report (1928) represents one of the earliest as well as one of the most influential critiques of ideas and practices exercised in the education of Indian pupils throughout the United States. More recently, ethnographic teams at the Bureau of Applied Research in Anthropology have taken a lead role in examining the impact of formal Western education upon the Indigenous groups of Arizona (Officer 1956; Kelley 1967). Additionally, the works of Knack (1978) provide insights into the educational experiences of contemporary Southern Paiutes, and Archuleta et al. (2000), Huff (1997), Lomawaima (1994), and Spring (2001) have been instrumental in identifying critical issues surrounding the education of Indigenous children through Western paradigms of thought.

This retrospective chapter explores how federal, state, and regional educational policies have impacted the lived experiences of the Paiutes and Western Shoshones of central Nevada from the late nineteenth century through the early twenty-first century. While the primary focus is placed on ethnographic and historic accounts of the early years (1890–1928), a brief chronology spanning from 1928 to 2015 is included as a means of bringing the story up to the recent past, and signposting major milestones, such as the successful nomination of the memory-laden cultural landscape known as the Stewart Indian School to the National Register of Historic Places. More recently, former school attendees, their descendants, and others have coordinated an annual Powwow on the Stewart Indian School grounds. This locus for commemoration activities allows people to pay homage to over a century of social memories of hardship and suffering, as well as forbearance and favor, in the wake of what were initially externally imposed enculturation processes.

Thereafter, I identify contemporary manifestations of historic educational policies within these communities. Throughout this analysis I demonstrate how governmental policies enacted at the Steward Indian School served as "instruments of social reproduction" (Willis 1977). Herein, Indian children were purposefully separated from traditional communities of knowledge and simultaneously prepared for jobs within economies derived from Western rather than traditional Indigenous philosophies of land and resource use. Building on the work of Willis (1977), Knack (1978), and Littlefield and Knack (1996), I illustrate how the vocational training that students received in boarding schools prepared them for the lowest paying jobs within local economies and thus served to reproduce rather than reduce social, economic, and political inequities extant between Nevada's Indigenous and non-Indigenous populations. I also provide narrative recollections of students attending Indian boarding schools within different periods, along with those of a former Shoshone student who attended a non-segregated day school in Warm Springs, Nevada, known as the Eden Creek School.

Throughout this analysis I describe the methods children and families utilized in order to mediate the risks that accompanied compulsory education. Risk reduction measures included the enactment of rituals of resistance, the display of varying degrees of compliance, the relocation of families to be near the schools of their children, and the development of support networks within educational institutions that sometimes muted traditional ethnic animosities and thus lay some of the groundwork for the late nineteenth and early twentieth century phenomenon of pan-Indian awareness. As a local analysis, this chapter is intended to complement a larger body of literature dedicated to the analysis of how Western forms of education have affected Indigenous groups throughout the United States. At the same time, the reader should bear in mind that the processes articulated through the oral histories presented within this chapter reveal patterns of risk perception, adaptation, and resistance that often parallel the experiences of Indigenous people exposed to Western forms of education in regions beyond the scope of the present study.

Federal Policies

During the late nineteenth-century relations between Indigenous and Euro-American groups were in the process of being reconceptualized and reconstructed within Nevada and throughout the United States. Although relations between these groups had never been static, the 1890s were particularly eventful. During this period federal policies were being enacted to "resolve" the "Indian Problem" (Berkhofer 1978, 169). One method of resolution was sought through measures of forced segregation. The dominant means of instituting this policy entailed placing people on reservations where they would remain under close surveillance and control (Berkhofer 1978, 170). The late nineteenth-century reservation policies helped Euro-Americans to gain greater control over aboriginal lands and resources as well as the dominant modes of production through which resources were utilized. Control over many mobile Indigenous populations was further augmented by the reservation system, which aimed to turn Indigenous people into farmers with fences. Cumulatively, reservation policies resulted in diminished access to land, traditional plants, animals, and water, and declines in population due to disease and starvation (Hittman 1973; Steward 1938; Stoffle et al. 1995; Stoffle et al. 2000; Zanjani 1994).

Although a growing majority of Indigenous people throughout the United States was being forced onto reservations by 1890, in Nevada, many Indigenous and non-Indigenous people initially resisted reservation legislation. While reservation boundaries were marked in Nevada as early as 1859 at the Pyramid and Walker Lake Reservations (Elliot 1987, 396), only 25 percent of Paiutes were living on reservations by 1890 (Logan 1980, 281). Much of the resistance stemmed from the fact that many Euro-American communities were already highly dependent upon the cheap labor pool ensured by the presence of Indigenous people near mining and ranching settlements. While living on ranches and on the margins of mining camps, many Numic people regularly performed menial labor for Euro-Americans in exchange for food or wages. However, work was frequently sporadic, and payment for labor was not always forthcoming (Zanjani 1994, 38).

A second means of resolving the "Indian Problem" occurred through the implementation of policies of compulsory education designed to eradicate the presumed "otherness" of Indigenous groups. "By the end of the century nearly half of all Native children attended school for some period of time" (Berkhofter 1978, 170). In Nevada, the Clear Creek Indian School, which was later renamed the Stewart Indian School, was established south of Carson City in 1890 (Elliot 1987, 397). Prior to its establishment, it is estimated that approximately 8 percent of Indians in Nevada were receiving some form of Western education.

Nineteenth-century and early twentieth-century educational policies placed Indigenous people in increasingly risk-imbued situations involving the disruption of family and community social systems, the interruption of traditional methods of education, language, and religious practices, and the exposure of children to multiple disease epidemics. Through nonreservation boarding schools, Indigenous youths from diverse linguistic, tribal, and cultural backgrounds came to share the same living spaces for extended periods of time. While living in these institutions, students were placed into biopower regimes, in which their behaviors were strictly regulated through ongoing surveillance, behavioral modification programs, and the liberal use of corporal punishment. Biopower refers to the "material, physical, corporal . . . exercise of power" (Foucault 1977, 57–58). Foucault indicates that "From the eighteenth to the early twentieth century . . . the investment of body by power [was] heavy, ponderous, meticulous and constant. Hence those formidable disciplinary regimes in the schools, hospitals, barracks, factories, cities, lodgings, families" (Foucault 1977, 57–58). Students attending these boarding schools learned that traditional ideas and behaviors resulted in punishments, while behaviors approved by the ideals of a white culture were rewarded.

The Early Years, 1890–1928

Designed, implemented, and maintained by the BIA and Indian Affairs, the juggernaut of educational reform began its tumultuous journey through the Indigenous communities of central Nevada during the last two decades of the nineteenth century. In the 1880s the reigning superintendent of Public Instruction, C. S. Young, made a recommendation to the Nevada legislature and BIA that an Indian industrial school be established (NSJ 1982). On January 25, 1887, the people of the state of Nevada passed an act supported by Senator William Stewart to establish "An Indian school for the purpose of training and educating Indian children . . . in Ormsby County" (Nevada Legislature 1887, 23). After gaining congressional funding, the Clear Creek Indian Training School was established on the outskirts of Carson City, Nevada.

Local newspaper accounts from Ely, Nevada reveal that the creation of the Indian School of Carson was represented to the local Euro-American community as an economic transaction rather than a social engineering program that would fundamentally refigure

Indigenous/Euro-American relations on a local as well as a national scale. According to the *White Pine News*, the Carson Indian School (as Stewart was earlier known) was expected to require appropriations of sixty-six thousand to seventy-six thousand dollars (*White Pine News* 1890). One week later, the story was discussed in terms of the potential economic benefits that local businesses would experience in conjunction with the creation of the Indian School in Carson City. According to one estimate, the presence of the Indian school would generate approximately three thousand dollars in revenues per month (*White Pine News* 1890). Unstated were the immediate and long-term economic impacts that would befall Indigenous families when their children were removed from their homes. Even less clear were the potential social ramifications of compulsory education.

While three Indian schools had been founded in Nevada by 1887, including the Pyramid Lake Boarding School (1887), Walker River Day School (1882), and McDermitt Day School (1886), a nonreservation school had yet to be established (Jackson 1969, 11). One of the principal reasons given for the creation of an off-reservation boarding school was that many youths living in rural locations were still unable to attend the available institutions (Scrugham 1935, 348–49). Furthermore, while elementary education was available through local schools, fewer facilities existed where Indigenous people could receive a high school education.

To address these issues, "H.M. Yerington, Jewett W. Adams and S.L. Lee [were] . . . appointed [to] a commission for the purposes hereinafter named, to be known as 'the Indian School Commission'" (Nevada Legislature 1887, 23). Through their organizational efforts and federal funding of the Carson Indian School, which was originally called Clear Creek Indian Training School, opened on December 17, 1890 (Margaret Wheat Papers n.d., 83-24/III/4, 29, 18). Other off-reservation boarding schools, which were to have equally profound effects upon the lives of Indigenous communities throughout North America, were established during one decade preceding and following the founding of Carson Indian School in 1890. Table 4.1 gives the dates of boarding school openings throughout the United States (Officer 1956, 16).

An analysis of enrollment and employment figures indicates that the Stewart Indian School experienced continuous growth from the late

Table 4.1: Opening dates of Indian boarding schools.

Date Established	School
1880	Chemawa Indian School, Salem, OR
1884	Chilocco Indian School, Chilocco, OK
1884	Albuquerque Indian School, NM
1884	Haskell Institute, Lawrence, KS
1886	Grand Junction School, Grand Junction, CO
1887	Pyramid Lake Boarding School (reservation), Nixon, NV
1890	Santa Fe Indian School, Santa Fe, NM
1890	Fort Mohave Indian School, Fort Mohave, AZ
1890	Clear Creek Indian Training School, Carson City, NV. Also known as Carson Indian School, Carson Industrial School, and finally Stewart Indian School*
1891	Phoenix Indian School, Phoenix, AZ

* Knack and Stewart (1984, 198, 200) and Thompson (2013, 5), note that Senator William Stewart, whom the Stewart Indian School was named after, expended considerable energy in later years to introduce legislation aimed at appropriating Northern Paiute Lands. Thompson notes, "Senator Stewart pushed for the opening of Indian Country in Nevada beginning in 1892, just a year after the school opened. He applied his considerable political pressure to introduce bills to completely dispose of the Walker River Reservation and to open the lands near Wadsworth on the Pyramid Lake Reservation to white settlement."

nineteenth to the middle twentieth century. When the Stewart School was originally opened in 1890, only thirty-seven Paiute, Shoshone, and Washoe youths were enrolled, and three teachers were assigned to instruct them in all subjects (NSJ 1982). However, by January 1891, ninety-one pupils were attending Stewart Indian School full time. This off-reservation boarding school continued to provide services to a population of students who were mostly from the Paiute, Shoshone, and Washoe communities within the state of Nevada. Between 1900 and 1901, 243 students attended Stewart, and by 1905, the student body had increased to 305 pupils with an enlarged staff of 25 employees. Enrollment continued to rise in smaller increments, as indicated by the 1919 figure of 371 students. In 1933, 637 students enrolled in grades one through ten at Stewart Indian School and in 1936, the school faculty added grades eleven and twelve. By 1939, the highest number of

Table 4.2: Indian student populations in Nevada, July 1939.

Number of Schools	Number of Pupils
Nixon, Pyramid Lake Sub-agency	94
Fort McDermitt McDermitt, Carson City Agency	31
Carson Boarding School, Carson Indian Agency, Stewart, Nevada	563
Reese River, Carson City Agency via Austin	7
Fallon, Fallon Sub-agency	28
Campbell Ranch Indian Agency, Yerington, Nevada	13
Walker River Walker River Sub-agency of Carson Indian Agency, Schurz, Nevada	55
Total	791 in school and on reservations July 1939

students continued to attend boarding schools; however, populations at day schools rose. Table 4.2, gives the number of students attending day and boarding schools in 1939.

Following World War II, more students began to attend Stewart from out of state and by 1947 the institute had admitted 147 Navajo students. The Navajo contingency continued to grow and by 1958, over half of the 613 students attending Stewart were Navajo. School counts taken seven years later indicate that 625 pupils were registered on a full-time basis (AT 1977). Although enrollment figures indicate higher student enrollments, after World War II, the number of students from within the state of Nevada continued to decline and progressively higher numbers of students chose to attend reservation day schools or public schools. Consequently, by the "modern period," begun in 1945, the boarding school's principal function had changed. Rather than serving as a primary education facility, the Stewart became known as an alternative educational center directed mostly toward meeting the needs of students who were experiencing difficulties in public schools.

Social Impacts

The implementation of compulsory education within the coeducational facilities at Stewart dramatically affected Indigenous children, families, and communities. In practice, the assimilation policies of the early years (1890–1928) and to a lesser extent in the reform years (1928–1945), translated into rational, systematic efforts to disrupt, and if possible, eradicate the transmission of Indigenous knowledge from elders to youths. Paiute Ed Johnson, former curator of the Stewart Indian Museum, reflects, "What they were trying to do was civilize the Indians, get the Indianness out of them" (Nevada 1990, 33).

Johnson's statement is illustrative of guiding principles underscoring federal policies of Indian education from 1869 to 1928. In practice, bureaucrats working under the aegis of the BIA, "remove the child from tribal influence by placing him in a federal boarding school; during his stay the school . . . teach him disrespect for tribal institutions, forbid the speaking of his Native language, expose him to Christianity, instruct him in skills related to a non-Indian, rather than Indian economy" (Officer 1956, 116).

In the place of Indigenous populations fluent in the languages, lands, religions, subsistence strategies, narratives, and social and political codes of each ethnic group, the schools endeavored to create a pool of "new Indians." These new Indians would be bereft of traditional knowledge, but much more malleable to the needs of a society structured by Western values and practices (Archuleta et al. 2000, 56). The founder of the Carlisle School, Captain Richard Henry Pratt, summed up the popular and brutal sentiment underscoring assimilation measures. Reading from a paper given at an 1892 convention, Pratt opened his talk with the claim that, "all the Indian there is in the race should be dead. Kill the Indian in him, and save the man" (Pratt 1892).

Once plans to open the Stewart Indian School had been confirmed in 1887, Indian Service agents working in conjunction with the BIA approached Paiute, Shoshone, and Washoe representatives to inform them of federal policies mandating Indian education. According to Jackson (1969, 22), tribal leaders actively voiced their concerns about sending their children to a nonreservation school. The Paiutes reportedly "complained bitterly over the fact that their children were being forced to attend a school situated so far from home." They also objected to the "unnatural environment of the White school." Furthermore, the Shoshones felt discriminated against, because their enrollment numbers were higher than those of the Paiutes, and the Washoes resented the fact that their children were not provided with meals because their settlement was near the school.

Although many families were reluctant to send their children to the Stewart school, they were lured by the hope that their children's economic futures might be improved if the children were exposed to Western forms of knowledge. Frequently, parents expressed the desire that their children would receive training that would prepare them for future occupations (see figure 4.1). Such hopes came at a time when Nevada was experiencing the repercussions of drought. In addition, Indigenous communities throughout Nevada were still endeavoring to find effective means of surviving in a world where subsistence economies were increasingly untenable. As the Western economies introduced by miners and ranchers became more powerful, many Indigenous people began to adopt mixed economic strategies that included traditional subsistence methods along with sporadically available wage labor. Given these circumstances it is not surprising that Western forms of education were perceived as one avenue through which the welfare of each community might be improved.

Despite a willingness to entertain hope in relation to federal policies of Indian education, the social memories of this period are infused with metaphors of disruption and powerlessness in the wake of educational reforms. Most poignant in many people's minds are the memories of children being "rounded up" and taken away by representatives of the same government that had allowed its citizens to take away aboriginal lands. Frank Rivers, who was among the first Washoes to attend Stewart, recalls, "they just came right in our camp and rounded us kids and took us to school" (REG 1962, 7).

Children were sometimes sent to Stewart when a parental figure died, or when there was no one within their extended family that could take care of them. Andy Vidovich, the son of Susie Crest who was of mixed Shoshone and Paiute ancestry and a Yugoslavian father, was born in Tule Canyon south of Lida. Vidovich recalls,

> After Mama died, we were sent to Stewart. Jerry an' I was little fellows, Jerry had a dress on when he was sent to Stewart, and I was about 6 years old. We was sent to Stewart because there was no woman to care for us, nobody around, you know. (Wheat 1959, AV tape 74, 7).

In a recent interview with Norma Nelson, this story repeats itself. Norma recalls how her mother was paid to take care of several children who had been orphaned. Upon reaching school age, they were taken to Stewart and taught to milk cows. In addition to sending orphans to Stewart, children were sent to Stewart during periods when food and clothing were scarce. The superintendent of Stewart Indian School in the first decade of the twentieth century observed a seasonal pattern to pupils' attendance:

> It is usually an easy matter to fill the school during the winter months when food is scarce and clothing needed, but during the summer months, when the parents are able to secure employment and little clothing is required it is hard to hold the pupils. (AT 1977)

Upon arriving at Stewart Indian School, the first generations of students were introduced into an institution driven by the purpose of assimilating the Indians into a white world. In practice this entailed labeling everything Indian "bad" and "forbidden" and everything white "good" and "desirable." In order to instill such counterintuitive lessons, school officials endeavored to keep children away from their families for extended periods of time.

> They'd just bring them in raw. They had to stay there for 3 years. They bring you in there, they sign you up for three years; you can't get out of there for three years, unless your father or mother come and take you. But after three years, like us, we lived way down to Lida, the government will pay our expense down there, and J. D. Oliver, or some of the big employees, would bring us home. And then, in the fall, they'd come down 'n get you. (Wheat 1959, AV tape 74: 10–11)

FIGURE 4.1. The Stewart Indian School smith shop. Nevada State Museum.

Disease

In addition to being placed in environments designed to undermine and destroy Indigenous ideas, values, beliefs, and practices, students attending Stewart were exposed to multiple life-endangering diseases. Ed Johnson, who authored *Walker River Paiutes* notes that "Students from kindergarten through the eighth grade . . . were subject to the ravages of diseases including measles, whooping cough, smallpox, and the flu. Soon after the school opened, students were afflicted with the mumps." (AT 1977). In addition, dysentery reportedly ran rampant (Jackson 1969, 36). Many of these diseases ended in death. Johnson reports, "Students died at the school. . . . In 1905 there were several cases of serious illness, mostly pneumonia, five proving fatal. [In addition], Superintendent James B. Royce and many students died during the 1918 worldwide flu epidemic" (AT 1977). In a recent interview Norma Nelson also reports that one of her sisters died of meningitis that she contracted while attending boarding school.

Mrs. Hershey, a white woman, was reared on a reservation in Utah, where her father was a minister. She remembers when she first came to Stewart there was much sickness. "It seems there was one epidemic after another then . . . but since we started giving immunization, we don't have much serious sickness anymore" (REG 1962, 7). By 1913, a hospital bed was added and children began to receive immunization shots, and in 1916 school officials opened the first Indian hospital and sanitarium in Nevada (NSJ 1916, 6).

Mistakenly, some reporters have attributed "a great deal of the sickness" that was evidenced among the students of Stewart to a "lack of medicines and food, and unhealthy living conditions on reservations" (REG 1962, 7). The lack of medicine, insufficient foods, overcrowding, and both physical and psychological trauma indicated in personal histories of former pupils and the BIA Meriam Report suggest that the spread of disease was catalyzed by conditions within the school itself. In response to these physical dangers, some children ran away. In addition, parents were known to remove their children from the schools (AT 1977).

Discipline

From the 1890s through the 1930s, and possibly later, Stewart was run as a semi-military institution in which Indian children's lives were closely monitored and controlled. "Although the rules gradually were relaxed, students once were required to wear uniforms, march to class, and attend drill instruction" (O'Brien 1990, 33). In addition to marching to class they were required to perform drills in front of the superintendent on a weekly basis. One former pupil maintains, "It was designed to break the morale of the Indians but it didn't work" (NSJ 1982).

Prior to the institution of reforms advocated by Lewis Meriam and John Collier, the use of corporal punishment extended to all aspects of the boarding school experience. Strict behavioral regimes were designed to "physically, ideologically, and emotionally remove Indian children from their families, homes and tribal affiliations" (Archuleta et al. 2000, 19). When Vidovich went to school at Stewart, Asbury was the agent and J. D. Oliver was the disciplinarian. Vidovich recalls,

> His word was law all the time . . . that was during the days when they were trying to make Indians white overnight, you know what I mean? And they beat that Indian tradition out of 'em . . . All that pride was taken out of 'em. They broke him. (Wheat 1959, AV tape 74: 10)

Measures of noncompliance were regularly met with extreme force. "In the first 30 years . . . discipline was immediate—and often brutal. Girls were locked in the attic of the girl's dormitory. Students were forced to carry railroad ties around the grounds. Some were shackled. Children who ran away—and many did—were returned in leg irons and chains. Even in the late years, students were subject to severe punishment" (RGJ 1994). Stories of student resistance abound. Not uncommonly, children ran away from the school. However, "If a child brought to the school ran away, he was rounded up and brought back, sometimes in chains, and put on detention and watched" (O'Brien 1990, 34).

Language

Speaking in one's native tongue was a common source of punishment. While such policies were justified as methods for catalyzing assimilation, many contemporary writers describe these measures as cultural genocide (e.g., Archuleta et al. 2000, 19). The lack of fluency in English was initially one of the greatest barriers separating the students of Stewart and their teachers as well as the students from different reservations. In an article from the BIA on why Indian boarding schools failed, the author writes,

> Ignoring completely the tribal differences which have been discussed in earlier issues of Indian Education, the infant representatives of hundreds of tribes were thrown together indiscriminately. The better to encourage the learning of English, the speaking of tribal languages was forbidden. The ban was enforced through corporal punishment—occasionally of a brute nature. Little children barely seven years old were torn from their parents, shipped sometimes thousands of miles from home, without understanding what it was all about, and then housed in vast ugly, friendless dormitories where sixty to a

> hundred and more children shared a single room. Bathing and toilet facilities were . . . inconvenient and unsanitary. . . . Thus did we undertake to "civilize" our wards—in an atmosphere which must have made the most primitive of Indian homes appear as paradise in comparison. (Bureau of Indian Affairs 1936, 6; cited in Officer 1956, 17)

Paiute-Shoshone Ned Crutcher of Herlong, California, seventy-one years old at the time of his recollection, was sent to Stewart Indian School in 1924. This was four years before the writing of the Meriam Report, which called for a series of reforms ranging from increasing the quality and quantity of food given to students to decreasing the menial work that students were required to perform outside of the classroom. Like many of his peers, Crutcher recalls that he was prohibited from speaking in Paiute or Shoshone. "You learn quick. The idea was you were not to speak your language. I got caught I got punished for it" (Nevada 1990, 36).

One Indigenous woman who was forced to attend a boarding school in Covelo recalled,

> I was eleven year[s] old [when I went to Covelo] and every night I cried and then I'd lay awake and think and think and think. I'd think to myself, If I ever get married and have children I'll never teach my children the language or all the Indian things that I know. I'll never teach them that, I don't want my children to be treated like they treated me. That's the way I raised my children. (Margolin 1993, 182).

Although punishment awaited the Indian pupil who was caught speaking anything but English, some of the older students at Stewart chose to employ rituals of resistance that allowed them to keep their languages alive while also ensuring that younger students would have the opportunity to speak in their native tongue. Effie Dressler recollects, "The older girls would come get us little ones and take us off behind a building so we could speak our language" (Nevada 1990, 36).

Given the severity of the corporal punishment that awaited those who chose to speak Paiute, Shoshone, or Washoe, the courage of this measure of resistance is worthy of note. In an interview with Margaret Wheat, Andy Vidivich recalls how he was treated when he spoke Paiute. Wheat asked, "Didn't you tell me one time that the kids were not permitted to speak Paiute or any other Indian language?" Vidovich responded,

> If you do, they break your head open. See, they call it blacksnake rule. The disciplinarian and the night watchman, the big officers, had black snakes on 'em. They catch you talkin' Indian, boy! They jus whale on you 'til you can't move.... Anytime... day or night, or anywhere or any place.... So as to break that Indian language, so they'll acquire the English language. (Wheat 1959, AV tape 74)

While the details of the "blacksnake rule" are perhaps lost to history, this statement by Northern Paiute Andy Vidovich, recorded by anthropologist Margaret Wheat, parallels descriptions of corporal punishment of boarding school students at other schools. At Rainy Mountain Boarding School among the Kiowa, for example,

> The most draconian punishment was whipping. Students genuinely feared such occasions, because they occasionally ran out of control. "The men ... do it," Annie Bigman recalled. "When they whip 'em, some would half kill them ... order and discipline, then, lay at the core of the boarding school experience. (Ellis 2006, 77).

Social Reproduction

In addition to creating an atmosphere that was designed to strip Paiutes and Shoshones of their cultural identities, the Stewart Indian School curriculum was designed to create a cheap pool of wageworkers that would service local economies. During the first forty years of its existence, the Stewart Indian School approximated a work camp in which the labor of the students was required to keep the institution afloat. Within this system, children were required to work half the day and attend school during the other half of the day. O'Brien (1990, 38) writes, "Vocational training predominated in the early years because the school, which fed and clothed itself, used its residents for production of food and clothing and for maintenance of the grounds and building."

Johnson states that in 1895, the school raised 1 1/4 tons of sweet corn, 32 1/2 tons of hay, 1 1/2 tons of rye, 15 tons of beets, 32 1/2 tons of potatoes, 1 1/2 tons of carrots, and 1 1/2 tons of other vegetables. These were stored for winter use (AT 1977). In spite of a heavy workload, however, the labors of students were not always sufficient to provide enough food for all of the pupils. "Former students have said that they raided the fields, vegetable cellars, Genoa and Carson orchards, milked the cows, caught rabbits and cooked their own stew because they were often still hungry after meals were served" (AT 1977).

Critics of prereform policies have disparaged this system's heavy emphasis of menial labor, the small amount of funds that were allocated for this institution in comparison to the cheapest non-Indigenous boarding schools, and the low academic standards that were set in comparison to non-Indian schools from the same period. After the Meriam Report was published in 1928, the quality of care and instruction in all BIA affiliated institutions came under closer scrutiny. Shortly thereafter, BIA-officials went to Stewart to assess the quality of instruction as well as the general welfare of students. In response, they recommended a number of reform measures including the institution of vocational training. Consequently, programs were revised and students were "given instruction and a choice of jobs in animal husbandry, farming, ranching, baking, blacksmithing (later auto mechanics), laundry, plumbing, carpentry, stone masonry, home economics, nursing skills, and bookkeeping skills, sewing, tailoring, printing, and cobblery" (O'Brien 1990, 38).

Achuleta et al. (2000, 34) writes, "The school's vocational training reflected federal intentions to fit Indian people into the lower economic sectors of American society as small-scale farmers, manual and unskilled laborers, or domestic workers." One method of reinforcing vocational habits while simultaneously reinforcing the cultural values of Euro-Americans occurred through the practice of placing children in white families over summer vacations. While living in these settings, students were required to help the families by doing physical tasks ranging from washing clothes and babysitting to engaging in agricultural and ranching duties. Summer placements served to prolong the period of time in which students were separated from their families; a practice that school officials believed would expedite their assimilation goals. Although there are multiple detractors of vocational training, there are those who support these measures as well. Not infrequently, former students cite the vocational training that they received as the most valuable aspect of their time spent at the Stewart Indian School.

Rituals of Resistance

Among former students within our study, far less value was attributed to the disciplinary structure under which the students' daily affairs were organized. In response to the rigors of a semi-military institution that was designed to "take the Indianness out of Indians," students employed innovative strategies to protect themselves and maintain a sense of cultural identity. Children would sequester themselves behind buildings where they would speak in their native languages. Older students often took the lead in ensuring that younger students had the opportunity to practice speaking their own languages. Students also developed "elaborate codes of slang and became expert note passers to circumvent school rules that impeded communication" (Archuleta et al. 2000, 26).

Some students also created strategies to ensure that they had ongoing contact with siblings within an institution that forbade socializing between male and female students. The Vidovich children went so far as to disguise their younger brother as a girl before arriving at the school:

> Jerry was a little baby. When he was going to Stewart he had a dress on him. And they put him in the big girls' dormitory, and they got to bathe him and dress him, and fix him up. See, I tell you, that's the reason we [Vidovich children] are so close together, on account of that. (Wheat 1959, AV tape 74, 15)

The enforced segregation of male and female students is described in the following passage. Vidovich recalls, "They have places called the 'dead line.' Places where big girls can't come over from their place across a certain sidewalk there. And the little girls can't come over certain place this side" (Wheat 1959, AV tape 74).

While adherence to "the dead line rule" was strictly enforced, children of all ages were known to "cross the line,"

> An' Jerry here, get pretty lonesome, you know, and used to come on over to the little girls' side, and he'd git over there, and he'd just bawl, you know. We had tough matrons there, too, them times, you know; boy, they really were rough. They used to come over there, and they'd say, "You-u-u shut up now, you." And they'd keep a-crying. "You little black devil, you. You shut up!" And they'd go over there and just whale the devil out of them. Gee, I used just figure if I could only get me a big branch of something, I'd go right in and beat her head off. I used to walk over, and then I'd get a good whaling. I'd try to put my arms around 'im you know. (Wheat 1959, AV tape 74)

The decision to separate children by sex disrupted sibling relationships as well as courting relationships that had sometimes begun before the students arrived at the school. Rather than acknowledging the cultural appropriateness of allowing youths to participate in tribally sanctioned rites of passage, however, school officials endeavored to curb these behaviors entirely. The most effective means of stopping cross-sex relationships was to frighten students into submission. This was affected by introducing the Judeo-Christian concepts of sin, hell, and damnation (Jackson 1969). Although such indoctrination curbed culturally instilled behaviors, students who left school and then returned again were notorious for reverting back to ideas and practices of their own ethnic groups.

Running away was another ritual of resistance that occurred with some frequency. In oral histories collected in the Zion/Pipe Springs Ethnographic Project, a woman from Koosharem talked about the places where some of the children hid within the Virgin River Gorge area:

> Sham people [Shivwits Reservation] used to go over there to hunt Mountain Sheep. Ray Mose and Norbert Zungia ran away from school at Ft. Mohave and hid out in the Virgin River Gorge area. They found a cabin with food in it and lived in this. The school never found them. (Stoffle et al. 1977, 84)

The parents of Indigenous students were often equally critical of the processes of indoctrination that children were exposed to in their stay at Stewart Indian School. In an interview with John Kennedy, Western Shoshone cultural representative from Lida, Nevada, he relates the story of how his own father as well as his extended family acted in concert to remove John and his two siblings from Stewart:

> The government tried to take every children. They don't want them to learn their language. Take them from their Indian ways. One train picked up all the little kids. Dad got us out of the school. Picked up all three kids in a Model T Ford. Took him to Telescope Peak with his aunt—Hide him out—Skipping him from here to there, family to family to miss school. To grandparents, stayed in Lida, with other grandfather in Lida. (Carroll 2003)

Boarding School Alternatives

Although many Paiute, Shoshone, and Washoe children from throughout Nevada attended the nonreservation Stewart Indian School from 1890 until the end of World War II, others were given the option of attending local reservation schools or public schools (NSJ 1982). By 1887, four Indian schools had been founded in Nevada including Pyramid Lake School (1887), The Walker River School (1882), the Western Shoshone School (1882), and the McDermitt School (1886) (Jackson 1969, 11).

In central Nevada, a public elementary school attended by Euro-American and Indian children was established in Round Mountain in 1907 (figure 4.2). In addition to establishing an elementary school, the residents of Round Mountain started a library in April 1907 and a newspaper in June 1906 (Berg 1941). While the library was short-lived, the newspaper, *The Round Mountain Nugget*, was regularly printed between June 1906 and November 1910.

Although the school was established in 1907, construction of building did not begin until August 1908. For a total of $1,500, the residents built a one-room schoolhouse measuring twenty by thirty feet. Other notable features included large windows and a seven-foot porch. The first teacher of this school, Mrs. W. R. Gibson, taught students of all ages in this one-room school. Berg (1941) reports that at times Indians comprised half of the student body. Although the number of children attending classes eventually swelled to as many as forty or fifty, Berg

(1941) reports that there was usually only one teacher to instruct all pupils; however, in 1935 two teachers were briefly employed. Until November 1937, the Round Mountain School served as the official elementary school and unofficial high school. Thereafter, teachers and students relocated to a four-room school that was used jointly as an elementary and high school facility.

In 1915 yet another small public school attended by Euro-American and Indian children was established south of Warm Springs, Nevada (figure 4.3). This one-room school, known as the Eden Creek School, was founded shortly after the Fallini family took over the ranch near Warm Springs. In a recent ethnographic interview, a Shoshone elder who was born and raised in the south Kawich Range reflected upon his educational experiences at the Eden Creek School as well as his experiences at the Stewart Indian School, which he attended in the early 1930s.

The educational experiences of Curtis Pete are similar as well as distinct from many of the experiences previously relayed by students attending the Stewart Indian School. Pete was born in Eden Creek in 1929. Pete came from a large family of five brothers and four sisters, of whom many moved away upon reaching adulthood. One of his brothers entered the Air Force, his sister Daisy Smith married a man from Duckwater and settled in Reno, and his oldest brother, Richard, moved to Ohio. Although the paths of their lives diverged in adulthood, as children they shared many experiences that were closely linked to the land of the Kawich Range, the communities that formed in Eden Creek, and the education they received as children in Warm Springs.

Pete describes himself as a Shoshone from a very independent family. Unlike many of the Shoshone families living in the southern Kawich range, the Pete family had their own ranch in Eden Creek upon which his great grandfather built a permanent house of stone. Each year the Pete family would travel to White Rock east of Gold Reed. Curtis recalls that his folks "wanted to get away from cold, and there was plentiful game and pine nuts down there. Then in the spring they would head back up to Eden Creek." While living in Eden Creek his grandfather and father worked for cattle ranchers in the area. One of the ranches that Curtis's father cowboyed for was owned by the Fallini family. He also worked for the United Packing Company.

In 1915, the Fallini family donated money to establish a public school for all children within the Warm Springs area. In order to provide the opportunity for their children to attend public school, the entire Pete family relocated themselves to Warm Springs, whereupon they built a simple shack to live in. This act of relocating families in order to keep a family together occurred repeatedly among Paiute and Shoshone communities throughout the state of Nevada and in neighboring states as well. For example, in 1908 officials of the Mission Agency ordered the roundup of the Chemehuevi children of Twenty Nine Palms, California. The children were taken to Banning, California and forced to attend school at Saint Boniface. As the removal of the children from their families was compulsory, many families felt compelled to move their entire households in order to be closer to their children. In practice this entailed moving to "the Malki Agency or the Morongo Reservation near Banning . . . Some scholars have argued that movements like this were natural and not forced . . . the circumstances surrounding the abandonment of Twenty-Nine Palms by Chemehuevis was not voluntary. . . . In the minds

FIGURE 4.2. Eden Creek Ranch school, circa 1935. Pictured (left to right), man standing far left, Fallini; back row: Ethel Argoni, Esther Siri (teacher), Eveleen Argoni, Aldo Argoni; front row: Hazel Argoni, Lawrence Argoni, Curtis (Pete) Littlebeaver, Daisy Williams, Bert Williams, Dick Pete, Alice Pete, Mabel Pete. File 337, Central Nevada Historical Society.

of parents and grandparents, aunts and uncles, they had no choice but to remain with their children" (Trafzer et al. 1997, 85–86).

In the case of the Pete family, living in Warm Springs with the family intact proved to be beneficial for the nine Pete children who attended school along with their Euro-American peers. While living there, the Pete children attended school in a one-room schoolhouse along with the Fallini children, several kids from Sharp, including Bert Williams and Daisy Williams, and a local white family known as the Argomes. In an interview Curtis Pete, Western Shoshone cultural representative, remembered his teacher Helen Humphrey with fondness, but was quick to note that not all of the children were equally disposed. After attending Warm Springs, which in his words had "nothing to do with Indian school," Pete transferred to Carson Indian School to attend high school classes (Carroll 2003).

Pete's recollections of Carson Indian School were decidedly less favorable than his memories at Eden Creek. Pete attended Carson in the late 1930s after the federal government had already mandated a series of reforms. Nonetheless, Pete's descriptions resonate with depictions of the school in the prereform period, which suggests the basic culture of behavioral control and anti-Indianness had not been fundamentally altered. Pete viewed Carson as a military-like institution where rules and condemnation prevailed. Pete believes that many of the youths he met at Carson did not like school and did not want to "go the white man's ways too much." He recalls, "They'd go to school for a little while and drop out, you know how it is, reading, writing, that's good enough for us, that was the attitude." Pete indicates that while this attitude prevailed among his peers, the parents of many children felt that "it would be best for them to get an education." Although Pete attended unwillingly and ran away, he comments, "As far as education for a youngster to know what's going to come ahead—living in a white person's world and we work for them, so it is better to speak English and have education" (Carroll 2003).

Pete's statement reveals an uneasy compromise with a system of education and socialization that failed to meet his needs as well as the needs of many of his peers. With all of its limitations, however, Pete still maintains that Indigenous youths need Western forms of education in order to understand and engage others in a world dominated by Euro-American ideas and interests. When one considers that Pete is an individual with a thirst for knowledge that he feeds through historical research and writing, the gap between the potential ideals of education, and their at times impoverished manifestations, is clearly evidenced (Carroll 2003).

Indian Education Policies and Historic Chronologies

The Bureau of Indian Affairs' and the general public's idea of Indian education has changed several times over the course of 125 years. As a result, the curriculums utilized by nonreservation boarding schools, reservation schools, and public schools have altered as well. Officer (1956, 116–17) has identified three periods in which Indian education policies as well as the enactment of these ideas have been modified. The earliest of these periods, extending from 1890 to 1928, is characterized by cultural destruction and forced assimilation. The second period, from 1928 to 1945, references the Indian Reform Movement that ensued in the wake of the Meriam Report; during the third, from 1945 to 1956, the federal government endeavored to remove itself from Indian affairs (see table 4.3). To this list, I add a fourth period, characterized by the theme of cultural revitalization. The latter allows us to bring the reader up to date with primary changes in education for Native peoples in Nevada from 1956 until 2015.

If the 1920s and 1930s were shaped by the Indian Reform Movement spurred on by the incriminatory findings cataloged in the Meriam Report (e.g., Meriam et al. 1928; Crum 2006, 156), the assimilation of Natives into the dominant economy as blue-collar workers is evidenced from the opening of Stewart Indian School in 1890 through at least the 1940s. This economic focal point of white enculturation began with speculation over the impact of an Indian school on the future economy in Ormsby County (Jackson 1969, 12). It continued with Native students being held responsible for producing all the food consumed and clothing required while attending boarding school. The provision of vocational options within the school, and the development and continuation of "outing" programs placing Native students as domestic and agricultural labor in white homes furthered this aim. Notably, the shift toward vocational training from 1935 to 1940 reflected a change of curriculum supported by tribal governments from Pyramid Lake,

McDermitt, and Western Shoshone Reservations (Jackson 1969, 83). Through on campus vocational training classes coupled with outing programs, host families and policymakers gave life to various economic, assimilationist, and moralistic agendas. Jacobs writes,

> in 1918, the BIA hired Bonnie Royce, wife of the superintendent of the Stewart Indian School in Carson City, Nevada (often referred to as the Carson Indian School), to place young Indian women from the surrounding area in domestic service. The Commissioner of Indian Affairs stipulated that Royce "give special attention to procuring [employment in] homes for Indian girls after they have left school or for any other Indian women of Nevada and Northern California . . ., in order that they may be protected from the degrading moral conditions which are found in the small mining towns of Nevada and the country adjacent thereto." (Jacobs 2007, 172)

The outing programs reputedly assisted Native children in becoming more assimilated to the Calvinist influences underscoring the dominant economies of Nevada and neighboring states. Many of the schools developed what came to be called "outing" programs, ostensibly to aid in the children's assimilation, which placed the children for part of each day and usually for entire summers with local families. Boys were usually set to work doing farm labor, while girls were to be employed in domestic service within the home. Even while in school, much of the education Indian children received revolved around training them for such menial positions, a process officials often characterized as making them "useful" (Jacobs 2007, 166).

From the 1930s through the 1940s, many young men and women from Stewart Indian School (then named the Carson Indian School) participated in outing programs in the San Francisco Bay Area of northern California, which resulted in them remaining away from their families for extended periods during summers and holiday breaks.

During the summer of 1929, for example, of forty-one Indian girls outed for the summer, twenty-seven were from the Carson school. Of the eighty young Indian women permanently outed in the Bay Area in 1929, twenty-eight were from the Carson school (Jacobs 2007, 173).

In part because of the dire economic strains that characterized the Depression a decade later, many Native men and women sought out domestic employment situations that contributed to their permanent or semi-permanent removal from Native communities either while enrolled in Stewart, or as graduates of this and other formal learning institutions. Jacobs writes,

> When the Depression hit, Indian women's options narrowed further as their need to earn money became even greater. "Wynona," a Mono Indian, wrote in search of a position because "I am quiet [sic] interested, as we certainly feel the depression. I will quit school in a minute to secure a job for fifty dollars per month as a cook." Some supported family members. "Daisy," a Shasta Indian who had three children, wrote to one of the matrons, "[I] have left my husband, he is worthless and cruel . . . . I tried to stay with him for the children's sake but he is just impossible. I am at home with mother now . . . . Must get some work to do soon as my three children and I are without shoes or clothes." During these hard times, many Indian women might have viewed domestic service as one part of an overall economic strategy. Many young Pomo women, for example, often worked picking hops in the summers and serving in white women's households in the Bay Area for the remainder of the year. (Jacobs 2007, 177)

Some Native American young men identified yet another niche for themselves in the arena of sports. Andrew McGregor (2013, 41), for example, reports that from 1935 to 1948, amateur boxing garnered a lot of public attention. Though controversial, such programs flowered in part because they expressed the "muscular Christianity concept" that linked physical education with assimilationist goals (McGregor 2013, 43). During this same period, particularly around World War II, former students such as Andrew Vidovich began enrolling in the US military in growing numbers. In some cases, students joined the military after graduating from Stewart Indian School. However, many older students also dropped out of school to join the military during the same time period (Jackson 1969, 87). Among many attendees and

Table 4.3: Federal Indian policies 1890–present.

Period	Federal Indian Policy	Policy Implementation
1890–1928	Destroy Indian Cultures Incorporate Indians into the General Cultural Stream of the United States	Remove the child from tribal influence by placing the child in a federal boarding school Teach the child disrespect for tribal institutions Forbid the child from speaking native languages Expose the child to Christianity Instruct the child in skills related to non-Indian, rather than an Indian economy
1928–1945	Acknowledge the values of Indian cultures Permit Indians to proceed at their own pace towards incorporation into the general stream of the United States	Let the child attend school near home and allow the child to be with family at night Teach respect for tribal institutions Encourage retention of select elements of Indian cultures Bring Indians into the planning of the school program Provide training in skills useful away from the reservation for those Indians who desire to live elsewhere
1945–1956	Remove the federal government from the "Indian business" as rapidly as possible	Encourage Indian attendance at public schools When educating Indian children in federal schools concentrate on preparing the Indian child for eventual off-reservation employment so as to help make Indians self-supporting Relieve the pressures of increasing reservation populations Prepare Indians for federal withdrawal
1956–present	Cultural Revitalization American Indian Education Foundation Act 1999	Increase Cultural Awareness Promote Educational Advancement Address Language Loss Catalyze Student Retention

former attendees of Stewart Indian School, educational policies as well as individual choices thus contributed to Native students electing nontraditional roles that often resulted in them remaining away from their families and cultural communities for extended periods of time.

From the 1940s through the 1960s, the façade of Stewart Indian School continued to change. In 1941, for example, Stewart opened its doors to Native students outside of Nevada, which resulted in a rise in enrollment to five hundred students during the fall semester of 1941 (Jackson 1969, 87). Eight years later, Stewart enrolled 148 Navajo children as part of the Special Navajo Program that sought to provide formal education for 13,000 Navajo children. Alongside changes in student populations, Native Americans began to assume greater control and responsibility in the teaching and administration of Stewart Indian School:

> In 1944 and 1949 inservice school was held at the Carson Indian School. The 1949 classes had the largest attendance of any Indian inservice programs in the United States. Thirty-six Indian tribes were represented, and twelve Indians were on the teaching staff. (Jackson 1969, 69)

As Native peoples moved into positions of authority within the boarding school, the climate and perception of this institution also shifted; however, changes did not sit equally well with all the tribal constituents. Jackson (1969, 22) reports that tribal animosities sometimes arose over staff and curriculum choices,

> Washoes and Shoshones were disgruntled over the fact that Indian teachers were frequently chosen from the Paiute tribe. When the first few out-of-state Indians teachers were brought in, all three of the Nevada tribes threatened to withdraw their children. Because the Washoes were readily available, groundskeepers and maintenance personnel were chosen from their ranks. Paiute and Shoshone attendance dropped to a new low.

Alongside changes in staff and curriculum, expectations around formal education for Native students also began to undergo transitions in the 1940s and 1950s. Crum (1989, 22) reports that in 1949, tribal communities of Nevada created an organization, Confederated Indian Tribes of Nevada:

> The participants wanted the Stewart Indian School, located adjacent to Carson City, to become an Indian junior college. But these ideas went nowhere because they were proposed in a period when the federal government started formulating its "Termination" (assimilation) policy for Native America. As had been earlier, the objective was to amalgamate the Indians into mainstream America. It was this kind of thinking which prevented the creation of an Indian college or university in the immediate postwar period. (Crum 1989, 22)

Although this did not come to pass, a Navajo College was established shortly thereafter, and during this same time frame, policies developed to integrate Native students into the public schools of Nevada (Haglund 1966). By 1963, Stewart accepted six hundred enrollees from fourteen tribes, children from Nevada, Utah, Arizona, and New Mexico. At this time, the Department of Indian Affairs praised Stewart as a "school of major importance" (Jackson 1969, 99). Despite such high praise, federal budget cuts resulted in Stewart Indian School closing its doors in 1980 (Stewart Indian School 2012). Shortly thereafter, Stewart was successfully nominated to the National Register of Historic Places (Stewart Indian School 2012). Currently an annual powwow is held at Stewart Indian School on Father's Day that includes "traditional competition dancing, Stewart School alumni recognition, arts and crafts, special events and exhibits" (Stewart Indian School 2012).

Contemporary Manifestations of Historical Processes

Throughout this chapter I have explored how the creation and enactment of federal education policies have shaped Native education in Nevada. In this final section, I examine the enduring legacies of Native education policies among the Paiute and Shoshone of central Nevada. In oral histories and personal narratives recounted by elders in interviews conducted in central Nevada in 2001, former students' responses suggest levels of significance associated with Indigenous education policies to which this chapter can only allude. At the same time, those who have personally experienced educational mandates during different historical periods have expressed collective themes that continue to have tangible social impacts in the present. First, I identify several social issues collectively raised over the course of these interviews. Specifically, these issues revolve around two core themes: loss and adaptation. Due to the nature of these experiences these themes are not mutually exclusive.

Language Loss, Language Gain

The rigid enforcement of English within Indian schools in Nevada has resulted in immeasurable losses as well as significant gains. The modern Paiute and Shoshone of central Nevada are without exception fluent in the English language. As a result, the Indigenous people of central Nevada are able to communicate with people outside of their original speech communities. While the speech communities acquired through fluency in English clearly extend to persons associated with the dominant "white" culture, fluency in English has also created channels for communication between and among Indigenous groups that previously shared no common language. The boarding school experience of the late nineteenth century thus laid the linguistic foundations for pan-Indian affiliations that have continued to evolve over the course of the last century. Although tribal histories and traditional alliances and animosities were never erased by a growing awareness of pan-Indianness, the development of cross ethnic Indigenous alliances has held and continues to acquire new social, political, and economic significance.

While the acquisition of English has empowered Paiutes and Shoshones in realms outside of their immediate communities, participation in Western forms of education has simultaneously undermined Native languages to such an extent that very few people remain who consider themselves to be fluent speakers of their Native languages. Among those who still speak Shoshone and Paiute fluently there is a growing conviction that they are among the last. In a recent interview, Shoshone elder Curtis Pete affirmed that he is fluent in Shoshone and "never gave that up." While he can speak "every word of it," he is distressed by the fact that "there is no one left to talk to." Similarly, Homer Hooper, son of Alice Hooper and grandson of Chief Kawich, revealed that while he still speaks his own language, he had a hard time finding people with whom to speak because none of the young people speak Shoshone. His wife, Nancy Hooper, maintained that hardly anyone still speaks Shoshone. When asked how many people were fluent, she estimated that she knew of only five to ten people (McCracken 1990, 10–11).

Bertha Moose, an Owens Valley Paiute, and daughter of Elsie Bowers and George C. Collins, had the fortune of being taught her Native language in a time when growing numbers of children were exposed to more English than Paiute. Bertha's mother attended boarding school at the Sherman Institute along with her sister, Lillian. Bertha recalls that her mother never lost her language and made a conscious decision to teach it to her children. Bertha also spent a lot of time with her grandmother, who spoke very little English. When Bertha began school, she was fluent in her Native language, but had to be taught English. As she grew older she recalls that truant officers would come to her grandmother's house and ask why Bertha was not at school. Although her grandmother spoke no English, Bertha taught her grandmother one phrase to get the truant officers to go away, "Go away. Bertha is sick!"

In a telling moment Homer Hooper asked the rhetorical question, "Now they want people to go to school to learn the Indian language and . . . I wonder why that is?" (McCracken 1990, 10). The poignancy of Hooper's question lies in its capacity to reveal the arbitrariness of Indian educational policies. Whereas federal policies of the late nineteenth century and early twentieth century were purposively designed to promote English and eradicate the use of Native languages, today the same languages that were systematically undermined are the centerpieces of language enhancement programs. Those who have the greatest stake in preserving Native languages are faced by multiple challenges, not the least of which is how to keep languages alive when the speech communities where a child previously learned the language are rapidly disappearing.

Dual Cultural Awareness

Participation and membership in more than one speech community and cultural group has also led many elders to express sentiments about acquiring fluency in more than one culture. When reflecting about the life of a sister who died of meningitis while living at the

Stewart Indian School, Norma Nelson, cultural representative from Owens Valley, Nevada, raised the issue of cultural fluency. At school Nelson's sister was introduced to one culture, and at home another. She reportedly enjoyed going to church and singing. "But when she came home my grandma and grandpa told us stories of the land, so she got both." In reflecting about her own education, Nelson recalls that she went to school in Bishop and later finished school in Yerington. Her family, like many families, was compelled to move around to wherever work was available. Nelson's father was a truck driver, and later went to work on the Hoover Dam, building roads. During this time, Nelson and her mother lived with him in a tent they had set up nearby. Due to the frequency with which they moved, Nelson says she "hardly got education" (Carroll 2003).

Nelson's statement appears to reflect a perception of being less fluent in the Western cultural constructions and practices than in the cultural matrixes of her own Indigenous community. Although she reports that she "hardly got education" she qualifies her statement saying, "Then again, my dad taught me everything about the land." In other words, Nelson received a traditional education, and as a consequence became well-versed in a type of knowledge that has until recently received little recognition among non-Indigenous people.

The sense of dual cultures is also raised by Alfred Stanton and by Curtis Pete, the latter of whom maintains that although Western education has a history of failing to meet the needs of many Indigenous children, the children nevertheless need Western forms of education to survive in a world of Western practices and beliefs. Pete also discusses the concern he noted among his peers of "becoming too white." His statement indicates that there is tension between learning enough about the ideas and practices espoused by non-Indigenous communities to be able to successfully negotiate cross-cultural encounters without becoming accommodating to the point of compromising or negating a sense of cultural identity. Alfred Stanton, on the other hand, expresses with conviction that he "got the best of both worlds."

The theme of conflicting cultural values is raised in Knack's (1978) analysis of the educational and work experiences of Southern Paiutes. Knack maintains that while educational institutions steeped in Western values and ideas promote behaviors stemming from competition and individualism, Numic people have traditionally emphasized cultural values of cooperation and community. These ideals thus appear to represent polarized rather than parallel values. At home they may be taught to privilege the group above the individual, yet at school they are socialized to view the community as secondary to the individual. Children exposed to competing sets of values often experience dissonance that is most easily resolved by selecting one set of values at the expense of the other. From 1890 to 1928, Indian education policies espoused a replacement theory of culture. Consequently, Indigenous children were encouraged to embrace the cultural values of Euro-Americans at the cost of Indigenous knowledge practices and beliefs. Following the Meriam Report in 1928, policies gradually moved toward acknowledging certain aspects of Indigenous cultures. Today collective efforts to revitalize and honor Indigenous cultures are having an effect upon the way in which both Indigenous and non-Indigenous communities view the existence and value of Indigenous knowledge. What remains to be seen is what role Indigenous knowledge will play in the classroom.

Vocational Skills

Former students of Stewart maintain that the vocational skills they learned while attending this nonreservation boarding school represent some of the most tangible benefits of their educations (see figure 4.4). The introduction of formal vocational programs followed recommendations from a member of the U.S. Board of Indian Commissioners in 1928. After visiting Stewart Indian School, this representative recommended more vocational and academic instruction: "The commissioner also reported that students did too much menial labor and stated that more employees should be hired so that the students could be given more classroom instruction" (AT 1977). Following this visit, the school developed a vocational emphasis which included the creation of industrial departments such as auto mechanics, carpentry, plumbing, heating, painting, electricity, masonry, plastering, and shoe repair. Additionally, the school assumed an agricultural emphasis that included the production of hay, beef, veal, hamburger, and milk. Many people who attended Stewart experienced a sense of empowerment in relation to the vocational skills they acquired while attending school. Homer Hooper recalls that when he was at Stewart he was trained to,

> work in the laundry . . . [and] in the paint shop . . . [Later he] took up a little bit in mechanics and welding . . . took up poultry—raising chickens—and farming, like planting vegetables and working in the dairy . . . I was just back and forth, looking for different trades. . . . That's when I took up all these different things that would help me out through the later years. (McCracken 1990, 8–9)

The importance of vocational training is also indicated in the life of Shoshone elder Helen Eben. Eben was born in Cottonwood and later lived in several places including Warm Springs, Carson City, and Duckwater. Like many of her peers, Eben moved to Stewart Boarding School to attend high school. Eben shared the experience of attending boarding school with her brother and sister; however, Helen viewed her stay from a somewhat different angle than her peers. She recalls that her brother disliked the school because of all the rules and strict discipline. While Eben did not particularly care for the way in which the institution was run, she was motivated to stay and graduate from Stewart so that she might successfully pursue her career goals. Eben attended school for four years. After graduating, Eben married Nebs Jackson from Reese River.

Thereafter, she obtained a job as a nurse. Throughout the rest of her working life, Eben remained a nurse. Consequently, in her recollections of boarding school, Eben emphasizes the training she received at Stewart as well as the friends she made from Elko, Carson, and Reno.

Throughout this chapter, I have talked directly as well as indirectly about people's personal and social memories of attending Indian schools. In this final section, I explore how the need to keep memories alive can be expressed in relation to the places where the memories were originally created. The importance of particular places in terms of social memory was made evident when Interior Secretary James Watt and Governor Robert List made plans to transfer the Stewart Indian School back to the State of Nevada. The *Nevada State Journal* reported

Figure 4.3. Woodshop at Stewart Indian School Social Memories, undated.

that under this agreement fifty central acres of the former school would be transferred back to the state for the purpose of establishing a prison. In response, petitioner Sferrazza wrote,

> To permit the federal government and the state of Nevada to turn a historic monument with so much meaning to Indians throughout the southwestern United States into a prison constitutes a travesty of justice and an affront to Native Americans throughout the United States. (NSJ 1982)

Some former pupils responded to these plans by creating a petition to protest, and if possible prevent federal employees and the state of Nevada from turning the Stewart Indian School into a prison. A reporter for the *Nevada State Journal* indicated that more than 6,200 signatures were gathered in response to List's proposal (NSJ 1983).

From the vantage of social memory, the Stewart Indian Boarding School represents a critical landmark in the lives of many Paiutes, Shoshones, Washoes, and other Indigenous groups. Historically, representatives from these communities experienced some of their darkest and most traumatizing hours in Indian boarding schools. In this chapter, I investigated how nineteenth- and early-twentieth-century educational policies placed Indigenous people in increasingly risk-imbued situations involving the disruption of family and community social systems, the interruption of traditional methods of education, language, and religious practices, and the exposure of children to multiple disease epidemics. Through nonreservation boarding schools, Indigenous youths from diverse linguistic, tribal, and cultural backgrounds came to share the same living spaces for extended periods of time.

While living in these institutions, students were placed into biopower regimes in which their behaviors were strictly regulated through ongoing surveillance, behavioral modification programs, and the liberal use of corporal punishment. Students attending school during the late nineteenth and early twentieth century soon learned that the expression of traditional ideas and behaviors resulted in demerits and the loss of individual privileges and freedoms, whereas behaviors approximating the ideals of a white culture were rewarded. Within these contexts, students endeavored to mediate risks through rituals of resistance and displays of varying degrees of compliance. Over time, some of the children and faculty of the Stewart institution, particularly returning graduates, endeavored to transform the Stewart Indian School from a place to be feared to a region of refuge.

The preservation of the Stewart Indian School stands as a collective effort to honor the social memory of all those who personally underwent the experiences of "becoming educated" according to Western standards of knowledge. In 1981 the state advisory board nominated the Stewart Indian School to the National Register of Historic Places, thereby halting any immediate measures to convert this site into a prison. Ellen Moose Brock, "a Southern Paiute/Western Shoshone whose grandparents, Dave and Lillian (Tootsie) Moose, attended Steward in the early 1900s," affirms this collective need when she says, "Everyone has some kind of connection to this school" (RGJ 1994).

Works Cited

AT (Apple Tree). 1977. "Native Language Was Forbidden: Discipline Was Strict for Stewart Students: Interview with Ed Johnson: Nevada Reveal." *Apple Tree*, February 13.

Archuleta, Margaret L., Brenda J. Child, and K. Tisanina Lomawaima. 2000. *Away from Home: American Indian Boarding School Experiences 1879–2000*. Santa Fe. NM: Museum of New Mexico Press.

Berg, Lucile Rae. 1941. "History of South-Central Nevada." Master's thesis, University of Nevada, Reno.

Berkhofer, Robert F., Jr. 1978. *The White Man's Indian*. New York: Vintage Books.

Carroll, Alex. 2003. "Unpublished Fieldnotes." Archived at Bureau of Applied Research in Anthropology. University of Arizona, Tucson.

Crum, Steven J. 1989. "The Idea of an Indian College or University in Twentieth Century America before the Formation of the Navajo Community College in 1968." *Tribal College: Journal of American Indian Higher Education* 1, no. 1 (May 15): 20–23.

———. 2006. "Rare Exceptions: Some University Professors and the Teaching of Native American History, 1900–1970." *The History Teacher* 39, no. 2 (Feb.): 153–73.

Elliot, Russell R. 1987. *History of Nevada*. 2nd ed., revised. Lincoln, NE: University of Nebraska Press.

Ellis, Clyde. 2006. "'We Had a Lot of Fun, but of Course, That Wasn't the School Part': Life at the Rainy Mountain Boarding School, 1893–1920." In *Boarding School Blues: Revisiting American Educational Experiences*, edited by Clifford E. Trafzer, Jean A. Keller, and Lorene Sisquoc. Lincoln, NE: University of Nebraska Press.

Haglund, E. A. 1966. *Indian Integration in Nevada Public Schools*. Carson City, NV: Nevada State Department of Education.

Hittman, Michael. 1973. "The 1870s Ghost Dance at the Walker River Reservation: A Reconstruction." *Ethnohistory* 20, no. 3: 247–78.

Huff, Delores J. 1997. *To Live Heroically: Institutional Racism and American Indian Education*. Albany, NY: State University New York Press.

Jackson, Nicholas D. 1969. "A History of the Stewart Indian School." Master's thesis, University of Nevada, Reno.

Jacobs, Margaret D. 2007. "American Indian Domestic Servants in White Women's Households in the San Francisco Bay Area, 1920–1940." *Frontiers: A Journal of Women Studies* 28, nos. 1 and 2: 165–99.

Kelley, William H. 1967. *A Study of Southern Arizona School-Age Indian Children 1966–1967*. Tucson, AZ: Bureau of Ethnic Research, Department of Anthropology, University of Arizona:.

Knack, Martha. 1978. "Beyond a Differential: An Inquiry into Southern Paiute Indian Experience with Public Schools." *Anthropology and Education Quarterly* 9: 59–66.

Knack, Martha C., and Omer Call Stewart. 1984. *As Long as the River Shall Run: An Ethnohistory of Pyramid Lake Indian Reservation*. Reno: University of Nevada Press.

Littlefield, Alice, and Martha C. Knack, eds. 1996. *Native Americans and Wage Labor—Ethnohistorical Perspectives*. Norman, OK: University of Oklahoma Press.

Logan, Brad. 1980. "The Ghost Dance among the Paiute: An Ethnohistorical View of the Documentary Evidence 1889–1893." *Ethnohistory* 27, no. 3: 267–88.

Lomawaima, Tsianina K. 1994. *They Called It Prairie Light: The Story of Chilocco Indian School*. Lincoln, NE: University of Nebraska Press.

Margaret Wheat Papers. N.d. Special Collections Department, University of Nevada Reno Knowledge Center.

———. 1959. Tonopah Oral History Project. Special Collections Department, University of Nevada Reno Knowledge Center.

Margolin, Malcolm, ed. 1993. *The Way We Lived: California Indian Stories, Songs & Reminiscences.* Berkeley, CA: Heyday Books/California Historical Society.

McCracken, Robert D., ed. 1990. "An Interview with Andy Thompson." Nye County Oral History Project, Nevada.

McGregor, Andrew. 2013. "Amateur Boxing and Assimilation at the Stewart Indian School Carson City, NV 1935–1948." In *The Native American Identity in Sports: Creating and Preserving a Culture*, edited by Frank A. Salamone, 41–56. Toronto: The Scarecrow Press.

Meriam Report. 1928. *The Problem of Indian Administration: Report of a Survey Made at the Request of Honorable Hubert Work, Secretary of the Interior, and Submitted to Him, February 21, 1928.* Brookings Institution. Baltimore, MD: The Johns Hopkins Press.

Nevada Reveal. 1990. "Interviewing Ed Johnson Regarding Cultural Practices at Steward Indian School," 33.

Nevada Legislature. 1887. An Act to Establish and Provide an Indian School. Thirteen Session Chapter XII—Approved January 25, 1887. *Statutes of the State of Nevada Passed at the Thirteenth Session of the Legislature.* Carson City, Nevada. https://books.google.com/books?id=cWVHAAAAYAAJ&dq=statutes%20of%20the%20state%20of%20nevada&pg=PR1#v=onepage&q=school&f=false.

NSJ (*Nevada State Journal*). 1916. "Items from Over the Entire State: News Notes of Interest from Various Cities and Counties of Nevada. Indian Hospital Open." March 12, 6.

———. 1982. "Stewart Indian School Retrospective Account: Interviews with Wamble and Oliver." April 4.

———. 1983. "Account of List Proposal to Turn Stewart Indian School into a Prison." April 25.

O'Brien, Colleen. 1990. "Stewart School Days: Graduates of Stewart Indian School Recall the Hardships, Friendships, and Lessons Learned." *Nevada* (September/October): 23, 34.

Officer, James E. 1956. *Indians in School: A Study of the Development of Educational Facilities for Arizona Indians.* Bureau of Ethnic Research: Department of Anthropology, University of Arizona.

Pratt, Richard Henry. 1892. "'Kill the Indian, and Save the Man': Capt. Richard H. Pratt on the Education of Native Americans." Speech available at History Matters. http://historymatters.gmu.edu/d/4929/, accessed November 5, 2018.

REG (*Reno Evening Gazette*). 1962. "Frank John Rivers Early Graduate of Stewart Indian School: Alma Mater of the Wa-Pai-Shone." January 17, p. 7, cols. 1 and 3.

RGJ (*Reno Gazette-Journal*). 1994. "Former Students of Steward Indian School Recount their Experiences." November 8.

Scrugham, J. G. 1935. *History of Nevada*, Vol. 1. Carson City, NV: State Printing Press.

Spring, Joel H. 2001. *Deculturalization and the Struggle for Equality: A Brief History of the Education of Dominated Cultures in the United States*. Boston: McGraw Hill.

Steward, Julian H. 1938. "Basin-Plateau Aboriginal Sociopolitical Groups." *Smithsonian Institution Bureau of American Ethnology Bulletin* 120. Reprint 1997, Salt Lake City: The University of Utah Press.

Stewart Indian School. 2012. Stewart Indian School website, http://stewartindian-school.com, accessed August 4, 2015.

Stoffle, Richard W., Diane E. Austin, David B. Halmo, and Arthur M. Phillips, III. 1977. Ethnographic Overview and Assessment: Zion National Park, Utah and Pipe Spring National Monument, Arizona. Prepared for Rocky Mountain Regional Office, National Park Service. Tucson: Bureau of Applied Research in Anthropology, University of Arizona.

Stoffle, Richard W., Kristine L. Jones, and Henry F. Dobyns. 1995. "Direct European Transmission of Old World Pathogens to Numic Indians During the Nineteenth Century." *American Indian Quarterly* 19: 181–204.

Stoffle, Richard W., Lawrence Loendorf, Diane E. Austin, David B. Halmo, and Angelita Bulletts. 2000. "Ghost Dancing the Grand Canyon: Southern Paiute Rock Art, Ceremony, and Cultural Landscapes." *Current Anthropology* 41: 11–38.

Thompson, Bonnie. 2013. "The Student Body: A History of the Stewart Indian School, 1890–1940." PhD diss., Arizona State University.

Trafzer, Clifford E., Luke Madrigal, and Anthony Madrigal. 1997. *Chemehuevi People of the Coachella Valley*. Coachella, CA: The Chemehuevi Press.

Willis, Paul. 1977. *Learning to Labor: How Working Class Kids Get Working Class Jobs*. New York: Columbia University Press.

WPN (*White Pine News*). 1890. "Times Review cited in White Pines News." March 15.

Zanjani, Sally. 1994. *The Ghost Dance Winter and Other Tales of the Frontier*. Reno: Nevada Historical Society.

CHAPTER 5

History and Daily Life at the Stewart Campus

Bonnie Thompson-Hardin

The Stewart Indian School was an American Indian nonreservation boarding school located in Nevada. The Nevada legislature authorized the building in 1890 for the state's Native inhabitants: the Washoes, Northern Paiutes, and Western Shoshones. The federal government developed nonreservation boarding schools to Americanize Indian children by removing them from their homes and tribal environment, requiring them to communicate in English, teaching skills or a trade for economic support, and insisting on a Christian work ethic as a replacement of Native value systems (see chapter 4). Indian Service educators utilized a strict military regimen and vocational labor to teach children the perceived need for order and self-discipline. This approach was in keeping with neoevolutionary approaches in vogue at the time, exemplified by anthropologist Julian Steward's faulty assumptions that Shoshones were incapable of self-governance (see chapter 1). As David Wallace Adams describes in *Education for Extinction: American Indians and the Boarding School Experience*, the underlying theory held that "Indian children, once removed from the savage surroundings of the Indian camp and placed in the purified environment of an all-encompassing institution, would slowly learn to look, act, and eventually think like their white counterparts" (Adams 1995, 335).

During the early boarding school period, from 1880 to roughly 1928, the federal government endeavored to wipe out Native culture in one generation. Colonel Richard Henry Pratt created the blueprint for the federal boarding school program in 1879, when he opened the

Carlisle Indian School in abandoned military barracks in Carlisle, Pennsylvania. Pratt believed that removing Native children from their "uncivilized" home communities, and placing them in a strictly controlled environment would assimilate them into mainstream society. Pratt's educational mission began in Fort Marion, Florida, where he supervised Kiowa prisoners from the Red River War. Rather than incarcerate the prisoners he endeavored to teach them the values of white society. Pratt instructed them in English, craftsmanship, soldiering, arts, and labor. Several of the prisoners even volunteered to attend Hampton Institute to further their education. Proud of his achievements, Pratt believed that American Indians could be Americanized in one generation just like European immigrants (Littlefield 1993, 46; Pratt 1964, 271).

Platt's plan to divest students of their Native identity started by instructing them in the tenants of white civilization, which included English classes and a basic public school education. Vocational training also played an important role in the school curriculum. Students spent half of the day in the classroom and the rest of the day doing institutional work and training (Adams 1995, 100). After several years of training at Carlisle, Pratt placed Indian students in white households during the summer months so they could experience the benefits of Anglo-American culture first hand. The Carlisle Slogan was "To civilize the Indian, get him into civilization. To keep him civilized, let him stay" (Pratt 1964, 283).

Using Carlisle as a model, the federal government built an additional twenty-four nonreservation boarding schools in the next two decades (Adams 1995, 57). Built in 1890, Stewart was the only nonreservation boarding school in the nation created by an act of the state legislature. Senate Bill Number 33, approved by both houses of the thirteenth Nevada State Legislature on January 25, 1887, appropriated ten thousand dollars for the purchase of land and the construction of a boarding school (Jackson 1969, 4; Littlefield 1993, 50). The Nevada legislature thus gambled that the Indian Department would reimburse them and assume responsibility for the school. The state purchased a triangle shaped parcel of 240 acres, including two houses and several barns and sheds, three miles south of Carson City (BIA 1892, 883–85;

Jackson 1969, 13). The legislature contracted for the construction of the necessary buildings, including an impressive Victorian schoolhouse, and then relinquished its rights to the property when the federal government bought the campus in 1890 (Jackson 1969, 14).

The Stewart Indian School has a complicated legacy. During the early boarding school era, school administrators adhered to the federal government's goal of cultural genocide outlined by Pratt. However, as national Indian policy transformed over the next half century, school administrators adapted to the changing tides of reforms that alternated between support and encouragement of Indian culture and a return to the repressive policies of the early era. By the 1970s, many Native children actively sought an education at Stewart, which had gained a reputation as an institution that fostered a sense of Indian solidarity and pride. Students weathered these policy changes with amazing resilience and when provided the opportunity found enjoyment in activities such as sports, bands, and parades.

The Early Years: Living and Working at Stewart

In the early years, the majority of children at Stewart were kidnapped, taken miles and miles from their homes, and transplanted to another world with little contact with home, family, and culture. The children endured trauma as they were separated from their families and communities, often suffered homesickness, and struggled to adjust to a new environment. One of the first students, Frank Rivers, remembered that when Superintendent Gibson arrived at his Washoe camp, neither he, nor any of his family, spoke English and they had no idea what was going on. Rivers recalled that "They just came right into our camps and rounded up us kids and took us to school." The practice of taking children from their homes by buckboard was often referred to as "wagoning," and was common at all federal boarding schools (McCue 1962a; Vogel 2000).

The first class of thirty-seven students arrived on December 17, 1890. By the end of the first school year the student population had increased to 105 (BIA 1891, 571). Thereafter, student numbers continued to increase, and by the 1940s the school consistently enrolled between four hundred and six hundred students at a time. While the Stewart Indian

School was not a flagship boarding school like Carlisle Indian School or Haskell Institute, nor a particularly large school like the Phoenix Indian School or the Chilocco Indian Agricultural School, which both enrolled upward of a thousand students per year, during the ninety years that Stewart operated, over thirty thousand Indian children attended before it closed in 1980 (Riney 1993, 14; Lomawaima 1994, xv).

When it opened, the school enrolled Paiutes from the Pyramid Lake and Walker Lake Reservations, Western Shoshones from what is now called the Duck Valley Indian Reservation, and Washoes from Carson Valley.

Indian Agents also used many other tactics to compel parents to send their children to school. Agents threatened to withhold rations, supplies, railroad passes, and other benefits to force attendance (Johnson 1975, 88). Congress condoned the policy of using any force necessary to compel compliance. In addition, Nevada passed its first compulsory education laws in 1913 and 1919, which demanded the enrollment of all Indian children in school (BIA 1920, 1).

Arrival at a boarding school was a traumatic experience for children in the early years. The first step in the assimilation process involved removing all outward signs of tribal identity from the students' bodies. Children had their hair cut, which was considered a traumatic event among Great Basin communities. Anthropologist Julian Steward (1943, 281; as cited in Dean and Marler 2001, 35) documented that cutting hair traditionally only occurred with the death of a close loved one. According to Dean and Marler (2001, 35), cutting hair is called *nadegqa'se*, which means "taking or killing oneself—where the mourners are literally sending a part of themselves to be with the dead." Children entering the school in the early years also had their clothing and adornment taken from them. This would have included the removal of medicine bags that children wore to protect them (Teeman personal communication; see the concept of *puha*, chapter 7). Sprayed down and washed in lye to remove any lice, the new pupils dressed in European-style uniforms. Finally, children picked new European names from a chalkboard and were punished for speaking their Native languages (Adams 1995, 100–10).

Many Native families were deeply concerned about any type of federal school, because they understood and opposed the government assimilation agenda. Some parents went to great lengths to keep their children out of school. The family of Eunice Silva of Battle Mountain moved constantly around so that Silva would not be captured and placed in school (Crum 1994, 68). Winona James spent one year at Stewart, but the following year when Indian Agents came recruiting students her grandmother hid her because her family did not want to part with her again. James recalled that "my grandmother didn't want me to come back to Stewart because she thought I would never, ever go back home again, I guess. They hid me and they wouldn't let me come back to Stewart so I never came back" (James 1984, 8).

Other Indian families advocated for education so that children would be better equipped to function in a white world. Day schools on the reservations supplied only a primary education. To continue their schooling children had to travel hundreds of miles to Stewart. Ray Thacker, a Paiute from the Duck Valley Shoshone-Paiute Reservation in Owyhee, saw a Stewart education as an opportunity. Thacker arrived at Stewart in 1921 at the age of seven or eight. He wanted to attend the school because his older brother and many friends were already students there. At the age of eighty, Thacker remembered an afternoon when he and his friends left school to cook hamburger over an open fire. One of the children said he was going to run away because they were starving him. Thacker replied, "Why you think your folks send you here? To be a fat Indian with a big belly? Or you come to get fat up here?" and pointed to his head (O'Brien 1990, 35).

To learn these new skills, children spent half the day in the classroom and half the day performing manual labor. To disrupt traditional cultural practices and persuade graduates to permanently abandon their reservations the boarding school system trained boys and girls to be workers in a wage economy. Young children were not encouraged to dream about careers as doctors or lawyers, instead the school trained them become part of a working class. Unlike other schools, Stewart never operated an extensive agricultural program because of lack of water and unfarmable land. Stewart had 686 acres of farmland in addition to the 240-acre campus, but only 40 acres were under cultivation in 1914, although that had expanded to 100 acres by 1925 (BIA 1914, 2). Another 160-acre farm several miles away in Jacks Valley produced much of the vegetables and grains needed to feed the campus and the livestock; Stewart leased farms in Jacks Valley until 1939 when several farms were purchased (Hale 2011; Perry 1925).

Stewart Superintendent James K. Allen argued that farming was impractical in Nevada. Agricultural training, he wrote, "is not best in a locality where every foot of land has been secured by white settlers and every inch of water for irrigating already appropriated." He continued, "In this section not one Indian in a hundred is able to obtain even a small parcel of land for a garden and secure 'water rights' with it" (BIA 1899, 407) The schools grew some crops to feed the students, but not enough to make any profit.

By the time Stewart opened in 1890, a substantial number of Washoes, Western Shoshones, and Northern Paiutes lived off of reservations and survived by working as farm or ranch hands and domestics (Crum 1994, 31; Knack and Stewart 1984, 51). Most male Stewart students could expect a career working with livestock on ranches. Similarly, Stewart trained young Indian women for careers as domestics on ranches or in the homes of white families, a placement program that put older children to work in white homes or farms just like Colonel Pratt's original system. The outing program situated young Indian women in the homes of white families in Reno and Carson City and the San Francisco Bay Area, California, and enlisted the help of white employers to "uplift" and train Indian women (Jacobs 2007, 166).

While at Stewart, boys worked as blacksmiths, stonemasons, carpenters, harness makers, cobblers, tailors, mechanics, and farmers (Snyder 1923). Male students also maintained herds of cattle and dairy cows, worked in the dining hall and bakery, and helped manicure the school grounds. Female pupils labored in the laundry, kitchens, sewing rooms, and chicken coops, and worked on dorm-cleaning crews. Many teenage girls also learned nursing skills in the hospital and sanatorium (*The Indian Advance* 1901, 1903; BIA 1900, 493).

Daily routine at Stewart centered on military training. Students marched from dorm to classroom to dining hall. The military nature of the drilling stood out for Daisy Smith, who arrived in 1939 from Tonopah. She remembered, "I was given the number nine, and had

FIGURE 5.1. Child-sized loaves of bread made by male students in the bakery. Courtesy Nevada State Museum, Carson City, Nevada Department of Tourism and Cultural Affairs.

to use this number like it was my name. We would have to line up by numbers and march to the dining room, to the dorms, and to the school buildings. We had to march everywhere" (Smith, n.d.). Seventy years after attending Stewart, Winona James vividly recalled that "They got you up at 5:00 in the morning and put your uniform on, and you had to go out in the cold and drill before breakfast and then you'd come back to the dorm and change your clothes and get ready for school." (James 1984, 29) Hillman Tobey, a member of the Pyramid Lake Paiute Tribe, recalled the incessant marching and the military routine. "Back then," he recalls,

> We had to wear uniforms and everything was very structured, like the military. I remember having to march in a line to the dining hall and to our classrooms. Before we could march to the dining hall our hands were inspected. If they weren't clean we would have to go back in and wash again. (Tobey, n.d.)

The military routine continued in the dining room. Boys and girls entered through separate doors and ate at gender-segregated tables. A typical breakfast included cream potatoes, oatmeal, milk, syrup, bread, and coffee. Lunch consisted of roast beef, mashed potatoes, gravy, and bread. Dinner was often beans, beef stew with potatoes, macaroni, bread, and milk. Students enjoyed dessert frequently, if not daily. Sweets consisted of bread pudding, cake, apple pie, or a serving of fruit such as apples or prunes (Records of Carson Indian School 1915). Students were so starved for fresh produce that they would save their money to buy peaches from a wagon vender who visited from California. Still hungry, many children raided the fields, orchards, and cellars, and caught rabbits to stew (*The Indian Advance* 1899; Johnson 1977a).

Effie Dressler, a woman of both Washoe and Basque heritage from Topaz, California, remembered that "if you were young and shy . . . there was never enough food. There would be six at a table. A bowl of beans would be set out, and if you didn't move quick, you didn't get anything to eat" (Johnson 1977a). Other children remember raiding surrounding fields and vegetable cellars, and even Genoa and Carson orchards to supplement their diets (Johnson 1977a).

The Amusements of Boarding School Life

Students did enjoy some extracurricular and leisure activities at Stewart, especially in the later decades. During breaks or holidays, students often played outside on the campus or sunned themselves by the pool. Superintendent Fredrick Snyder built an Olympic-sized pool in the 1920s for baptisms, swimming lessons, and a reservoir in case of fire. It was located in front of the main administration building. Although the photo at right shows children solemnly assembled for a baptism, the pool was also a vivacious center of fun and relaxation for the children (McCue 1962b; O'Brien 1992).

Sporting events, concerts, and parades became a source of pride for Stewart students and their families, who embraced the chance to show off the athletic and musical skills learned at Stewart. Stewart had championship basketball, football, and boxing teams. Almost all federal boarding schools formed their own bands. Bands served as good public relations for the Indian Service. Watching neatly dressed Indian children playing familiar songs on familiar instruments provided visual evidence of the changes wrought by a white education. The first Stewart band of twenty-one boys assembled in 1896 under the instruction of Edwin Schanandore, an Oneida employed as a disciplinarian at

FIGURE 5.2. A baptism in the school pool circa 1920s. Courtesy Nevada State Museum, Carson City, Nevada Department of Tourism and Cultural Affairs.

the school. Joining the band became so popular that it deterred children from running away and students strove to earn a place in the group. Superintendent Mead expressed his delight in the new program in his annual report to the Commissioner of Indian Affairs. "Such was the effect on the general moral tone and the contentment of our pupils that we have not a single runaway recorded for the year" (BIA 1897, 358–59).

Indian School bands played at a variety of community venues, including rodeos, political rallies, sports games, concerts, parades, graduation ceremonies, burials, and club meetings. Stewart alumni especially take pride in the school's longstanding tradition of marching in the parades celebrating Nevada Day. The Stewart Indian School had a float or marching entry every year until the school closed and alumni continue the Nevada Day Parade tradition to the present day (Johnson 1977b; Vogel 2000). The Stewart band remains a source of pride for Stewart pupils.

Physical education served as a core component in the federal Indian boarding school program from its earliest days. Educators hoped that by encouraging physical fitness through calisthenics and group sports, students would also learn moral and intellectual lessons (Bloom 2000, 35). Again, this assertion demonstrates early educators' ignorance of Great Basin cultures' value systems that already incorporated physical activity and hard work with moral lessons.

FIGURE 5.3. Stewart Indian School band marching south on Carson Street in the Nevada Day parade circa 1945–1949. Courtesy Nevada State Museum, Carson City, Nevada Department of Tourism and Cultural Affairs.

Nevertheless, many students enjoyed a wide variety of sports at the school. Stewart formed its first boy's football, baseball, and track-and-field teams at the turn of the century. The players competed under the name of the Stewart Braves, playing non-Indian teams in the vicinity. One of the earliest rivalries sprang up with Carson High School. The school newspaper happily reported that Stewart boys had won the most points during a track-and-field competition in 1902 against their arch rivals (*The Indian Advance* 1902). Gaining more and more notoriety and experience in all sports, the Braves by 1905 were competing against college teams including the University of Nevada, Reno (UNR). Stewart enrolled many young adults, a common practice among boarding schools since many Indian pupils did not have the same access as white pupils to an early childhood education (Deloria 2004, 132). Older male students made the Braves competitive on the college and professional level. Huge crowds of white and Indian spectators attended the games (*Reno Evening Gazette* 1905, 3).

Another popular sport, basketball, started around 1910 under Coach James Oliver, a Fond Dulac Chippewa, who had earned great acclaim playing football at Haskell Institute. Like the football team, the basketball team played high school teams around the state. Stewart won several state championships in the 1910s. Dewey Sampson, a star player on the basketball team, went on to play semiprofessionally. In later years, the team competed in the state championship in 1938 and 1939, and won the title in 1966, beating Moapa Valley sixty-two to fifty-nine (Johnson 1977b; Albright 2003).

Basketball was one sport that Stewart girls also got to play competitively in the early years. Educators encouraged girls to play on swing sets, adorn maypoles, and play games that fostered cooperation rather than channeling raw aggression through football and boxing. Federal curriculum stressed drills and exercises for female students rather than contact sports. Girls joined basketball and tennis teams throughout the boarding school system but played under rules designed specifically for female teams to promote feminine qualities (Bloom 2000, 36, 87; Trennert 1988, 128–29).

Boxing came to dominate the sports arena at most boarding schools in the late 1930s. Stewart had a top-rated team and produced many famous boxers who competed against other Indian schools, local colleges, high schools, and amateur boxing clubs. Stewart had a distinguished boxing program from 1935 to 1948 and won ten Nevada Golden Glove team titles (O'Brien 1990). In 1974, Stewart administrators built a modern athletic center on the grounds and it was quickly dubbed Moccasin Square Gardens (Johnson 1977b).

The School Campus

These children lived, worked, and played in an ever-evolving landscape of buildings. The Stewart Indian School campus that survives today is a collection of over ninety years of construction. When the school first opened, the campus consisted mostly of Victorian-style wood-framed buildings. The massive colonial revival school building constructed by the legislature in 1890 dominated the grounds (Ashbury 1910). The building contained dorms, employee quarters, schoolrooms, playrooms, a kitchen, and a dining room. The imposing structure

FIGURE 5.4. Main school building, undated.
Courtesy Nevada State Museum, Carson City, Nevada Department of Tourism and Cultural Affairs.

conveyed the grandeur of civilization, to be obtained if the students worked hard. A large lawn, gravel walkways, carriage drive, and shade trees ornamented the front of the building. All visitors and students had to enter through either the front door or the kitchen. Thus, almost all entered through the formal entrance and walked under the arch over the double front gate which read "Indian Industrial School" and "Visiting Day, Wednesday 9 a.m. to 12 p.m." (BIA 1891, 571).

Additions to the main school building added more space for dorms but the school population quickly outgrew the main building. In 1900 a separate dorm was built for the girls (BIA 1900, 544). With school enrollments growing and no funds for new facilities, children were crowded into dorms, sleeping two or three to a bed. Boarding schools constantly needed repairs because Congress appropriated very little money to keep them running. Repairs and additions allowed Stewart's buildings to survive far beyond their expiration dates, but upkeep was often the first thing to be neglected.

A radical overhaul of the campus began in 1919 with the arrival of Superintendent Frederick Snyder. Snyder held the position of superintendent for over fourteen years. His inspiration for Stewart's distinctive

FIGURE 5.5. Early view of the Stewart campus. Courtesy Nevada State. Museum, Carson City, Nevada Department of Tourism and Cultural Affairs.

architectural style came from a chapel in Arizona that was made out of native colored rock. Stewart's architectural style consists of single-story buildings made from randomly shaped native stones of brown, red, green, and black set in dark mortar. Using the soft colors of Nevada stone, Snyder re-created his inspiration over and over on the Stewart campus. Students spent two years collecting the stone from across the state in Snyder's old Ford truck (McCue 1962a). Much of the stone came from the Christopher quarry along the Carson River. He recruited Hopi stonemasons to erect the new buildings and hired the local contractor firm of James and John Christopher. Students helped with the construction under the guidance of the master masons (Seavey 1982, item 7, p. 1).

Snyder also expanded upon the existing landscape and turned the campus into a horticultural showpiece. The first superintendent, William D. C. Gibson, had planted dozens of stately Lombardy poplars along the streets. The trees served as a wind block, provided shade, and beautified the campus (*Carson City Chronicle* 1941). Snyder added more shade trees along the major walkways, and the students planted extensive flower beds of petunias, asters, marigolds, verbenas, and sweet peas (McCue 1962a; Perry 1925). An inspector wrote, "the grass is beautifully kept. The miles of borders of flowers along walks, drive-ways, and flower beds . . . were gorgeous and charming in appearance.

All who passed by must involuntarily stop to admire the extensive floral bloom on the Carson school campus surrounded by a desert of sage brush and other desert growths" (Coon 1926).

When Snyder retired in 1934, the next superintendent, Alida Bowler, continued his architectural legacy. The Construction Division of the Department of the Interior took an active role in the design and implementation of the new buildings, staying true to Snyder's vision. Almost all stone construction halted at the beginning of World War II. A few modern buildings such as a classroom building were constructed in the 1960s and 1970s (Seavey 1982, item 7, p. 2; item 8, p. 3).

Changing Indian Education Policy

Early policymakers believed that they could transform the bodies, hearts, and souls of Indian children. By 1900, they had started to realize that their plan was not working as expected. Rather than graduating, leaving the reservations, and renouncing their tribal identity, most students returned home and used their educational and vocational skills to help their people. The Indian Service closed many schools in the early 1900s and started pushing for Indian students to attend reservation day schools or public schools at substantial cost savings. Yet, policymakers, politicians, and the general public continued to question why the Indian "problem" seemed to be getting worse, not better. Business as usual had created systemic poverty and inequality for Native peoples on reservations.

The Meriam Report, officially titled the *Problem of Indian Administration*, condemned federal policy for creating these inequalities and making Indians wards of the government. Published in 1928, the Meriam Report included a searing condemnation of the Indian Service's failure to fulfill its objectives and criticized the assimilationist agenda of the school system. Spurred by these criticisms, reformers, led by the newly appointed commissioner of Indian Affairs, John Collier, passed the Indian Reorganization Act of 1934. The Act gave tribes and communities the ability to form their own tribal governments, encouraged tribal institutions, and reversed longstanding policies of land allotment to individual Indians under the Dawes Act of 1887. The political reforms of the mid-1930s are often referred to as the "Indian New Deal" (Washburn 1988, 308–10).

By the 1930s the Stewart Indian School had become a model of progressive education under the Indian Reorganization Act of 1934. Commissioner Collier appointed Alida Cynthia Bowler superintendent at Stewart on September 1, 1934. Bowler became the first female superintendent in the Indian Service and under her leadership the Stewart Indian School embraced the reform ethos of the Indian New Deal. She encouraged Native languages, dances, and crafts at Stewart and helped dozens of tribal colonies and reservations in the state to become federally recognized tribes under the Indian Reorganization Act. Bowler was only the third woman to be appointed to a high-ranking government position during the New Deal (*Milwaukee Journal* 1934). Contemporary Nevada Indian Country reflects the changes made under the Indian Reorganization Act. Today there are thirty-two different colonies and reservations in Nevada. Twenty recognized tribes in Nevada have a binding relationship with the United States government through treaties, acts of Congress, or executive orders (Nevada's Indian Territory 2013).

Many of these recognized tribes are called "colonies." Acknowledging that a large Native population resided off reservation, the federal government set aside colonies starting in 1917 for Washoes, Western Shoshones, and Northern Paiutes. These colonies were small tracts of land, often just a few miles wide, on the fringes of towns or right in the middle of the urban areas of Reno and Carson City (Hittman 1984, 33, 41; Makley 2007, 156–57). This colony system is unique to the Great Basin, although the Indian Service created similar small reserves in other states, including what are called "Rancherias" in California. This contributed to a patchwork of Indian lands across the region (Crum 1994; Knack and Steward 1984, 51).

Just as the entire landscape of Indian Territory in Nevada changed dramatically in the 1930s, so did the tribal backgrounds of the Stewart student body. The Stewart Indian School transformed from a local nonreservation boarding school serving nearby Washoe, Paiute, and Western Shoshone communities to a hub in the federal Indian education system with students attending from all over the West. Stewart's students hailed from at least 335 different hometowns, including three dozen reservations across the West, and represented over sixty different tribal groups (Thompson n.d.).

Stewart followed a similar trajectory to other nonreservation boarding schools by expanding its extracurricular activities and adding high school grades. Students participated in sports and band, watched movies, enjoyed socials and dances, and joined the YMCA. Stewart students enjoyed the expanded leisure activities (Johnson 1977b). Stewart provided a high school education and continued intensive vocational training to meet the expressed needs of Native communities.

Termination Era and Closure

After World War II, the Indian Service underwent a major policy reversal, with the arrival of what is called the Termination Era. Rather than celebrating Indian culture and heritage, education policy turned once again to assimilating Indian children into white culture. Federal boarding schools started training students for jobs in urban areas so that they could ultimately leave their reservations. Stewart was also swept up in the wave of new education policy. In 1947 the federal government selected Stewart as one of seven boarding schools to participate in the Navajo Special Education Program to provide additional educational opportunities to Navajo students. About thirteen thousand Navajo children had no access to government schools. Their vast reservation did not have enough schools and many children lived too far away from them for daily busing to be a good option. World War II had convinced many tribes, particularly the Navajo, that education was absolutely imperative for their survival. The Navajo people, who had stayed relatively isolated prior to World War II, demanded that their children receive the education promised them in their 1868 Treaty. Returning veterans had learned the importance of a bilingual education on the front lines, and many communities saw the infrastructure improvements made by the Indian Civilian Conservation Corps and Works Progress Administration during the Depression.

In 1948, Stewart opened its doors to 148 children from the Navajo Nation. Over the next decade Navajo children accounted for over two-thirds of the Stewart population, which had reached almost six hundred. The Navajo Special Education Program consisted of a five-year intensive program that taught basic academic skills, including two years of specialized vocational training in a profession of the student's choice. With little previous access to mainstream schooling, many of the children had to start from scratch, and communication caused many initial difficulties. Pupils who could translate between English and Navajo occasionally had to interpret entire lessons for the new students (Jackson 1969, 88–90).

Ten years after the start of the Navajo Special Education Program, Stewart began accepting Hopi and Apache students as well. This enrollment pattern lasted for another four years until 1962, when newly constructed schools in Arizona and New Mexico enabled more students to be educated in their home states. Because of the influx of students from the Southwest from 1947 to 1962, Stewart has a strong alumni community in the Southwest (Jackson 1969, 96–99).

Many Southern Paiute children also began attending Stewart from Southern Nevada. The Southern Paiutes live in the area stretching from Salt Lake City, Utah, through the southern part of the state and along a strip on the northern part of Arizona and into Nevada through Moapa and part of Las Vegas. The Moapa Band of Paiutes lives within the boundaries of the state of Nevada in Clark County just north of Las Vegas. While they may be located in Nevada, jurisdiction over the Southern Paiutes fell under the Utah Indian Agency in Salt Lake City until the 1940s. Moapa children started to attend Stewart in the 1940s (Jackson 1969, 96–99; Knack, 1980, 12–13).

By the 1960s, the school had eliminated elementary grades and become an Indian high school rather than a vocational training center (McCue 1962a). This corresponded with waves of Indian activism, including the American Indian Movement (AIM) and self-determination. Moving away from assimilation and termination once again, Indian peoples across the country demanded their rights to have a real say in their children's education. Congress and Indian leaders pushed the Indian Service to adopt an educational structure responsive to the needs of individual communities and run by Indians themselves (Szasz 1977, 141–45).

In her dissertation, "'The little skingin that could': An Autobiographical, Affirmative look at Native American Off-Reservation Boarding Schools between 1970 and 1980," Roberta Whitlock Baeta (Salt River Pima/Maricopa) recounts her experiences as a student at the Stewart Indian School from 1970 to 1980 (2008, 117–69). Baeta attests that in 1972 when she went to Stewart the school had one of the best elective vocational programs in the country, which included auto body shop, agriculture, house painting, food service, heavy equipment operations, nursing, and college preparatory classes. Extracurricular activities included speech competition, fashion design, field trips, photography, drama, voice, and public speaking.

Baeta also investigated the experiences of her fellow alumni through oral histories and a twenty-one-question survey. The twenty participants in her survey unanimously claimed to have enjoyed their time at Stewart, and all of them declared that they would have chosen a boarding school over a public school. Off-reservation boarding schools, she argues, "came to be seen no longer as institutions of oppression, but as places where tribalness, Native culture, and Indian solidarity could be strengthened" (Baeta 2008, 226–28, 234).

In 1980 the federal government closed Stewart after ninety years of operation because the buildings did not meet current earthquake standards. The closure occurred the same year that Chilocco Indian Agricultural School in Oklahoma and Inter-mountain Indian School in Brigham City, Utah, shut their doors. Thus, Stewart was part of larger cuts to nonreservation boarding schools. Today only Chemawa in Salem, Oregon, Riverside Indian School in Anadarko, Oklahoma, and Sherman Indian High School in Riverside, California remain open (Baeta 2008, 20).

The quitclaim deed that conveyed the school campus to the state of Nevada from the federal government included a provision that "The State of Nevada wishing to perpetuate the 90 years history of the Stewart Indian School will reserve Building 1 and Building 3 to house and display the crafts, artifacts and the memorability relating to the Stewart Indian School." If the state of Nevada fails to fulfill this requirement the title will be forfeited and the land reverted back to the federal government. As part of that obligation, the Nevada Indian Commission (NIC) has its offices in the house that Superintendent Snyder built for himself and his wife in the 1920s. Several other state agencies including the Nevada Department of Corrections, and the Division of Forestry have offices in a variety of the old stone buildings as well (Mose 1986).

Boarding schools as institutions have left deep scars in Native communities. In the earlier years, the government removed generations of children from their families, thereby interrupting the transmission of traditional knowledge and language, and causing long-term historical trauma for tribes and communities. In later years, some students experienced additional hardships, while others found opportunities for education and friendships. Life at the Stewart Indian School was an interwoven tapestry of both trauma and opportunity that has left a complicated story for the institution and the students who lived there.

Works Cited

Adams, David Wallace. 1995. *Education for Extinction: American Indians and the Boarding School Experience, 1875–1926*. Lawrence, KS: University Press of Kansas.

Albright, Willie. 2003. "Native American School May Reopen as Museum." *Sparks Daily Tribune*, June 20.

Ashbury, Calvin H. 1910. "Map of the Carson School, attached to a letter from Superintendent Calvin H. Ashbury to the CIA, June 2, 1910." File 27639-2-1910, box 101, Carson 820-820, Central Classified Files, 1907–1939, Record Group 75, NARA, Washington, DC.

Baeta, Roberta Whitlock. 2008. "The Little Skingin that Could: An Autobiographical, Affirmative Look at Native American Off-Reservation Boarding Schools Between 1970 and 1980." PhD diss. University of Southern California.

BIA (Bureau of Indian Affairs). 1891. "Carson Indian School." Superintendents' Annual Narrative and Statistical Reports from the Field Jurisdictions of the BIA Section 3, Schools. Washington, DC: Government Printing Office.

———. 1892. "Carson Indian School." Superintendents' Annual Narrative and Statistical Reports from the Field Jurisdictions of the BIA Section 3, Schools. Washington, DC: Government Printing Office.

———. 1897. "Carson Indian School." Superintendents' Annual Narrative and Statistical Reports from the Field Jurisdictions of the BIA Section 3, Schools. Washington, DC: Government Printing Office.

———. 1899. "Carson Indian School." Superintendents' Annual Narrative and Statistical Reports from the Field Jurisdictions of the BIA Section 3, Schools. Washington, DC: Government Printing Office.

———. 1900. "Carson Indian School." Superintendents' Annual Narrative and Statistical Reports from the Field Jurisdictions of the BIA Section 3, Schools. Washington, DC: Government Printing Office.

———. 1913. "Carson Indian School." Superintendents' Annual Narrative and Statistical Reports from the Field Jurisdictions of the BIA Section 3, Schools. Washington, DC: Government Printing Office.

———. 1914. "Carson Indian School." Superintendents' Annual Narrative and Statistical Reports from the Field Jurisdictions of the BIA Section 3, Schools. Washington, DC: Government Printing Office.

———. 1920. "Carson Indian School." Superintendents' Annual Narrative and Statistical Reports from the Field Jurisdictions of the BIA Section 3, Schools. Washington, DC: Government Printing Office.

Bloom, John. 2000. *To Show What an Indian Can Do: Sports at Native American Boarding Schools.* Minneapolis, MN: University of Minnesota Press.

Carson City Chronicle. 1941. "Stewart Indian School to Observe Anniversary; Founded Fifty Years Ago." April 25.

Coon, W. W. 1926. "Inspection Report of W. W. Coon, Supervisor. November 2, 1926." File 52206-1926, box 99, Carson 806-806, Central Classified Files, 1907–1939, Record Group 75, NARA, Washington, DC.

Crum, Steven J. 1994. *The Road on Which We Came: A History of the Western Shoshone.* Salt Lake City, UT: University of Utah Press, 1994.

Dean, Patricia A., and Clayton F. Marler. 2001. "Shoshone Spirituality and Enhancing Archaeological Interpretation in Southeast Idaho." *The SAA Archaeological Record* (March): 34–36.

Deloria, Philip J. 2004. *Indians in Unexpected Places.* Lawrence, KS: University Press of Kansas.

Ellis, Clyde. 2006. "'We Had a Lot of Fun, but of Course, That Wasn't the School Part.'" In *Boarding School Blues: Revisiting American Indian Education Experiences,* edited by Clifford E. Trafzer, Jean M. Keller, and Lorene Sisquoc, 65–98. Lincoln, NE: University of Nebraska Press.

Hale, Larry. 2011. Interview conducted by Bonnie Thompson. Audio recording and transcription in the possession of Bonnie Thompson, Truckee, CA. June 16.

Hittman, Michael. 1984. *The Yerington Paiute Tribe: A Numa History.* Yerington, NV: Yerington Paiute Tribe.

Jackson, Nicholas D. 1969. "A History of the Stewart Indian School." Master's thesis, University of Nevada, Reno.

Jacobs, Margaret D. 2007. "Working on the Domestic Frontier: American Indian Domestic Servants in White Women's Households in the San Francisco Bay Area, 1920–1940." *Frontiers: A Journal of Women Studies* 28, nos. 1 and 2: 165–99.

James, Winona. 1984. Interview, conducted by R. T. King. Reno: Oral History Program University of Nevada, Reno.

Johnson, Edward C. 1975. *Walker River Paiutes: A Tribal History.* Schurz, NV: Walker River Paiute Tribe.

———. 1977a. "Discipline Was Strict for Stewart Students." *Apple Tree,* February, 13.

———. 1977b. "Stewart Indian School Has Progressed." *Apple Tree,* March 13.

Knack, Martha C. 1980. *Life Is with People: Household Organization of the Contemporary Southern Paiute Indians.* Socorro, NM: Ballena Press.

Knack, Martha C., and Omer Call Stewart. 1984. *As Long as the River Shall Run: An Ethnohistory of Pyramid Lake Indian Reservation.* Reno: University of Nevada Press.

Littlefield, Alice. 1993. "Learning to Labor: Native American Education in the United States, 1880–1930." In *The Political Economy of North American Indians*, edited by John. H. Moore. Norman, OK: University of Oklahoma Press.

Lomawaima, K. Tsianina. 1994. *They Called It Prairie Light: The Story of the Chilocco Indian School.* Lincoln, NE: University of Nebraska Press.

Makley, Matthew Stephen. 2007. "'These Will be Strong': A History of the Washoe People." PhD diss., Arizona State University.

McCue, Myra. 1962a. "Alma Mater of the Wa-Pai-Shone." *Reno Evening Gazette*, January 17.

———. 1962b. "History of the Rock Houses at Stewart and Their Builder." *Reno Evening Gazette*, January 27.

Milwaukee Journal. 1934. "Third of 'First' Women Gets Job Among Indians." August 3.

Mose, Elwood. 1986. Memo. "Stewart Indian School." State of Nevada Indian Commission, May 22. Clipping File, Nevada Historical Society.

Nevada's Indian Territory. N.d. *Nevada's Indian Territory.* Carson City, Nevada. http://www.nevadaindianterritory.com/wp-content/uploads/2015/01/255-4018-IT-BROCHURE-ONLINE.pdf, accessed November 5, 2018.

O'Brien, Colleen. 1990. "Stewart School Days: Graduates of the Stewart Indian School Recall Hardships, Friendships, and Lessons Learned." *Nevada Magazine* (Sept/Oct): 35.

Perry, J. G. 1925. "Perry to the Commissioner of Indian Affairs, October 19, 1925." File 50235-1926, box 92, Carson 730-737, Central Classified Files, 1907–1939, Record Group 75, NARA, Washington, DC.

Pratt, Richard Henry. 1964. *Battlefield and Classroom: Four Decades with the American Indian*. New Haven, CT: Yale University Press.

Records of the Carson Indian School. 1915. "Menu, Monday 15th, 1915." File "Menus," box 270, Administrative Files, 1909–1923, Record Group 75, NARA, San Bruno, CA

Reno Evening Gazette. 1905. "Indians to Meet Second Eleven." November 9.

Riney, Scott. 1999. *The Rapid City Indian School, 1898–1933*. Norman, OK: University of Oklahoma Press, 1999.

Seavey, Kent L. 1982. "Nevada SP Stewart Indian School." National Register of Historic Places and National Historic Landmarks Program Records: Nevada, National Register of Historic Places and National Historic Landmarks Program Records, 2013–2017, Records of the National Park Service, 1785–2006, Record Group 79.

Smith, Daisy. N.d. "Stewart Indian School Walking Trail. #5 Auditorium." Podcast. Stewart Indian School, Nevada Indian Commission. http://stewartindianschool.com/walking-trail/, accessed November 4, 2018.

Snyder, Frederic. 1923. "Frederic Snyder to the Commissioner of Indian Affairs, July 25, 1923." File 88479-1922, box 92, Carson 730-737, Central Classified Files, 1907–1939, Record Group 75, NARA, Washington, DC.

Steward, Julian. 1943. "Culture Element Distributions: XII Nevada Shoshoni." *Anthropological Records* 8, no. 3: 263–92.

Szasz, Margaret Connell. 1977. *Education and the American Indian: The Road to Self-Determination since 1920*. Albuquerque, NM: University of New Mexico Press.

Thompson, Bonnie. 2013. "The Student Body: A History of the Stewart Indian School, 1890–1940." PhD diss., Arizona State University.

Tobey, Hillman. N.d. "Stewart Indian School Walking Trail. #12 Shops (Carpentry)." Podcast. Stewart Indian School, Nevada Indian Commission. http://stewartindianschool.com/walking-trail/, accessed November 4, 2018.

Trennert, Robert A. 1988. *The Phoenix Indian School: Forced Assimilation in Arizona, 1891–1935*. Norman, OK: University of Oklahoma Press.

Vogel, Ed. 2000. "Historic Indian School Falls under Scrutiny." *Elko Daily Free Press* 117, no. 78 (April).

Washburn, Wilcomb E. 1988. *History of Indian-White Relations*. Vol. 4, *Handbook of North American Indians*, edited by William C. Sturtevant. Washington DC: Smithsonian Institution.

CHAPTER 6

Stewart Indian School Methods and Research Results

Ashley M. Long, Sarah E. Cowie, and Ian Springer

This chapter provides an overview of the methods and results of historical and archaeological research undertaken for the Stewart Indian School Collaborative Historical Archaeology Field School project (for more complete data see Long 2015 and Springer 2015). We intertwine standard archaeological data reporting with details of our efforts specific to conducting a collaborative, Indigenous archaeology project. Thus, in addition to providing specific information archaeologists are accustomed to seeing (e.g., artifact counts, dates, and illustrations), we also provide select examples of our efforts to decolonize our methods and interpretations throughout the project. Our work in this regard is guided by a vast body of literature (see chapters 1, 2, and 8), and particularly inspired by Indigenous scholars in decolonizing methods and Indigenous archaeology (e.g., Atalay 2006; Smith 1999; Watkins 2000).

We describe the methods used for completing historical research, those used during fieldwork, and those used for artifact analysis in the lab. Collaborative methods are also described in this chapter although collaboration is discussed throughout the volume.

Historic Research Methods

Historical research on the Stewart Indian School included photographs, documents, news clippings, and other archival sources. A collection of historical photographs and documents was provided to the project courtesy of the Nevada State Historical Preservation Office and the Nevada Indian Commission (NIC). Historical documents in the Special Collections Department at the University of Nevada, Reno (UNR) Knowledge Center were also consulted. Additional historical photographs were also examined online through Nevada State Museum virtual tours. Nevada newspaper clippings and articles were consulted online through the Cooperative Libraries Automated Network and the Online Newspaper Archive through UNR.

Field Methods

Prior to the field school, project archaeologists and Darrel Cruz, the Washoe Tribal Historic Preservation Officer (THPO), walked the site to discuss potential areas for excavation. A precontact-period Martis-style projectile point was discovered on the ground surface near Clear Creek and was later photographed, drawn, and returned to its location. Although not the focus of this investigation, the presence of this and other precontact-period artifacts illustrates the presence of Native people in this area for thousands of years.

As part of the field school training and to better address the potential surface and subsurface deposits at the site, we completed a partial pedestrian survey. We are hopeful that the information gained during the pedestrian survey will be useful to the Stewart Indian School community for future planning and preservation needs. This could assist in locating areas for future excavation but also to avoid sensitive areas that should not be disturbed. The original focus of the pedestrian survey was on areas described above that show potential for subsurface components. Additionally, based on the results of an earlier field visit, other culturally sensitive areas were determined to be a priority for pedestrian survey.

In July 2013, James T. Daniels, Jr., of ASM Affiliates, conducted ground-penetrating radar (GPR) with assistance from UNR archaeologists (Daniels 2013). The GPR was used to locate subsurface anomalies that could potentially be archaeological features. The GPR was conducted according to grids laid out over areas of interests, including in front of the new gym, an area where a swimming pool was once located, an area south of the campus infirmary, and in the lawn north of Gibson Avenue. These grids were used to locate archaeological anomalies potentially associated with the original school building and the swimming pool once located on the site.

Fieldwork was conducted in July and August 2013 as part of the Collaborative Historical Archaeology Field School of the University of Nevada, Reno. Sarah Cowie was principal investigator and Diane L. Teeman (an enrolled member of the Burns Paiute Tribe), Chris LeBlanc, and Ashley Long served as field supervisors. Numerous volunteers also assisted in the fieldwork as part of the public archaeology component of the field school.

During the field school, one meter by one meter test units (TUs) were excavated at the site. All of the locations of the TUs were recorded with a total station. The TUs were excavated with trowels and shovels in arbitrary ten-centimeter levels or with the natural stratigraphy. Due to extremely compact soils in Grid D, rock picks were used in addition to shovels and trowels during the excavation. Grids B, C, and EF required the removal of sod before the TUs could be excavated; the one meter by one meter squares of sod were placed on large sheets of plastic and watered over the course of the field school. Standardized TU level forms, feature forms, profile forms, artifact bag logs, and photo logs were used to thoroughly record the results of the excavations. All of the soil was screened through eighth-inch wire screens and all of the historic artifacts were collected, unless stated otherwise. Some materials, such as concrete and asphalt, were sampled and the remaining materials returned to the TUs. Features were additionally recorded on feature forms and photographed. The TUs were terminated at the discovery of sterile soil or due to time constraints as the field school was reaching an end. After excavation of a unit ceased, at least one of the profile walls was drawn onto a profile form and photographed. TUs were backfilled at the end of the project.

Due to the collaborative nature of the project and at the request of project stakeholders, the NIC and the Washoe THPO, and in accordance with the Nevada State Historic Preservation Office (SHPO), artifacts potentially associated with a precontact occupation, such as lithics or other artifacts considered more sensitive in nature (i.e., flaked bottle glass), were not collected and only minimally recorded in the field. These items were recorded on a separate artifact log during the field school. If lithics were found in a TU, they were analyzed and photographed in-field, with the exception of a basalt biface tip that was illustrated by a Washoe tribal member during the field school. Upon discussion with some tribal members on the project, it was determined that the biface tip should be recorded with additional care since it was representative of a tool and potentially of a more sensitive nature. Lithic analysis was conducted for material type, tool type, and stage of production. Artifacts were then temporarily placed in plastic bags labeled with the associated provenience information.

In the initial research design, flaked materials were to be placed in plastic bags and returned, in the bag, to their appropriate TU during backfill. However, as part of the collaborative process, several group discussions were held among the students, staff, and volunteers on the project, as to the appropriate treatment of the lithic artifacts. As a result, it was determined that flaked artifacts would be returned directly to the TU without the plastic bag. The intention here was to restore certain artifacts to the earth, so as not to disrupt things that should remain in place (see discussions of *puha* and power, throughout this volume).

After the flaked materials were returned to their respective units, the TUs were backfilled and the sod was replaced. Some flaked materials were not identified in the field and mistakenly brought to the lab. These artifacts were recorded in the lab under the same requirements of the in-field analysis and were reburied in their associated TUs after the artifact cataloguing was finished. The TUs were relocated by identifying differences in the sod associated with its removal and replacement. The sod from the northwest corner of each TU was lifted and the artifacts placed immediately under the sod in the soil. Among these artifacts was a flaked bottle glass sherd that was reburied along with the other flaked materials.

Another collaborative attribute of the field methods came from the public archaeology component of the field school. Stakeholders expressed a serious interest in raising public awareness about the status of the campus and its contentious history. As such, students developed talking points in coordination with the NIC, Washoe THPO, and other Native stakeholders to discuss as they gave tours of the campus and excavations. Students also participated in interviews with various media outlets as another aspect of raising public awareness.

Oral History

The recording of oral histories was initially planned as a component of the field school at the request of several community members and research partners. Interview forms were adapted from the Oral History Program at the University of Nevada, Reno, and a Native student of the field school, Patrick Burtt, was designated as the interviewer and assistant oral history coordinator (see Burtt essay in chapter 7). However, many of the elders who participated in the interview process hesitated to have their testimony formally recorded. Over the course of the project, several tribal members pointed out the long history of anthropologists publishing Native stories, which has questionable repercussions for intellectual property issues. Given these discussions, Patrick Burtt determined it was best to orally record these stories in a more traditional way, and share them less formally with non-Natives. Thus, the oral histories referred to in this volume either came from the Under One Sky oral history database (conducted by the Nevada State Museum and maintained by the Oral History Program at the University of Nevada, Reno), or oral histories provided by tribal members that were not formally recorded (cited as personal communication). One project participant, A. J. Johnson, a Native archaeological technician and an alumnus of Stewart Indian School, shared his thoughts in an essay for this volume (see A. J. Johnson essay, chapter 7).

Laboratory Analysis and Curation

Artifacts were treated with care following their removal from the site and were temporarily housed in a secure location in UNR's Historic Archaeology Laboratory where they were cleaned, cataloged, and analyzed. Glass and ceramic artifacts were wet brushed, while all other artifacts were either dry brushed or not cleaned. As part of the analysis, artifacts were separated into two categories: diagnostic and nondiagnostic. If determined to be nondiagnostic, the artifact was analyzed by artifact type, material, quantity, weight, and function (if known) and recorded on a nondiagnostic form.

If considered diagnostic, the artifact was analyzed by artifact type and recorded on a separate form. The categories and associated forms included ammunition, bottles/jars/jugs, buttons, cans, ceramics, faunal, nails, and other diagnostics. The latter category included all diagnostic artifacts that could not confidently be placed in any of the other categories. Diagnostic artifacts required more extensive analysis; special attention was paid to buttons, toys (marbles, toy dolls, toy cars, etc.), and miscellaneous school items. In addition to function and material type, diagnostic artifacts were researched online and analyzed according to maker's marks or other inscriptions, temporal features, and design.

The primary functional categories used for this analysis were adapted from Stanley South's list of functional groups (South 1977, 95–102). These included architectural, arms, communications, domestic, faunal, food/drink, indulgences, landscape, mining, other, personal, sanitation, transportation, unknown, and utilities. Then, when possible, a secondary function was assigned based on the identification of a primary function. For example, a nail may be assigned the primary function of architectural and the secondary function of structural material. Functional categories were assigned conservatively to the artifacts; if the function could not be determined with a high degree of certainty, it was labeled as unknown.

Comprehensive data for each artifact, including its provenience, artifact type, material, functional categories, and all other important information, was recorded on paper catalog forms and then digitally recorded in a Microsoft Access database (Long 2015). The catalog includes all of the historic artifacts collected, which also includes the flaked bottle glass sherd. All other flaked materials were recorded on a separate log during fieldwork. We separated flaked materials (glass and lithics) at the request of the Washoe THPO Darrel Cruz, as these items required more sensitive treatment (see chapter 7).

Faunal Analysis

Ashlee Younie separately analyzed faunal remains found at the site (Long 2015; Younie 2015). The faunal remains were initially catalogued on nondiagnostic forms and assigned individual catalog numbers. Younie conducted a separate analysis on all of the remains and recorded them on diagnostic faunal forms and a digital spreadsheet. She conducted analysis on the taxa, element, and presence of modification of each artifact. Careful attention was paid to elements that could be rabbit bone, because a number of oral histories suggested the traditional importance of rabbit hunting in this area and that Stewart Indian School students also participated in rabbit hunting unbeknownst to school staff.

Nail Chronology

Due to the dearth of dateable artifacts in this assemblage, nails were used to determine change over time and to estimate general dates for individual TUs. The number of cut nails and wire nails were tallied for each level of a unit and the total for each unit was recorded as well. This count only included complete nails and incomplete nails with the head still attached. The totals were then compared by level and by TU. According to Adams (2002), the theory behind this analysis is that a larger volume of cut nails within a level or unit would suggest an earlier date than would a large volume of wire nails. A large percentage of cut nails might imply a mid-nineteenth-century date, while wire nails might suggest a twentieth-century date. An equal number of both types might indicate a date around the turn of the nineteenth century, which is around the date for the transition from cut to wire nails (Adams 2002).

Curation

Artifacts recovered during our work were cataloged in UNR's Historic Archaeology Laboratory and prepared for long-term storage following the Secretary of the Interior's curation standards and guidelines (36CFR79.9). Artifacts were labeled according to current standards, including nondestructive "reversible" techniques (e.g., lacquered acid-free catalog numbers on lithic artifacts, acid-free tags for perishable artifacts). The UNR Department of Anthropology agreed to provide permanent curation in the UNR Anthropology Museum, free of charge, for collections from the 2013 summer field school at the Stewart Indian School site. The artifacts remain the property of the state of Nevada, but many stakeholders on the project are hopeful they could someday be curated on-site.

Results of Historical Research

A great deal of historical research had already been conducted for this site (see chapters 4 and 5), but some historical research was necessary to support specific archaeological questions. For example, historical photographs provided by the NIC aided in the placement of

TUs during the field school. Archaeologists carefully examined photographs of the original school building for landscape features, such as mountain peaks, and lined them up with the modern landscape. This provided a new location (Grid EF) for the building since it was previously believed to have been located across campus. Further investigation of historic maps shows that Grid EF is in close proximity to where the school building once was (figure 6.1).

Historic photographs and newspaper articles also provided information about life at Stewart during its formative years (see chapters 4 and 5). For example, a newspaper clipping describes the lives of Harry and Dewey Sampson who attended Stewart in 1910 and experienced firsthand what it was like to be forcibly taken from their homes. Dewey went missing from his village one day, and as Harry went searching for his brother, he was also taken and enrolled at Stewart (Albright 2003). Since this was a common occurrence, the children's parents would frequently camp out along a ridge just south of the campus (Vogel 2000).

As is common on community-based and public archaeology projects, professionals and members of the public who visited our project provided valuable historical insights into the site. For example, Larry Hale, a graduate of Stewart Indian School and retired Stewart facility supervisor, and Ron Bodnar, current Stewart facility supervisor, visited the project periodically to offer assistance and important information about the campus grounds. Conversations about our work and project goals led to the realization that their office had the only known copies of campus maps from the 1930s and 1940s, which provided invaluable information on the location of historic buildings on campus. They graciously provided access to the maps and other knowledge of the grounds, all of which contributed significantly to the project. The maps are on file at the Stewart Facility Office and are incorporated into GIS layers presented in figures below.

Results of GPR

Grid A was not investigated after historical photographs showed the original school building to be located in a different area (Grid EF), which was also suggested by some of the oral histories provided by staff at the NIC. Grids B, C, D, and EF became the locations of the excavation units during the field school (figure 6.2). Grids B and C

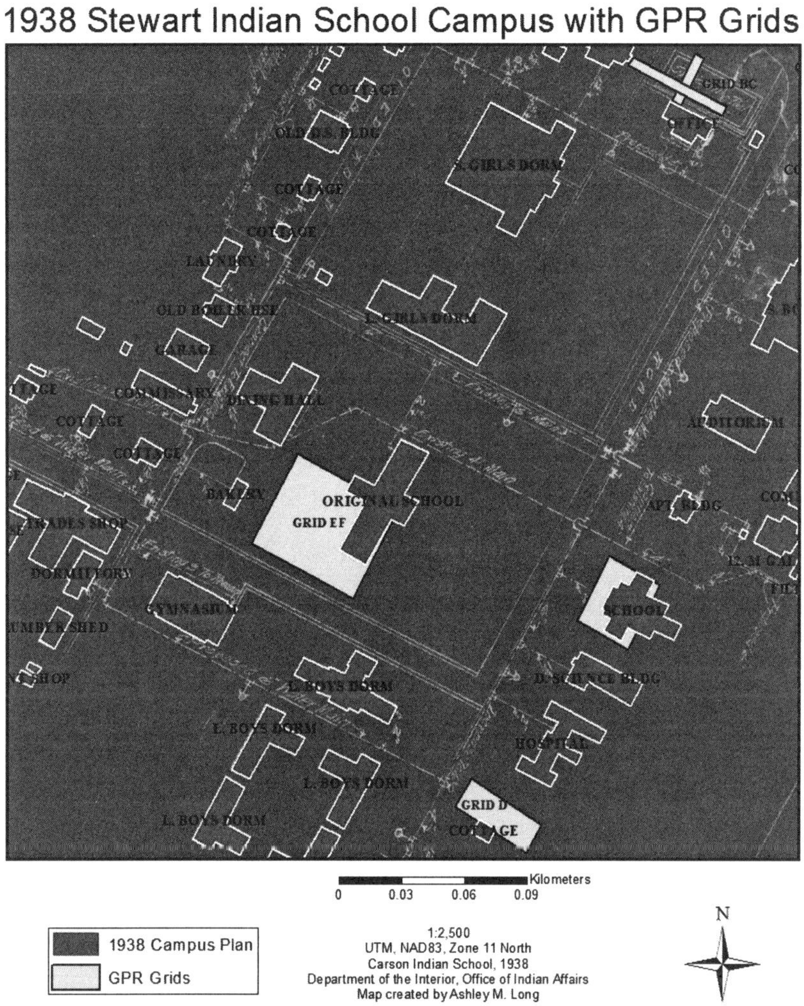

FIGURE 6.1. Historic map with GPR grids.

showed several linear alignments that may correspond with the foundation of the pool, which was investigated during the field school. Grid D showed a few small circular anomalies and Grid EF showed several large anomalies potentially associated with the original school building; all of which were investigated. The GPR report (Daniels 2013) provided data that informed excavation decisions presented in this volume.

Figure 6.2. Location of GPR grids.

Artifact Descriptions and Analysis: Historic Artifacts in the TUs and Features

In total, there were 12,826 artifacts collected from the excavations at Stewart Indian School. The assemblage includes ecofacts, modern materials, and historic artifacts. Functional categories applied to the artifacts include architectural, arms, domestic, faunal, food/drink,

Table 6.1. Historic artifact count by function for Grid EF.

Function	TU 1	TU 2	TU 3	TU 4	TU 5	TU 6
Architectural	508	660	1609	1823	554	268
Arms					1	
Domestic	6	10	15	7	5	3
Faunal	37	18	22	22	37	
Food/drink	9	18	19	4	29	3
Indulgences						
Personal	27	28	52	62	12	6
Sanitation	1	1		1	10	
Transportation						8
Utilities	14	60	29	28	97	47
Unknown	179	274	736	1036	406	193
Total count	781	1069	2482	2983	1151	528

Table 6.2. Historic artifact count by function for Grid BC.

Function	TU 9	Grid BC
Architectural	32	32
Arms		
Domestic	1	1
Faunal	3	3
Food/drink	1	1
Indulgences		
Personal	2	2
Sanitation		
Transportation		
Utilities	7	7
Unknown	98	98
Total count	144	144

Table 6.3. Historic artifact count for Grid D.

Function	TU 10 Feature 5	TU 11	TU 12	TU 13	Grid D
Architectural	122	37	40	149	354
Arms					0
Domestic	1	1		1	3
Faunal	2				2
Food/drink	87	1		3	91
Indulgences	1				1
Personal	7	4		2	13
Sanitation					0
Transportation		32		1	33
Utilities	3	3			6
Unknown	1128	186	70	80	1464
Total count	1351	264	110	236	1968

FIGURE 6.3. South profile of Test Unit 4.

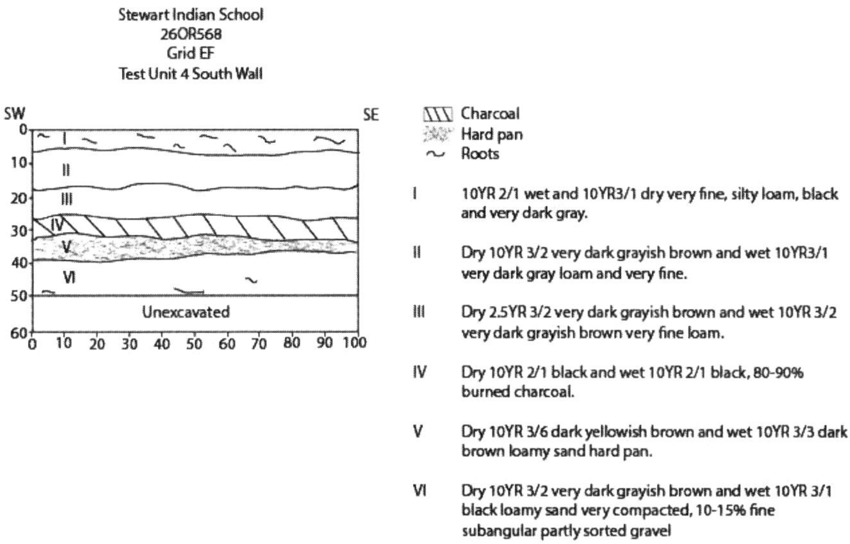

FIGURE 6.4. South profile of Test Unit 4. Figure by Eric Terzich and Ashley Long.

indulgences, other, personal, sanitation, transportation, unknown, and utilities. A variety of materials were represented including asphalt, bone, caulk, ceramic, cloth, coal/charcoal/clinkers/slag, concrete, glass, leather, metal (such as aluminum, copper alloy, ferrous, lead, and tin), mortar, paper, plastic, rubber, shell, styrofoam, stone, and wood.

Artifact Patterns and Site Formation Processes

This section will discuss the interpretations of TUs and individual artifacts, with emphasis placed on diagnostic artifacts, as well as interpretations of site formation processes and other land use practices. As discussed earlier, excavation units were opened following a GPR survey that identified potential archaeological features, in combination with areas of interest identified by stakeholders and in historical sources. Thus, excavations in Grid EF explored potential remains for the original 1890 school building, Grid BC was overlain on the historic swimming pool that had also been used as a baptismal, and excavations in Grid D attempted to locate remains of an early single-room building that had been near the infirmary.

Original School Building (TUs in Grid EF)

All of the TUs located in Grid EF were placed in order to determine the location of the original school building at Stewart Indian School. As a result, it was presumed that the majority of artifacts collected from those units would be of architectural materials. This was found to be true for all of the units. However, the materials were all extremely crushed and presumably represent repeated movement of the materials by heavy machinery. A more detailed account of architectural materials is discussed for each individual unit.

TU 1 and Feature 2

As mentioned, the purpose of TU 1 was to locate possible remains of the original school building. The thin strata and soil inclusions indicate that the soil was heavily mixed and likely pushed around with heavy machinery. There is also evidence of multiple rodent disturbances at various depths. The majority of the artifacts recovered from the unit were architectural materials, of which twenty-two were cut nails. The cut nails were primarily found in the lower levels (Level 3 and Level 4) and the wire nails were mostly found in the upper levels. This possibly indicates that some stratigraphic integrity was preserved even with the continuous mixing and moving of soils, since cut nails more often date to earlier time periods than wire nails.

Dateable artifacts collected from this unit included two prosser buttons—one complete, black, four-hole dished prosser button found in the mix from Level 3 and Level 4; and one broken, white, dished prosser button found in Level 2—which give an earliest possible date of 1840 (Sprague 2002, 113). A glass marble found in Level 2 has an earliest possible date of 1926, since there is no cut-off mark visible and this is when glass, machine-made marbles were made completely spherical (Carskadden and Gartley 1990). Two yellow ware ceramic marbles found in Level 2, and in the mix from Level 3 and 4, provide a date range from 1860 to 1874. These dates are associated with the manufacturing dates of a single pottery in Ohio known to have made these types of marbles (Carskadden and Gartley 1990). Five copper alloy rivets, all found in Level 2, provide a possible date of 1873, as this was when Jacob Davis, of Reno, Nevada, patented copper rivets for the Levi-Strauss jeans company (Davis 1873). The Levi-Strauss maker's mark was found on two of these rivets. A glass fragment with a starburst design can possibly provide a date range from 1925 to 1940 (Florence 1995), and a crown cap found in the mix from Level 3 and 4 has a patent date of 1892 (Lief 1965, 17).

Other diagnostics that provide contextual information included four glass beads, three comb fragments, a small copper hinge, several fragments of a bone toothbrush, and a large ferrous handle. The glass beads are probably associated with clothing and adornments that belonged to the students at Stewart, especially after 1920, when the campus became significantly more lenient on the students' traditional practices and customs (Thompson 2013). Additionally, the ferrous handle is similar to those used on tools for cleaning out fireplaces, and it is known that there were stoves in each of the rooms to heat the original school building.

Feature 2 was identified as a linear soil feature most likely representing a previous irrigation line running through the unit. There is plenty of evidence of irrigation in Grid EF as the groundskeepers at Stewart have consistently maintained grass on the campus. This interpretation is

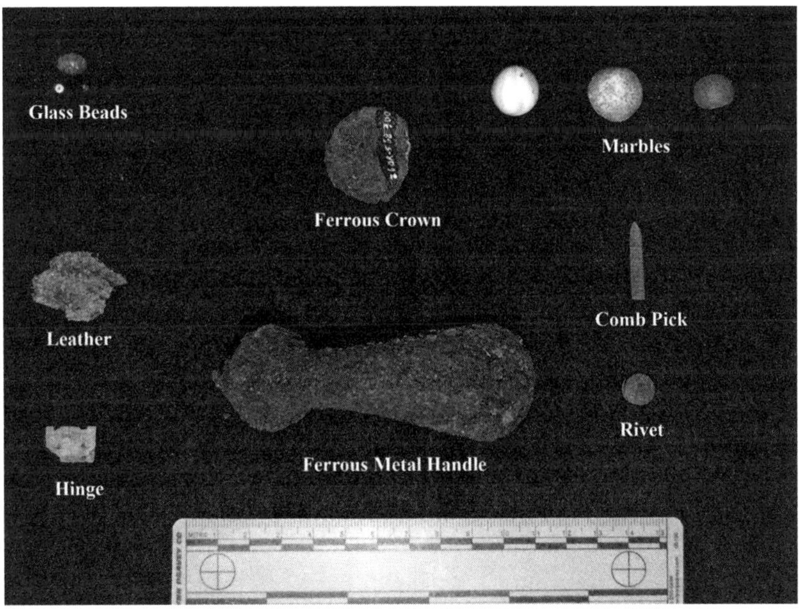

FIGURE 6.5. Diagnostic artifacts from Test Unit 1

further supported by the ceramic pipe fragments collected from the unit that resemble fragments of a sewage pipe. The feature was discovered at the base of Level 1, indicating that it predates the most recent earth moving activities in this area.

TU 2 and Feature 1

TU 2 was located in Grid EF and was very similar to TU 1 in terms of stratigraphy, the presence of a linear feature, and artifact categories. The strata were slightly less disturbed but still indicated the mixing of soils. The majority of artifacts collected from TU 2 were architectural materials and included thirty cut nails, of which the great majority was recovered from Level 1, suggesting the nails were reused or the original stratigraphy was mixed. Dateable artifacts collected from the unit included three ceramic marbles found in Level 1 and Level 2. A copper alloy rivet found in Level 1 with a maker's mark reading "LS & CO/ SF," which stands for the Levi Strauss jeans company, has a patent date of 1873.

Diagnostic artifacts that did not provide dates included a plastic bead, found in Level 1; a possible fastener from a military jacket—the object resembles something from a belt buckle or a buckle from a jacket; a copper alloy flat disk button that was possibly used as a collar button for a formal shirt; and finally, six metal toy car fragments with a possible red paint. All of these items are typical items lost or discarded on a school campus.

Figure 6.6. Copper rivet with maker's mark.

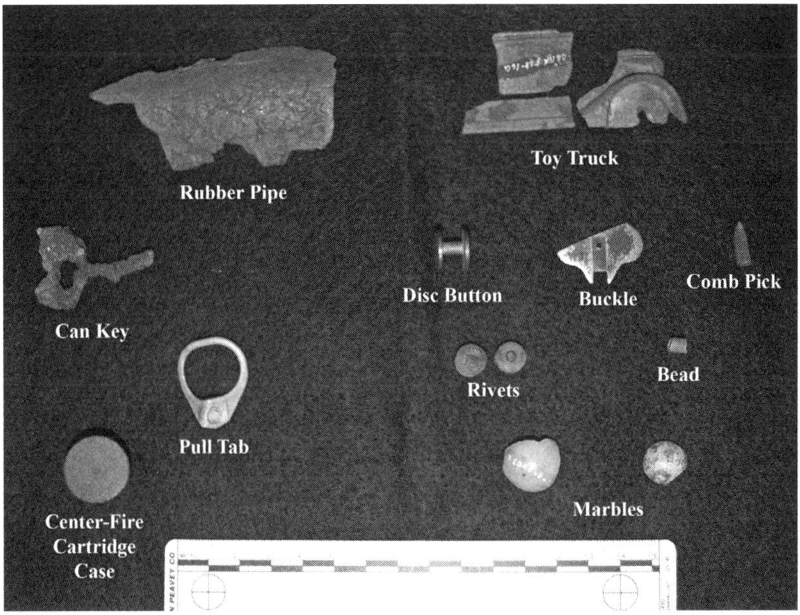

FIGURE 6.7. Diagnostic artifacts from Test Unit 2.

Feature 1 was identified as a linear soil feature discovered at the base of Level 1, which is possibly representative of a previous irrigation line. Considering that Feature 1 and Feature 2 were both linear features located at similar depths and the TUs were only a few meters apart, it is likely that the features both represent the same irrigation line.

TU 3

TU 3 was located in the southwest corner of Grid EF, located where the school building once was. The most noticeable attribute of this unit was the solid layer of charcoal and ash discovered at approximately thirty-five centimeters below datum. The stratum immediately below the charcoal layer was unique with yellow-brown burned earth. Additionally, the majority of artifacts recovered from this unit were found in the levels directly above and within the charcoal layer and the majority of them were architectural materials. Considering all of these elements, it is likely that this unit represents a burned trash pile, perhaps of materials left from the building. Most of the artifacts were extremely crushed, which was most likely caused by pushing the materials with heavy machinery. The types of artifacts recovered also support this interpretation since they mostly consisted of crushed architectural materials and items frequently lost such as buttons, broken doll parts, marbles, and miscellaneous clothing items. The preservation of the charcoal layer and the burned earth below it suggests that it was immediately covered with a soil deposit and was not disturbed, further indicating a degree of stratigraphic integrity for this unit.

Aside from cut nails, of which there were only two found in Level 3 and Level 5, dateable artifacts from this unit included five buttons made of various materials. The first button, found in Level 2, is made of plastic and appears to be slightly melted. It has an earliest possible date of 1940 and a range that continues into the present (Meikle 1995, 82–95). Another button found in Level 2 is made of wood and according to Rivers (1999, 30), early utilitarian bone and wood buttons were made by the same techniques and likely by the same artisans; therefore, allowing South's (1964, 115–21) date range of 1800 to 1865 for four-holed bone buttons to also be applied to wooden buttons. Of particular interest is a U.S. Army button found in Level 3. Historical documents state that male students were required to wear military uniforms upon arriving at the school and presence of this button supports the historical record. This particular button is made of zinc, and, according to collectors, was used as a trouser button for U.S. Army uniforms throughout World War I and World War II (World War II Impressions n.d.). Additionally in Level 3, there was a two-piece pressed metal button that Olsen (1963) dates to post-1870. Finally, a white prosser button was found in Level 4 and has an earliest possible date of 1840 (Sprague 2002, 113).

The marbles collected can also provide a date range for this TU. In Level 2 a single fragment from a machine-made glass marble yields a date range between 1901 to the present (Carskadden and Gartley 1990). Level 3 produced a variety of ceramic marbles, including two hand-rolled, whiteware marbles, two machine-made, yellow ware marbles, and a fragment from a brown salt-glazed, stoneware marble. All of these marbles together produce a *terminus post quem* date of 1910 for Level 3, since the whiteware marbles have a manufacturer date range of 1880 to 1910 (Carskadden and Gartley 1990). The date

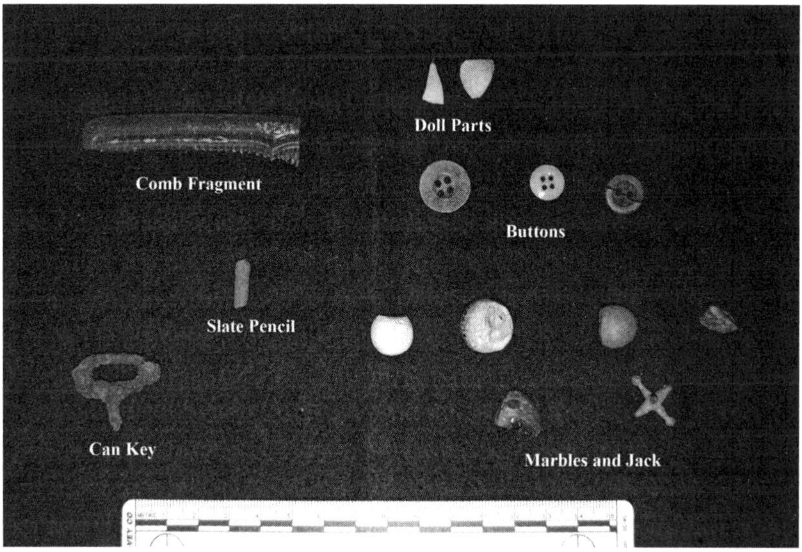

FIGURE 6.8. Diagnostic artifacts from Test Unit 3.

is further supported by the presence of a narrow, machine-made bottle finish, which must have been deposited after 1910, as this was when those bottles were first produced (Miller and MicNichol 2002).

The vast quantity and variety of artifacts collected from TU 3 is significant evidence of the unit being associated with a burn pile. It was possibly a trash pile from the original school building since many of the artifacts are associated with children and school items.

TU 4

TU 4 was located in the far southeast corner of Grid EF immediately adjacent to a large tree on the edge of the grid. Similar to TU 3, this unit also included a solid layer of charcoal that was discovered at approximately twenty-eight centimeters below datum. Directly beneath the charcoal was a layer of hard pan, or tightly packed soil, that was yellowish-brown in color—indicating burned earth. As with TU 3, TU 4 is most likely associated with a burned trash pile. The majority of the artifacts were extremely crushed and/or fire affected, making it even more likely that the items were pushed into a specific area and then burned as a method of disposal.

The presence of a U.S. one cent piece from 1944, found in Level 1, provides an approximate date for the last soil deposit in this unit. The buttons from TU 4 can provide dates for the charcoal layer and the artifacts associated with the burn pile. A military button from Level 3 with a maker's mark reading "Waterbury Button Co." provides a date range from 1849 to 1943, which is when the Waterbury Button Companies Inc., of Waterbury, Connecticut, was using that maker's mark (Luscomb 2006, 220). Another military button with the exact same maker's mark was found in Level 4, but unlike the former, this button shows signs of damage caused by fire. In addition to the button chronology, a zipper pull provides an earliest possible date of 1913 for Level 2 since this is when the zipper became a common addition to clothing items after improvements were made after its 1893 patent date (Panati 1987, 316–17).

Other items found in this unit would be expected at the school building, including artifacts such as a jewelry clasp, porcelain doll fragments, clothing items, and slate pencil fragments. It is very likely that the burn pile is directly associated with TU 3 and possibly with items discarded from the original school building.

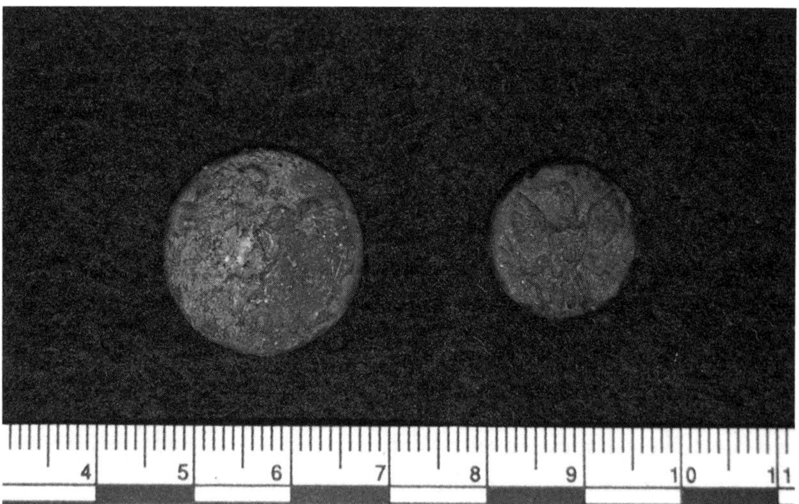

Figure 6.9. Military buttons from Test Unit 4

TU 5

TU 5 was located in the central western portion of Grid EF. Almost all of the artifacts were recovered from the first two levels and the remaining levels were mostly devoid of artifacts. It is possible that Stratum 1 and Stratum 2 represent a single soil deposit consisting of fill from a different area in the grid or elsewhere. The dateable artifacts were all collected from the mix in the first two levels and so they do not contribute to the stratigraphic interpretation, but they do provide general dates for the unit and Grid EF. Wire and cut nails were found mixed together in the first two levels. A Bennington stoneware marble fragment provides a date from 1870 to 1910 (Carskadden and Gartley 1990). A white prosser button has an earliest possible date of 1840 (Sprague 2002, 113), but given the marble, the *terminus post quem* is 1910.

Other diagnostics provided contextual information such as a glass privacy brick, faunal remains, cloth fragments, an eyelet, various school-related items, and milk glass and porcelain fragments. These items are similar to those found in the trash pile associated with TU 3 and TU 4, and so they are likely also associated with materials from the original school building.

TU 6

TU 6 was located in the central western portion of Grid EF, just slightly northwest of TU 5. It has similar stratigraphy to TU 5 in that most of the artifacts were collected from the first two levels, which represent a single deposit of mixed soil used as fill or moved from nearby to level the landscape. Of the 536 artifacts collected from this unit, over half of them were architectural materials and very few artifacts were found in general. The cut and wire nails were all mixed within the first two levels. Most of the dateable artifacts were collected Level 1 and included a utilitarian bone button, which has a production date range of 1800 to 1865 (South 1964, 115–21); a removable pull-tab from a tin can, which has a date range from 1963 to circa 1976 (Rock 1989, 18); and a colorless glass fragment with the letters "TER . . . T" embossed on the glass, which has a date range of 1856 to 1920 (Pullin 1986, 355; Fike 1987, 5). Therefore, the *terminus post quem* for Level 1 is 1976. The range of dates provided by artifacts found in Level 1 supports the interpretation of heavily mixed soils used for landscaping the area in Grid EF. Other diagnostics found in the unit included a cloth fragment, milk glass, school-related items, fragments of a handsaw, and white improved earthenware fragments.

TU 7

TU 7 was located in the northwest corner of Grid EF. Again, the stratigraphy indicates that the soil was heavily mixed, as the strata seem to blend into each other. The majority of artifacts came from Level 2 and architectural materials made up over half of all the artifacts collected. A significant number of complete cut nails was collected, and were found in the same context as wire nails as well. The dateable artifacts were all collected from the first two levels and included a removable pull-tab found in Level 1 with a date range of 1963 to circa 1976 (Rock 1989, 18); porcelain doll fragments from Level 2 that have a date range between 1860 to 1917 (Coleman et al. 1968, 74–78); and a rimfire bullet from Level 1, which is missing the cartridge case, but is most likely a .22 Short and therefore produces a range from 1857 to the present (Barnes 1989, 359). Considering the amount of mixing shown in the stratigraphy, it is likely that the artifacts from Level 1 and Level 2 are from the same deposit. The *terminus post quem* then is 1976, which may have been around the time the lot was leveled and relandscaped, perhaps for the installation of updated irrigation lines.

Other diagnostics include faunal remains, a safety pin, slate pencil fragments, and fragments of a lice comb. The safety pin is an interesting find as it could be associated with the sewing activities that female students are known to have participated in while attending Stewart Indian School. The pin, as well as the slate pencil fragments and lice comb fragments, are items commonly associated with schoolhouses and are possibly associated with the original school building.

TU 8

TU 8 was located in the far northwest corner of Grid EF. The stratigraphy in this unit is extremely mixed with no distinct stratigraphic layers. As with the other TUs in this grid, the majority of artifacts collected were of architectural materials. However, the materials found in TU 8 were much larger than materials found in other units. This included partially whole fragments of ceramic brick and a piece of milled lumber. It is very likely that the increase in size is related to this unit's proximity to the initial location of the original school building. Figure 6.1 shows TU 8 and its location in comparison to the location of the school building from a 1930 map of the campus.

Dateable artifacts from the unit included a significant number of cut nails, of which over half of those were found in Level 3. The number of cut nails reduced in the upper levels, possibly suggesting some chronological integrity in the unit, even without the noticeable strata. Most of the dateable artifacts came from Level 1 and included a fragment of amethyst glass, which has a date of anywhere between 1880 to 1914 (Newman 1970, 70–75; Miller and McNichol 2002, 4); a Bennington stoneware marble with a blue glaze that has a date range between 1870 to 1910 (Carskadden and Gartley 1990); and four fragments of a plastic shotshell hull that have the letters "I R D" on one of the fragments and date to at least 1958 (Ball 1997, 133). Therefore, the *terminus post quem* for Level 1 is 1958. Dates for Level 2 were provided by a ferrous, side-winding, can key that has a date range of circa 1895 to the present (Rock 1989, 78–79), and a cartridge case from a .22 caliber

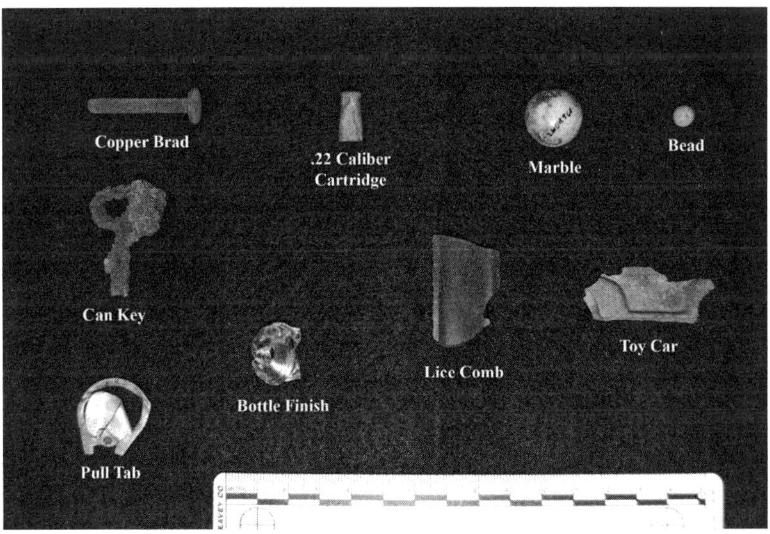

FIGURE 6.10. Diagnostics artifacts from Test Unit 8.

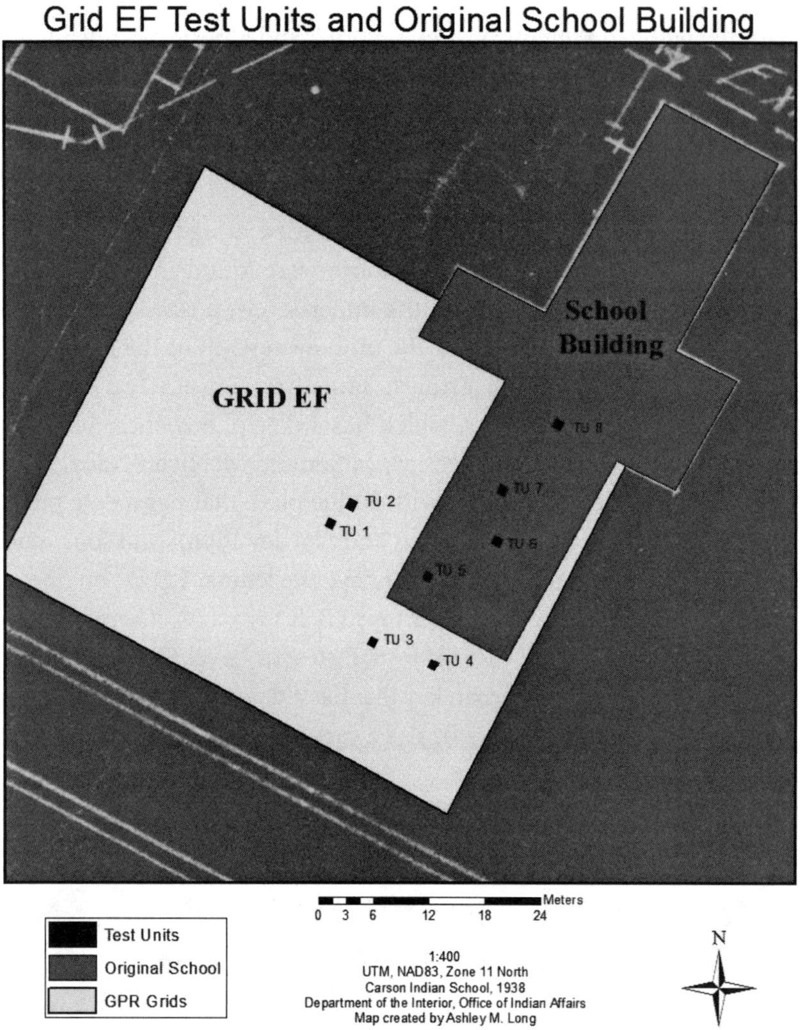

FIGURE 6.11. Grid EF Test Units and original school building.

rifle provides a date range of 1857 to the present (Barnes 1989, 359). According to these artifacts, the *terminus ante quem* for Level 2 is 1895.

Other diagnostics from TU 8 included a bead, a lice comb, parts of a toy car, a possible jewelry box hinge, and various ceramics. These artifacts further corroborate the interpretation of the unit as being representative of materials from the original school building since these are all items that would be expected to be found in a school.

Interpretations of Grid EF

The information gathered through TU 1 to TU 8 mostly all supports the interpretation of Grid EF as a site of a multiple episodes of soil being moved around with heavy machinery. The significant amount of mixed soils and crushed architectural materials from all of the units provides the main evidence in support of this interpretation, but there is also the presence of the burned trash pile found in TU 3 and TU 4, which appeared as an anomaly in the GPR. Therefore, it is possible that during the demolition of the original school building, and afterward, that materials were crushed and spread around the grid with heavy machinery; while the trash from in and around the building was likely piled into one area and burned. The preservation of the charcoal layer suggests that it was covered with soil shortly after the pile was burned.

The linear features found in TU 1 and TU 2 also provide evidence for irrigation efforts either after the building was demolished or around the same time period. The installation of the sprinkler system may also be responsible for some of the soil mixing found in the majority of the units.

Overall, it is most likely that the northwest portion of the grid provides the most substantial evidence of the school building due to the amount of large architectural debris collected and the proximity to the approximate location of the building on historic maps (figure 6.11). The *terminus post quem* dates for this grid indicate that the top layer of soil is most likely associated with a deposit made around the late 1970s, and the deepest subsurface levels are probably associated with deposits made from the late nineteenth century to the early twentieth century (table 6.4).

Also, artifacts recovered from this grid, including military buttons, lice combs, and various other comb fragments, correspond with oral histories referenced in earlier chapters regarding life at Indian schools (see chapters 3, 4, 5). The integration of oral histories provided particular perspectives on those items and what they may have represented to the students. For instance, Lowry (1993) discussed his familiarity with wearing military uniforms and associated it with the military formations and disciplinary actions at the Fort Bidwell Indian School. Although the mixing in Grid EF makes it difficult to positively associate the buttons to a particular time period at Stewart, considering the

Table 6.4. *Terminus post quem* dates for Grid EF.

	TU 1	TU 2	TU 3	TU 4	TU 5	TU 6	TU 7	TU 8
Level 1	n/a	post-1873	n/a	1944	n/a	1976	1976	1958
Level 2		n/a	1940–p*	1913–p*	1910	n/a	1917	1895
Level 3	n/a	n/a	1910	n/a	n/a	n/a	n/a	n/a
Level 4	post-1892	n/a	1840	1849–1943	n/a	n/a	n/a	n/a

* p = present.

history of the school, it is likely that these buttons are associated with the earliest years of the school's operation and can therefore be interpreted as a representation of the strict assimilation agenda adopted by the Bureau of Indian Affairs (BIA) and boarding school administration during the late nineteenth century.

Similarly, the lice comb fragments correspond with Millett's (n.d.) account of working in the Stewart Indian School infirmary as a student. The comb fragments may then be interpreted as representing the vocational work that students were required to do, but they can also speak to the concerns for personal hygiene and sanitation that were enforced at the school. Although Millett (n.d.) did not speak fondly of her experiences screening for lice in the infirmary, this may have been a familiar experience for some of the students and there is no way to determine whether the items are associated with the earlier, more restrictive years of the school, or the later, more progressive years.

The Swimming Pool (TU in Grid BC)

A single TU, TU 9, was placed in the cross-section of Grid B and Grid C, recorded as Grid BC. The purpose of the unit was to locate the remains of a large swimming pool that was once located on the campus and to ascertain its condition. The NIC wished to know more about the state of the buried pool to aid in planning future efforts to install a reflection pool at the location as part of the future Cultural Center. Excavations here were intended to assist with their planning work.

TU 9 was full of ferrous pipe fragments, rebar, and large pieces of concrete. As such, the stratigraphy shows three large strata before reaching the base of the pool, which was probably infilled all at once. There were a few miscellaneous diagnostic artifacts recovered from the unit. They do not seem to be associated with any sort of pool activity and most likely represent fill taken from another area to be used for filling in the pool. These artifacts included a fragment of milk glass stemware, a ceramic plate fragment, and a slate pencil fragment, none of which provided useful dates for the interpretation of this unit. Two U.S. quarters collected from Level 1 have dates of 1980 and 1979, possibly representing the date for the last episode of relandscaping or irrigating the lot. There were also three large fragments of butchered faunal remains retrieved from the unit, which further supports the interpretation of the soil coming from another area. Overall, the materials recovered from TU 9 provided information on how the pool was initially filled in. It also gives a definite location of the base, which will benefit the NIC if they proceed with plans for a reflection pool in that area.

Single-Room Building (TUs in Grid D)

TUs were placed in Grid D in an attempt to locate a single-room building that was once located in the area adjacent to the infirmary. This information was provided during the field school during a discussion with an alumnus of the Stewart Indian School. According to oral histories, the building was one of the earliest school buildings that was later used as a mock residence in training girls for domestic service.

TU 10 and Feature 5

TU 10 was originally identified as Feature 5 and was located just outside of Grid D. The feature was located on the surface as a concrete ring and was investigated to determine if it was a well. It was found that the circular concrete structure continued far under the surface and was eventually identified as part of a sewage pipe or drainage system. Similar to TU 9, the stratigraphy was interrupted by large pieces of rebar, concrete, and rock. There are, however, four apparent strata and some chronological integrity provided by various dateable artifacts. The range of artifact types and dates provided by those artifacts suggest that the pipe was repeatedly used as a trash pit.

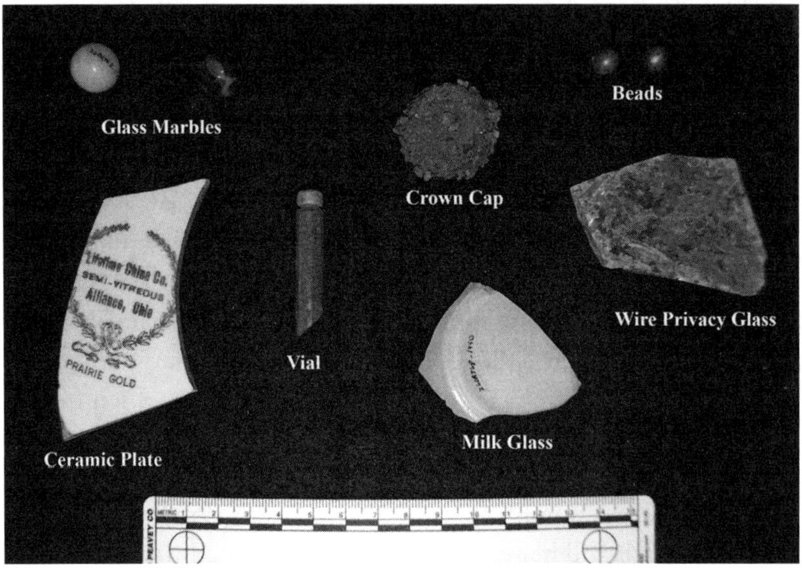

Figure 6.12. Diagnostic Artifacts from Test Unit 10, Level 1.

This unit had a large quantity of dateable artifacts since it was most likely used as a trash dump for several years. For Level 1, a cigarette filter can provide an approximate date of 1970, as this was when 33 percent of all cigarettes began to have filters (*Encyclopedia Britannica* 1973 (5), 767–68). A machine-made, glass marble from the same level has a range from 1901 to the present (Carskadden and Gartley 1990). There was also a large, ceramic plate fragment with a maker's mark reading, "Lifetime China Co. / Semi-Vitreous / Alliance, Ohio / Prairie Gold." The mark is associated with the Lifetime China Co., which was a distributor for the Homer Laughlin China Co. from 1953 to 1968 (Robbins n.d.). According to these artifacts, the approximate *terminus post quem* for Level 1 is circa 1970. In addition to these diagnostic artifacts, two medicine vials were recovered from Level 1. The vials resemble those used for extracting medicine with syringes. Although the vials could not be adequately dated, they do provide information about health practices at the infirmary, which was located across the street from TU 10 (figure 6.1).

There were no diagnostic artifacts retrieved from Level 2, and the majority of those found in Level 3 were various glass fragments with embossed letters. Most of the fragments only have partial letters or incomplete phrases that do not provide chronological information.

Dateable artifacts from Level 4 included eight sanitary cans, four of which were opened with a church key. Although sanitary cans were being produced as early as 1898 (Keen 1982, 316), church keys were not being used until around 1935 (Rock 1989, 194), which makes that the earliest possible date that the cans could have been deposited. There was also a felt marker collected from Level 4. The label reads, "Sanford's Marker Deluxe," and additional information printed on the marker states, "PAT APPL FOR / MADE IN USA / KEEP TIGHTLY CAPPED / Bellwood, ILL / NO 1100." The company moved to Bellwood, Illinois in 1947 (Reference for Business 2015), and according to the U.S.P.T.O. Full-Text Patent Database, the patent was applied for in 1960 and was officially patented in 1963. Therefore, the marker must date between 1960 and 1963.

The Sanford marker is of additional interest as it shows signs of modification. On either side of the marker there are small holes, apparently drilled or poked into the marker. There is additional evidence of the holes then being pried open by another tool. It is impossible to know what exactly the purpose of the holes were, but considering the object was found on a school campus, it is possible that it demonstrates the efforts of a resident to open the marker and inhale the fumes. Students elsewhere have been known to huff these types of markers (Patterson and Post n.d.), and this interpretation is made under the assumption that students at Stewart may have participated in the same behavior. Other

FIGURE 6.13. Sanford's Marker Deluxe from Test Unit 10.

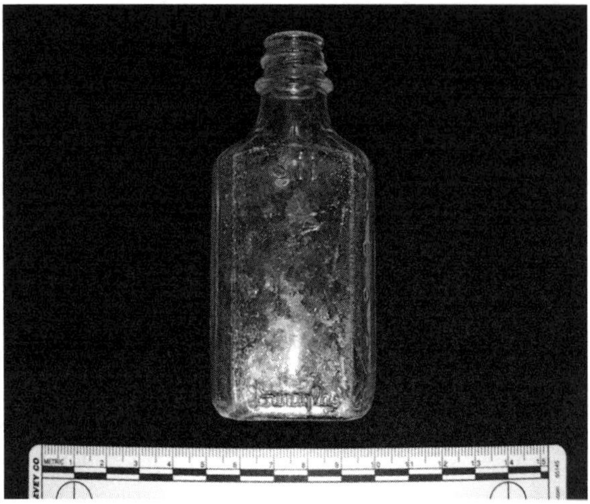

Figure 6.14. Duraglass medicine bottle from Test Unit 10.

interpretations of the holes may simply relate to curiosity or possibly someone's attempt to extract marker ink to be used in a different way.

Dateable artifacts were also collected from Level 5 and included a complete Duraglas medicine bottle that dates to around 1949. Duraglass was the name given to a bottle-making process used by the

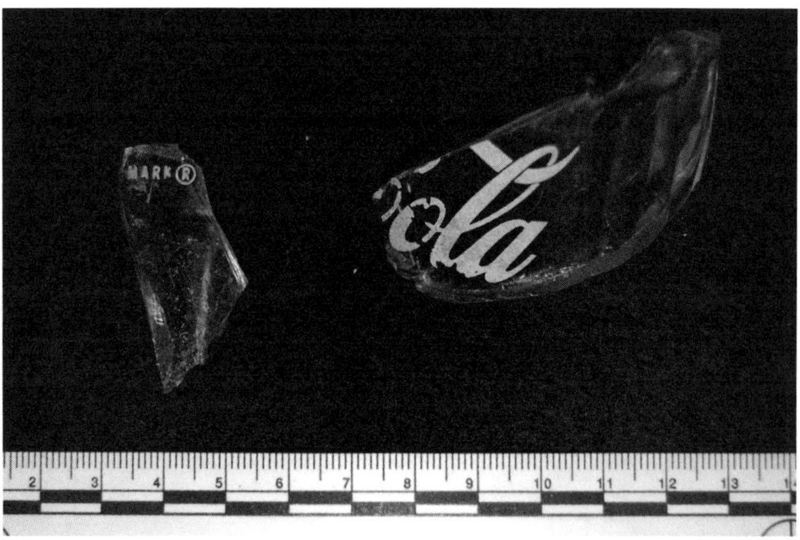

Figure 6.15. Coca-Cola bottle from Test Unit 10.

Owens-Illinois Glass Company. The name was embossed (in script) on bottles beginning in 1940 and continuing into the 1950s. This bottle had a maker's mark indicating that it was produced in the Oakland, California factory (Lockhart and Hoenig 2015), so its specific date range is from 1936 to circa 1950.

Fragments from a glass Coca-Cola bottle were also found in Level 5. The white applied color label (ACL) on one fragment, and the embossed, "MARK ®," found on another fragment, indicate that the fragments were from a bottle produced anywhere between 1960 and 1970 (Munsey 1972, 59, 61). In addition to the glass bottles found in this level, there was also a fragment of wire privacy glass found that dates to post-1892 (Encyclopedia Britannica 1898, 1408). Due to the numerous other artifacts from this level with later dates, the *terminus post quem* for this level is 1970.

Very few diagnostic artifacts were recovered from Level 6 other than two, ferrous crown caps that have a patent date of 1892 (Lief 1965, 17). The remaining dates come from artifacts found in Level 7.

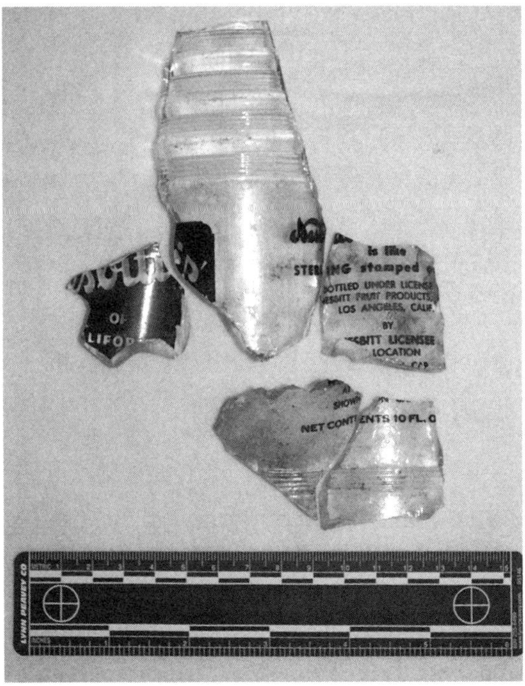

FIGURE 6.16. Nesbitt's Drink bottle from Test Unit 10.

Fragments of a glass Nesbitt's Drink bottle were found and possibly yield a date between 1940 and 1942 according to the angle of the ACL (Scott n.d.), and a machine-made, spherical, glass marble has a date range of 1926 to the present (Carskadden and Gartley 1990). Therefore, the approximate *terminus post quem* for this last level is 1942.

TU 11

TU 11 was located nearby the northern edge of Grid D and was placed over the approximate location of a one-room, wooden school building once located on the campus. Due to the unit's close proximity to a road, the soil was very compact and difficult to excavate. As a result, the unit is shallow in comparison to most of the previous units. Based on the presence of architectural materials, including three complete cut nails found in Level 2, and items associated with a classroom such as a copper brad and graphite pencil lead fragments, it is possible that the unit was placed near the location of the wooden building. Additionally, a ferrous metal adornment, possibly a broach or pendant, was collected from the unit. It is possible that it may have been lost or discarded by a faculty member while using the small school building. Green 7-Up bottle fragments found in Level 1 and Level 2 provided a date range of 1930 to circa 1980 (Hake 1992, 141).

TU 12

TU 12 was located in the central portion of Grid D, again, in the approximate location of the one-room school building. Out of two identifiable strata, Stratum 1 is very thin, while Stratum 2 makes up the remaining soil in the unit. Very few artifacts were collected, none diagnostic, and mostly consisted of crushed architectural materials.

TU 13

TU 13 was located in the southern portion of Grid D, south of TU 12. The upper strata were thin and included a charcoal smear in Stratum 2. The remaining strata indicate mixing, as the soil is mottled with various other soil inclusions. Most of the artifacts were architectural materials, and included six complete cut nails found in Levels 1 through 3. Additionally, slate pencil fragments found in Level 4 and graphite pencil lead fragments found in Level 3, support the presence of scholastic activities in that area. There was also a large rock located in the southeast corner of the unit. It is possible that the rock represents a foundation once used for the school building.

A broken butter knife found in Level 1 and a milk glass fragment found in Level 2 may suggest that the building was also used as an eating area, as a training area for domestic service, or as being associated with the trash deposits found in Feature 5.

Interpretations of Grid D

Grid D most likely represents the extremely crushed and scattered debris of a building said to have been located in the area. Alumni visitors to the site suggested it was the location of a one-room building original to the campus. Considering that most of the artifacts collected from the three units within the grid were architectural materials mixed with classroom objects such as pencil fragments, it is likely that the interpretation of the building's use for education is correct. It is also possible that much of the trash collected from Feature 5 is associated with the school building, and/or vice versa.

Additionally, many of the items found in TU 10, such as food wrappers and fragments of Coca-Cola bottles, correspond with some of the stories told by tribal members during the field school. For example, Jo Ann Nevers, a Washoe Tribal Elder (see Nevers essay, chapter 7) and an alumnus of the school, visited the field school and gave a public talk about her experiences as a student there. Among other things, she

Table 6.5. *Terminus post quem* dates for Grid D.

	TU 10	TU 11	TU 12	TU 13
Level 1	1970	c. 1980	n/a	n/a
Level 2	n/a	c. 1980	n/a	n/a
Level 3	n/a	n/a	n/a	n/a
Level 4	1963	n/a	n/a	n/a
Level 5	1970	n/a	n/a	n/a
Level 6	1892	n/a	n/a	n/a
Level 7	1942	n/a	n/a	n/a

spoke about purchasing sweet treats such as Coke and doughnuts. She recalled these experiences as positive and exciting for the children as they all enjoyed the treats and the change from their typical cafeteria menu (Jo Ann Nevers, personal communication). Therefore, it is possible to interpret some of the items from TU 10 as being associated with the students purchasing the treats for themselves from the commissaries on campus.

Interpretations of Faunal Remains

Of the identifiable faunal elements found in the excavation units, cow and bird elements were predominant. The remains are quite fragmentary but do provide some information. The large number of cow elements collected from the site is most likely a result of the frequent use of the animal for food. The presence of cut marks and other modifications on many of the elements further supports this interpretation. Furthermore, the majority of the cow elements were collected from TU 8 located in the far northeast corner of Grid EF, which also held the largest architectural materials. Considering the amount and size of the brick and wood fragments collected from this unit, it is possible that TU 8 represents materials from a stove, since they were known to have been in the original buildings.

However, the prominence of bird elements found at the site is less easily explained. It is possible that the birds represent natural processes or small-game hunting trips made by the students; historical documents and oral histories indicate that this was a common occurrence, although they mostly describe the hunting of rabbits. Another possibility for the large amount of Class 2 elements could be related to religious ceremonial practices performed by students in the privacy of their dorm rooms (see chapters 4 and 5).

There is also the possibility that the faunal remains are representative of the earliest days of the Stewart Indian School, and small game may have been an additional food source that was most easily acquired. According to stories from alumni and community members visiting the site, students supplemented their diets by catching wild rabbits, and sometimes their families camped nearby so they could occasionally see their children and give them additional food; this was more common in earlier years when attendance was mandatory.

Geochemical and Macrobotanical Analyses

This section summarizes geochemical and macrobotanical analyses performed on soil samples collected from two excavation units (for additional details, see Springer 2015). These units were in Grid EF, where the original school building is thought to have been, specifically from the areas thought to be possible burn piles from the building remnants.

Geochemical Analysis

Geochemical analysis for the Stewart Indian School samples was performed using x-ray fluorescence spectroscopy (XRF) and loss-on-ignition (LOI). The two methods were employed to help answer three fundamental questions about the school and the nature of burn features at the site: (1) Do the results support the preliminary site interpretation that the investigated features are designated burn piles, rather than the remains of structures burned in place? (2) Can geochemical methods be used to determine the parent material of the slag found in the potential burn piles? and (3) If the features are associated with burning events, can geochemical methods determine what materials were burned in the features?

In order to determine their geochemistry, two methods of geochemical analysis were performed on the soil samples from the Stewart Indian School: XRF and LOI. In each case, the results of the analyses were compared to a control sample taken near the school grounds to determine their validity.

X-Ray Fluorescence (XRF) Results

Soil sample number 68 contained elevated amounts of seven elements relative to the control sample, and in the case of calcium, relative to both the control and soil sample number 69. These elements are calcium, manganese, copper, zinc, arsenic, strontium, and lead. Each of these elements is significantly higher in concentration than what is found in the control. Barium is missing from this sample, although it is found in sample 69 and the control.

Soil sample 69 contains elevated amounts of six elements relative to the control sample. These elements are calcium, copper, zinc, arsenic, strontium, and lead. Calcium is found in lower quantities than in sample 68, but still in twice the quantity found in the control. Lead is found in a significantly higher concentration than in sample 68.

Analyses were also performed on slag samples for each TU in an attempt to identify the material (see figure 6.17). The slag was first analyzed using fragments selected directly from the soil sample bags. A second analysis involved pulverizing the slag samples in an attempt to obtain a more complete geochemistry for the slag. The process involved placing a few nodules of slag material into an agate mortar and pulverizing by hand using an agate pestle.

The XRF analysis suggests that seven elements found in TUs 3 and 4 are potentially anthropogenic. These elements are calcium, manganese, copper, zinc, arsenic, strontium, and lead. Each of these elements occurred in quantities significantly higher than that found in the control sample.

FIGURE 6.17. Slag example.

Table 6.6. Loss on ignition results.

Soil sample number	Sample weight	At 500° C	At 900° C	Organic matter % loss at 500°C	Carbonate % loss at 900°C	Total % loss
68	5.1571 g	4.6383 g	4.4554 g	10.06%	3.55%	13.61%
69	7.3882 g	6.9952 g	6.8828 g	5.32%	1.52%	6.84%

Loss-on-Ignition (LOI) Results

The LOI results will be described as a percent rather than in grams, as each sample began with different amounts prior to placement in the furnace. Each sample was subjected to two firings. The first firing ignites any organic matter present. The second firing ignites carbonate. See table 6.5 below for results.

Soil sample 68 was found to contain a significant percentage of its weight as organic matter and carbonate, while soil sample 69 contained roughly half the amount. In appearance, both samples are nearly identical, but these results clearly demonstrate otherwise. Burn features containing ash can be found to contain a significant amount of carbonate during loss-on-ignition; but in this case, ash was not present in the feature, leading to a relatively small percentage of carbonate content. Additionally, features containing seeds and a variety of organic matter tend to have high percentages of organic matter content highlighted during firing, yet soil sample 68 contained no seeds, and visibly approximately the same quantity of rootlets as soil sample 69. No explanation readily presents itself for this anomaly.

Interpretations of the Geochemical Analysis

The archaeological remains found in TUs 3 and 4 are likely to be the result of designated pile burning rather than a structure fire. However, the low levels of calcium identified in the XRF and LOI analyses do not make for a simple case. The calcium levels are significantly higher than what was found in the control sample. The presence of calcium indicates calcium carbonate, the primary component of some types of ash. While calcium carbonate is also the primary component of caliche, the Holocene geologic formations in Eagle Valley are too young for its formation (Pease 1980). If structural materials were burned in place, or if burned materials were brought in and dumped in the feature, significant amounts of ash should be present in either case, but neither soil sample from the Stewart Indian School contained visible quantities of ash. This suggests that the ash may either have been blown away or removed from the feature at some point after the burn event. High winds are common in this area, so this explanation is possible. It is also possible that much of the wood from demolition was salvaged prior to burning, and much of what burned was fueled by remnants of coal. Coal was used to warm the building for decades; chunks of it were found throughout the excavation units.

In this case, it was not possible to definitively identify the source material of the slag found in both soil samples. Comparisons were made with a library of slag chemical compositions (Bachmann 1982), but the results did not demonstrate enough similarity with any of the materials (see Bachmann 1982; table 6.5). The element that comprised the greatest percentage of the soil samples was silicon at approximately 15 percent, which is not high enough to determine that it is glass slag.

The geochemical analysis identified seven potentially anthropogenic elements in the samples, including the previously discussed calcium. Of those, several may be significant. The elevated levels of manganese may be associated with pigments (Erlandson et al. 1999, 520-521). The elevated strontium levels may have come from the animal bone fragments that were found in the unit levels. The source of the lead is open to interpretation, but at seven hundred to a thousand parts per million, it exceeds EPA standards for what is allowed in the soils of schools by four hundred to eight hundred parts per million (Tarrago and Demers 2010, 23). Soils normally contain less than fifty parts per million of lead (Tarrago and Demers 2010, 23), so the prevalence of it in these units may indicate waste disposal of items containing lead, such as coal, paint, or pencils.

Macrobotanical Analysis and Results

Macrobotanical analysis of the soil samples was performed using the bucket method of flotation, in order to identify plant macroremains and artifacts by separating the light remains from the heavy. The tables below summarize the results for both the light and heavy fraction

Table 6.7. Macrobotanical recovery results.

	Heavy Fraction			Light Fraction		
	Weight (g)	Quality	Color	Weight (g)	Quality	Color
Soil sample no. 68						
Seed bead		1	red/white			
Glass fragment		1	olive			
Glass fragment, flat	1.7		colorless			
Mortar fragment	5					
Ferrous conglomerate	8.1					
Burned rock	31.5					
Slag	306.2			0.4		
Coal/charcoal	183.5			283.2		
Pebbles very fine to med.	70.8					
Sedimentary rock	42					
Wood fragments				0.1		
Rootlets	0.1			0.5		
Fraction remainder	5.8			38.1		
Unknown material	1.0			11		
Soil Sample no. 69						
Coal/charcoal	24.8			90.8		
Glass fragments	2.4		colorless			
Ferrous material	0.2					
Slag	75					
Sedimentary rock	3.4					
Rootlets	0.1				1.1 g	
Pebbles very fine to med.	38					
Fraction remainder	172.5				6.5 g	
Unknown material	0.1				0.3 g	

analyses. No anthropogenic macrobotanical remains were found in the soils. Due to the presence of slag and coal/charcoal, the results are atypically weighted toward the heavy fraction. See table 6.6 for results.

The presence of large quantities of coal (both burned and unburned) and charcoal, and the lack of ash, indicate that at least some of the materials in the feature from TUs 3 and 4 were from the cleanouts of stoves, furnaces, or boiler fireboxes.

Few architectural materials were identified during the flotation analysis, although both wire and cut nails were recovered from the TUs in the field prior to soil sample collection. Food waste was also not recovered, although the temperatures could have been too high to preserve any evidence during burning. Glass fragments, seed beads, and buttons were found in the TUs prior to soil sampling, which suggests a general disposal of materials, such as in an incinerator, burn pile, and/or stove clean-outs.

Overall, despite the limitations in this case, the results of the geochemical and macrobotanical analyses demonstrate the applicability of these methods to a variety of features in historical archaeological sites.

Discussion of Archaeological Findings, Relative to Research Questions

One of the main focuses of this project is to demonstrate how collaborative methods in archaeology can not only further the reaches of this field, but may also help to bridge the gaps that exist between scientists and Indigenous communities. This discussion of collaborative methods was further supplemented by an analysis of artifacts through theoretical lenses based on the archaeological investigations of institutions and childhood. The analysis is therefore limited in that attention was spread out across all three of the major themes: collaborative archaeology, the archaeology of institutional life, and the archaeology of childhood. This section presents the initial results of these analyses through a discussion of the research questions.

The Archaeology of Institutional Life

The archaeology of institutional life offers several theoretical lenses that prove useful in illuminating many of the underlying implications behind the artifacts and the landscape at Stewart Indian School. It is possible to critically expand on life at Stewart, by observing how such issues as consumerism, market exchange, and power are reflected in the landscape and artifact assemblage.

Items such as Coca-Cola and Nesbitt's Drink bottles, ferrous crown caps, tin can fragments, and various aluminum and plastic food wrappers can represent the administration's efforts to influence students by exposing them to consumerism and market exchange through the presence of commissaries on campus. Many of the students may have already encountered such things before arriving at Stewart through experiences with the many mining towns all over Nevada, especially in later years. The opposite was also possible, and for some, it may have been the first time they had regular access to items such as Coca-Cola and wrapped candies.

While attending Stewart, students were required to participate in vocational work; in some instances, they were able to earn small wages for their work. This provided them with the means to purchase goods from the small shops on campus and around Carson City when they were allowed to take field trips off campus. The commissaries, with their sugary drinks and treats, were incentive for students to fulfill their vocational work so they may acquire these items. It was a system that directly exposed children to Euro-American values such as individualism, since the children were learning to work for themselves, to earn money for themselves, so they may purchase things that they wanted. This is in contrast to the community work ethic that is common among American Indian tribes (Lomawaima 1994).

It is also possible to examine the landscape and identify how these same concepts were put to use through the location of those commissaries and their proximity to other buildings such as classroom halls, dormitories, and buildings used for vocational work. By conducting a viewshed analysis in ArcGIS, it is possible to analyze what buildings the students would have been looking at most often, for example, what buildings the students could see from their dormitories and classrooms. The viewshed was applied to maps of the campus dating to 1938 and 1945. In both cases, the children would have had an almost constant visual of the commissaries, which may have increased their motivation to earn money and purchase items (Long 2015).

Additionally, an investigation of the landscape can also speak to the control over the students' daily movements as well. First, the boys' and girls' dorms were kept separate and were also distinguished by age, with younger boys and girls kept separate from the older boys and girls. Sidewalks and roads laid out in a grid-like fashion provided a structured path for residents to travel around the campus. Even though a Least Cost Path analysis of the campus shows several direct paths

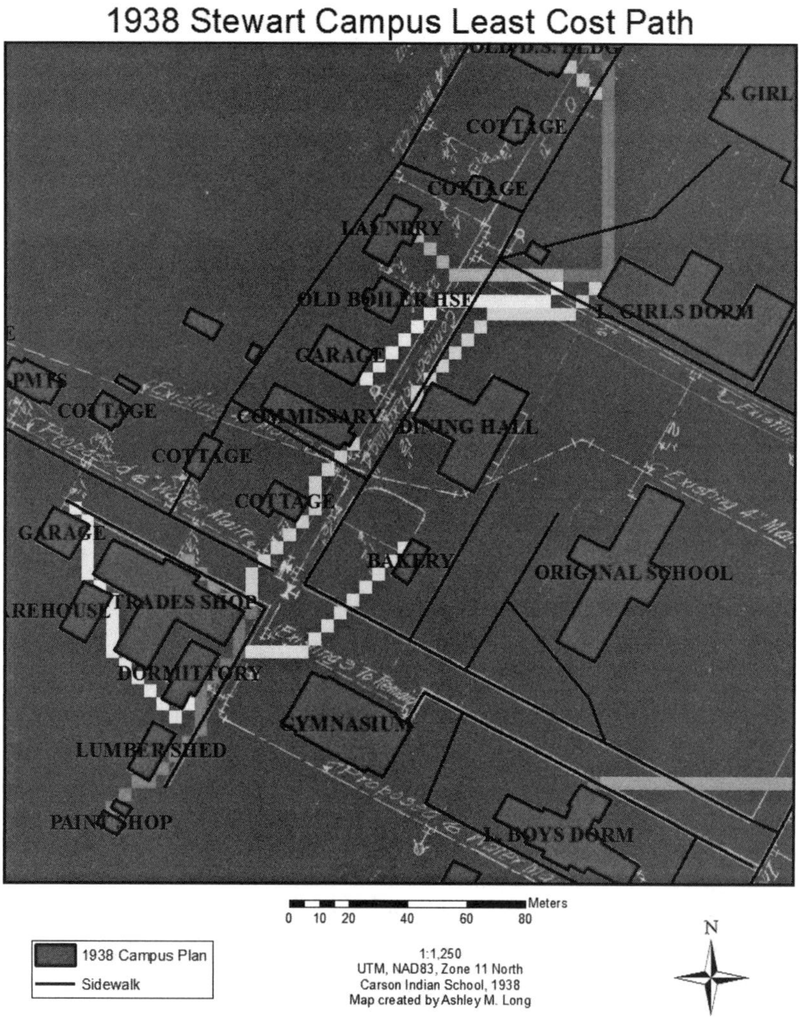

FIGURE 6.18. 1938 Stewart Campus Least Cost Path.

between buildings (figure 6.18), the children would have been directed to stay on sidewalks (although this may have not always happened). Evidence from Grid EF of extensive moving of soils and irrigation features in TU 1 and TU 2, further supports this interpretation of the landscape. Such effort to manipulate the landscape with grass, flowers, and trees, as well as the strict organization applied through the sidewalks and roads, illustrates the administration's efforts to control the residents' daily movements. Also, the Gregorian-style landscape represents the values and belief system of those that were imposing order on students at Stewart. In an argument that parallels Foucault's (1977) work on discipline, this imposition of power over the children through the landscape would have greatly influenced the residents and aided in their assimilation.

Items such as military buttons, lice combs, and bone toothbrushes recovered from the field school can also speak to issues of power at Stewart. As mentioned in chapter 3, during the earlier years of the school's operation, students were forced to change their appearance once they were enrolled (Adams 2006). This included wearing military uniforms and the act of cutting their hair (see chapter 5, for a discussion of this trauma). This process also included being searched for lice, often by other students, and in some cases, being assigned a toothbrush and hair comb if they did not already have these items. The military uniforms especially represent the assimilation efforts of the administration since this would have likely been a drastic change from what the students normally wore. According to Luther Standing Bear, "The fact is that we were to be transformed, and short hair being the mark of gentility with the white man, he put upon us the mark" (Standing Bear 1933, 189). The uniforms and short hair replaced the external signs of tribal identity with those associated with Euro-American values.

The children all came from diverse homes (e.g., reservations, ranches, farms) and some were accustomed to Euro-American practices. However, in some cases, the implementation of a strict personal hygiene routine may have also been a significant change in the daily lives of the children. This speaks to the concerns of the administration and the lengths taken to control the daily actions of those children who attended the school during the late nineteenth century.

The Archaeology of Childhood

As discussed in chapter 2, the identification of children as active agents in the shaping of material culture is a foundational concept of the archaeology of childhood. Viewing the artifacts from Stewart from this perspective allows for an alternative interpretation not based on assimilation, but rather the continuance of American Indian customs through the modification of artifacts and spaces.

The results of another archaeological investigation at the Phoenix Indian School in Arizona can also add to this discussion (Lindauer 1998). For example, at both the Phoenix Indian School site and the dump site at the Stewart Indian School, there was evidence of modification to comb and toothbrush fragments. In an earlier excavation at Stewart, Hattori (1978) found that one comb fragment appeared to have been shaped into a pendant; and both Hattori (1978) and Lindauer (1998) found that students had carved their names into the handles of combs and toothbrushes. The comb pendant and the name "Jack Winnemucca" (Hattori 1978, 24) carved into a comb handle suggest that students exhibited individual agency through the modification of historic artifacts. Since Winnemucca is a well-known Northern Paiute name (Hattori 1978, 24), it was possibly done so as an attempt to remain associated with their traditional beliefs. A possible flaked bottle glass fragment recovered from the Stewart field school may also be representative of this behavior. Lindauer (1998) found flaked ceramics at the Phoenix site, and the similar modifications from both schools could support ethnographic accounts of a pan-tribal community created by Native students living at Indian boarding schools (Lomawaima 1994, see chapter 2). Rather than fully assimilating to Western values, this is evidence that children acted as individual agents and made an effort to preserve their cultural practices. This type of "persistence" or "survivance" (Silliman 2008, 2014) is not uncommon at postcolonial Indigenous sites, as Native peoples actively continued to shape and reshape their daily practices in the face of oppression.

There is also the concept of "secret spaces" from the archaeology of childhood (Adams 1995, see chapter 2) that can add to the interpretation of artifacts found during field school mapping exercises designed to teach students the value of noninvasive archaeology (which is also in keeping some principles in Indigenous archaeology; refer to chapter 2). Students learned to record surface finds in between buildings on the edge of campus. They recorded a wide variety of artifacts, but noted a higher concentration of marbles and colorful bits of glass and rocks in between campus agricultural buildings near the creek. Students may have used these areas to engage in activities, intentionally away from the main part of campus and away from adults' viewshed. Similarly, there was a noticeable concentration of toys recovered from TU 3 and TU 4, as a burn pile possibly associated with the original school building. The abundance of marbles and porcelain doll fragments collected from those units could indicate that students were using hidden spaces in, around, or under the school building to play games. Also, fragmented faunal remains, some of which appear to be butchered rabbit, could suggest religious activity accompanying food consumption was occurring in those secret spaces. Oral histories from Stewart repeatedly state that students illicitly hunted rabbits near campus or secretly received rabbits hunted by their families who were camping nearby (chapters 2, 4, and 5). During fieldwork Richard Arnold (Arnold essay, chapter 7), chair of the NIC, gave a talk to field school students, including the relevance of butchered animal bones in archaeological contexts. He urged archaeologists to remember that faunal remains represent more than just calories consumed, but also indicate social and prayer activities surrounding food sharing (Richard Arnold, personal communication). The possibility that students did such rituals in secret is further supported by ethnographic evidence from the Chilocco Indian School in Oklahoma. There, Lomawaima (1994) found that students were practicing rituals in the dorm's rooms after their dorm supervisor had gone to sleep.

Collaborative Methods and Standard Methods

As discussed previously, the most apparent change to standard archaeological methods from taking a collaborative stance is obviously the inclusion of diverse stakeholders in the development of research design and all subsequent decision-making processes, including the interpretation of data and writing and publication. For the Stewart project, these stakeholders included elders from the surrounding tribes, Native students and staff, and prominent members of American Indian communities in Nevada. Participating in a collaborative project such as this requires flexibility from everyone since communities and individuals each have goals they wish to obtain through the research project. As such, the "standards" in archaeology become much more fluid, and changes to the methods begin immediately. It is necessary to archaeologists to remain open-minded about the validity of input from nonarchaeologists. This also means that collaborative projects can look very different from case-to-case, although there are standards for collaborative archaeology as well.

Collaborative projects will usually begin with an archaeologist approaching a community and posing the question of potential research (Nicholas 2012, 30). It is important to note that the archaeologist does *not* bring a developed research design to this meeting, as the goal is to investigate the concerns of the community, not to promote the interests of the researcher. For the Stewart project, UNR archaeologists approached the NIC and Washoe-THPO about their interest in an archaeological project and, through a series of meetings, numerous stakeholders agreed that a project at Stewart would be beneficial to many Native people. Stakeholders noticed possible potential in the Stewart project and agreed to work collaboratively alongside faculty, students, and volunteers during an archaeological field school.

A second major change to traditional methods is the required flexibility of all methods (Lightfoot 2008). Typically, during an archaeological project, the researcher will aim to follow the designated research design with as few deviations as possible. This is not the case for a collaborative project. Native partners may wish to alter certain research practices, and these changes may occur while the project is underway; hence, there is a need for flexibility during all aspects of the research process. The project at Stewart Indian School serves as an example of how these changes may occur and what they may look like.

For instance, it was initially agreed upon in the research design that all flaked materials (lithics and glass) would be returned to the units in plastic bags and the units lined with landscaping fabric before being backfilled. Returning artifacts to excavation units is uncommon in standard archaeological practices and was only agreed upon after consulting with the SHPO and the Nevada State Museum, which provides antiquities permits. However, during the field school, Native students expressed concern with the plastic bags and landscaping fabric, concerned that we were not treating precontact-period artifacts with as much sensitivity as we should; the artifacts needed to be returned close to the earth, without artificial barriers. Upon voicing these concerns, we halted backfilling procedures and began a discussion of alternate options and the reasons for them. Afterward it became clear that most of the students, both Native and non-Native, agreed that the plastic bags and fabric were unnecessary elements that further removed the artifacts from their original provenience, and likewise, their connection to the land. Even though the artifacts were only minimally recorded in the field, it did not reduce the amount of significant information that we were able to obtain from the analysis. This is a change that would more than likely not occur in a project that was not initially designated as collaborative and as such, represents an important method in collaborative archaeology. Likewise, with GPR and total station mapping, the lithics and TUs will still be possible to relocate should future researchers want to do so.

The discussion described above was typical for this project. When an issue arose, we often slowed or stopped data collection in order to sit in a circle, talk, and listen. This was often a time-consuming process that was necessary to allow and encourage input from each individual so we could be assured of relative consensus. Collaborative archaeology may result in a reduction in the amount of standard archaeological data that can be gathered. However, taking time to have conversations around particular practices and the meaning of particular classes of data ultimately offers new and more nuanced interpretations of the data. Thus, collaborative methods provide a net gain in terms of research.

In addition to changing the archaeological procedures, collaboration with Indigenous communities may also require the addition of various other anthropological methods such as public anthropology and oral histories. Involving the public during archaeological excavations can be a difficult thing to maneuver and will most likely require extended involvement and dedication beyond the usual realms of the project. Participating in media interviews, providing tours of the site, and mediating opposition to the project are all possible occurrences during a collaborative archaeology project.

Finally, the last major change to occur during these projects is during the writing and publication process. Instead of following general practices for writing an archaeological report, the focus was instead on including all of the many perspectives that contributed to the success of the project. Instead of only reporting the scientific data of a particular project, the goal here is to report on the concerns and/or interests of stakeholders as accurately as possible while demonstrating the upmost respect for their beliefs. Finally, a multivocal publication is necessary for this project, which is the reasoning behind this volume with numerous coeditors and coauthors.

Collaborative Methods and the Archaeological Assemblage

The effect of collaborative methods on standard archaeological data represents one of the primary concerns of archaeologists who are not engaged in collaborative projects. Indeed, it is one of the loudest arguments against collaborative methods. More often than not, this concern stems from the inclusion of Native interpretations for artifacts and from low-impact field methods that often include the reburial of artifacts and in-field recording. However, as the results from the Stewart project show, these methods did not significantly impact the data on this particular project. In fact, it was the alternate interpretations and additional information provided by Native community members that greatly aided the overall interpretation of the site. Sites with larger precontact components might yield different results.

Overall, public archaeology and collaborative methods generated more and diverse kinds of data that would not have been available without public involvement. Throughout the field school, Native visitors, Stewart alumni (thanks to the NIC), and other interested parties provided useful contextual information that aided in the discovery of the original school building and on the interpretation of certain artifacts found at the site. For example, Stewart Indian School groundskeepers, including tribal member Larry Hale, provided one-of-a-kind maps from 1938 and 1945 that allowed us to positively identify the location of the original school building. The maps also provided an approximate date range for when the school building was demolished, as it is present on the 1938 map and is absent on the 1945 map. Although we estimated the location of the building by lining up landscape features from historical photographs, these maps provided historical documentation of the location—information that we may have never gathered otherwise.

A similar experience provided information on a one-room schoolhouse that was possibly located in Grid D. An alumnus of Stewart Indian School visited our excavation and remembered a small school building directly south of the infirmary in what is now an empty lot. This information was valuable since the goal of the research project was to locate the original schoolhouse, but also any early, wooden buildings that had been demolished. Initially, it was uncertain whether or not Grid D would be excavated, but with this personal account and the discovery of Feature 5, the grid was excavated toward the end of the field school. Again, we may have never discovered this valuable information without the help of a Native community member. It was apparent that those people who gave out this information appreciated the collaborative and public nature of the project and seemed eager to participate because of it. Presumably, had the project not been collaborative, those same people may have never shared the information or have known that it would be useful.

When looking at the assemblage and considering how these low-impact methods may have affected the collected artifacts, it was determined that the only real effect was caused by the very specific research goal of locating the original school building and by the reburial of flaked materials. This specificity is not particular to collaborative archaeology. Any archaeological project is bound to have specific research interests, and those will inevitably dictate where excavation units are placed and how deep they are excavated. Since the purpose of the field school was to locate a specific building and the foundation of a pool, the units were only placed in areas where those structures may have been. Hence, the assemblage is representative of only those areas and, as expected, mostly consisted of architectural materials. Had the focus been placed on the daily lives of students at Stewart, then the TUs may have been located less regionally and may have produced a broader spectrum of artifacts (see Hattori 1978 and Lindauer 1998). Regardless, valuable information on life at Stewart Indian School was still obtained through the assemblage.

Collaborative Methods and Indigenous Communities

Historically, Indigenous communities have had little influence over decisions made regarding archaeological sites associated with their ancestors. Collaborative projects provide the opportunity for Indigenous communities to gain control over research on their material culture, their heritage, and the use of their ancestral lands and sacred places. This is not to say that Native communities ever lost their heritage, but rather, to illustrate how collaborative projects allow Native peoples more control over how, when, and why their heritage is researched by people outside of their community. It is undeniable that the relationship between archaeologists and tribes has largely been dictated by issues of power and control over heritage. Archaeologists have a reputation of taking an authoritative perspective on history and subsequently taking control over knowledge production. Nicholas and Hollowell (2008, 61) describe this relationship between archaeologists and Native communities as one characterized by "scientific colonialism" (see chapters 1 and 2). Collaborative archaeology seeks to dissolve this disparity, to place control over Indigenous knowledge production back with the communities, and to create an alternative approach to archaeological investigations. All of these may have a direct positive impact on Indigenous communities, since they can regulate every aspect of the archaeological research.

Even though there are increasing numbers of Native archaeologists, technicians, and monitors practicing in the country today, the field is still overwhelmingly practiced by non-Native individuals. And when considering the field's history of scientific colonialism, collaborative methods in archaeology provide an essential avenue for strengthening relationships between researchers and Indigenous communities. This not only impacts the field, but also Native communities, since many still understandably distrust archaeologists. By working in cooperation, there is the possibility for both sides to reach a greater level of understanding, and in doing so, create archaeological projects that produce truly holistic interpretations of the past.

The Stewart Indian School was, for many, a very traumatic place to live, especially during the earliest years of its operation. Although the school is now cherished by many Native communities for its significance, its history demonstrates the turmoil that has long existed between Euro-Americans and Indigenous peoples. That being so, it was essential to the success of this project that respect was given to all participants, at all times, and to earnestly consider beliefs and practices valued by each participant. For example, members of the field school demonstrated this respect by participating in a ceremonial smudging before excavations began and immediately after they ended every day. All participants opted into this practice after Mark Johnson, an elder who volunteered on the project, became ill (see Cowie essay, A.J. Johnson essay, and Mark Johnson essay, chapter 7, and chapter 8). Smudging cleansed the participants of their negative energy as to prevent the attraction of negativity that could have potentially caused harm. By participating in this ceremony every day for the majority of the field school, a bond was created among the members—Native and otherwise—that may have been absent under different circumstances. This is an example of social capital, valued relations with others, which promotes communication, generates ideas, and establishes long-term relationships that can have lasting benefits (see discussion of social capital in chapter 2). Furthermore, it is evidence that the field of archaeology is steadily becoming one that respects the beliefs and customs of Indigenous peoples. As the field continues to grow in this way, the potential for tribes to benefit from archaeological research will also continue to grow, as will the potential for archaeological research to benefit from the participation of Native peoples.

Even though the benefits of collaboration are plenty, there is still a possibility for a collaborative project to negatively affect a community or to simply not produce the required results. For instance, the initial research design may prove to be inadequate in accomplishing the research goals and therefore the community may not benefit from the project as much as they hoped. While this can be considered a typical concern for any research project, it is important to note that this sort of issue may have added repercussions in collaborative investigations; social capital depends on positive relationships. There may also be additional issues that arise during the course of a project, such as the inability to make adjustments to archaeological procedures during the course of excavations (e.g., certain procedures are necessary to remain in compliance with heritage legislation and permits). While this sort of mediation is typically structured into a collaborative research design, there is always the potential for unforeseen complications.

Longer-Term Benefits to Communities

Another prominent issue surrounding collaborative archaeology is whether or not the project will actually benefit communities after it has come to an end. In many cases, the project is designed to do just that. Collaborative archaeology acts as a tool for communities to reach certain goals or to alleviate certain issues. When UNR archaeologists approached the NIC and Washoe THPO about a potential research project, members of these organizations and other stakeholders expressed an interest in spreading awareness of the Stewart Indian School. The NIC is interested in the campus becoming a National Historic Landmark and also creating a Cultural Events Center that would feature exhibits on the school. Overall, the hope was to gather support for the preservation of the campus, spread awareness of the events that happened there, and illustrate its importance to Native peoples all over the state and beyond.

Therefore, the field school was designed to address all of these concerns and facilitate processes that will continue to benefit the community long after the research is published. For instance, a public archaeology component was included in the research design. As a part of this public component, students gave tours of the excavations and of the campus during the field school. Students were prepared with talking points that addressed specific topics that tribal members wanted to emphasize. This was an efficient way to spread awareness to the public and to also illustrate how important the preservation of the campus was to the Native communities. Interviews were also given with numerous different media outlets, which also increased the capacity of awareness for the school. News articles were published online and in local, regional, and national newspapers and magazines. Considering the digital age that we live in today, those articles published online will continue to reach interested people for years to come.

Furthermore, in the couple years following the field school, the Nevada State Legislature and Governor awarded substantial funding to help preserve buildings at the Stewart Indian School. Some of the funding is currently being used to establish a museum and cultural center, as well as to hire professionals for writing a National Landmark nomination. The NIC has worked tirelessly for years toward these and has coordinated extensively with professionals who have common preservation goals (see Rupert and Gibbons essay, chapter 7). It is our hope that artifacts from the excavation can someday be used in the museum, and that the public's fascination with archaeology helped raise awareness for this worthy cause.

It is important to note that the media attention not only benefits Native communities who want to preserve Stewart, it also benefits the archaeological community. Many people, all over the country, still do not have an accurate understanding of what archaeology is, and this provided an opportunity for the public to see firsthand what an archaeological project looks like. Related publications will help expose people to the history of Indian boarding schools and the field of collaborative archaeology.

Works Cited

Adams, David W. 2006. "Beyond Bleakness: The Brighter Side of Indian Boarding Schools, 1970–1940." In *Boarding School Blues: Revisiting American Indian Educational Experiences*, edited by Clifford Trafzer, Jean M. Keller, and Lorene Sisquoc, 35–64. Lincoln, NE: University of Nebraska Press.

Adams, William Hampton. 2002. "Machine Cut Nails and Wire Nails: American Production and Use for Dating 19th Century and Early-20th-Century Sites. *Historical Archaeology* 36, no. 4: 66–88.

Albright, Willie. 2003. "Infamous Indian School May Re-Open as a Cultural Center." *Sparks Tribune*, May 18.

Atalay, Sonya. 2006. "Indigenous Archaeology as Decolonizing Practice." *The American Indian Quarterly* 30, nos. 3 and 4: 280–310.

Bachmann, Hans-Gert. 1982 *The Identification of Slags from Archaeological Sites.* Walnut Creek, CA: Left Coast Press, Inc.

Ball, Donald B. 1997. "An Introduction to Metallic Cartridge Case Terminology, Identification, and Headstamps." *Ohio Valley Historical Archaeology* 12: 112–29.

Barnes, Frank C. 1989. *Cartridges of the World.* 6th ed. Edited by Ken Warner. Northbrook, IL: DBI Books.

Carskadden, Jeff, and Richard Gartley. 1990. "A Preliminary Seriation of 19th-Century Decorated Porcelain Marbles." *Historical Archaeology* 24, no. 2: 55–69.

Coleman, Dorothy S., Elizabeth A. Coleman, and Evelyn J. Coleman. 1968. *The Collector's Encyclopedia of Dolls*. New York: Crown Publishers.

Daniels, James. 2013. "GPR results for the Stewart Indian School Project, Carson City, Nevada." ASM letter report and data submitted to the Stewart Indian School Project, Department of Anthropology, University of Nevada, Reno.

Davis, Jacob W. 1873. Improvement in Fastening Pocket-Openings. Patent # US000139121.

Encyclopedia Britannica New American Edition. 1898. "Glass, Wire." vol. 3, 1408. New York: Werner Co.

Encyclopedia Britannica New American Edition. 1973. "Cigarette." vol. 5: 767–68. Chicago: Encyclopedia Britannica, Inc..

Erlandson, Jon M., J. D. Robertson, and Christophe Descantes. 1999. "Geochemical Analysis of Eight Red Ochres from Western North America." *American Antiquity* 64, no. 3: 517–26.

Fike, Richard. 1987. *The Bottle Book: A Comprehensive Guide to Historic Embossed Medicine Bottles*. Salt Lake City, UT: Peregrine Smith Books.

Florence, Gene. 1995. *Kitchen Glassware of the Depression Years*. Paducah, KY: Collector Books.

Foucault, Michel. 1977. *Discipline and Punish: The Birth of the Prison*. Translated by Alan Sheridan. New York: Vintage Books.

Frazier, Katie. 2006. Interview. Under One Sky Oral History Project, University of Nevada Oral History Program. Reno, Nevada.

Hake, Ted. 1992. *Hake's Guide to Advertising Collectibles: 100 Years of Advertising from 100 Famous Companies*. Radnor, PA: Wallace-Homestead Book Company.

Hattori, Eugene M. 1978. "The Archaeology of the Stewart Dump Site (26OR121)." Report to Carson City Department of Public Works, from the Carson City Department of Public Works and Nevada State Museum, Carson City.

Keen, Sharon. 1982. "Metal Container Artifact Class." In *Artifact Analysis for Historical Archaeology*, edited by Dana-Mae Grainger. Manuscript report. Parks Canada, Prairie Region, Winnipeg, Manitoba.

Lief, Alfred. 1965. *A Close-up of Closures*. New York: Glass Container Manufacturers Institute.

Lightfoot, Kent G. 2008. "Collaborative Research Programs: Implications for the Practice of North American Archaeology." In *Collaborating at the Trowel's Edge: Teaching and Learning in Indigenous Archaeology*, edited by Stephen W. Silliman, 211–27. Tucson, AZ: University of Arizona Press.

Lindauer, Owen. 1997. "Not for School, But for Life: Lessons from the Historical Archaeology of the Phoenix Indian School." Arizona State University, Office of Cultural Resource Management, Report of Investigations, no. 95, Tempe.

Lockhart, Bill, and Russ Hoenig. 2015. "The Bewildering Array of Owens-Illinois Glass Co. Logos and Codes." Society for Historical Archaeology. Last updated March 20, 2015. https://sha.org/bottle/pdffiles/OwensIll_BLockhart.pdf.

Lomawaima, K. Tsianina. 1994. *They Called It Prairie Light: The Story of Chilocco Indian School.* Lincoln, NE: University of Nebraska Press.
Long, Ashley M. 2015. "Better Together: Collaborative Archaeology at the Stewart Indian School." Master's thesis, University of Nevada, Reno.
Lowry, Leonard. 1993. Interview. University of Nevada Oral History Program, Catalog no. 179, 1999, Reno, Nevada.
Luscomb, Sally C. 2006. *The Collector's Encyclopedia of Buttons.* New York: Bonanza Books.
Meikle, Jeffrey L. 1995. *American Plastic: A Cultural History.* New Brunswick, NJ: Rutgers University Press.
Miller, George L., and Tony McNichol. 2002. "Dates for Suction Scarred Bottoms: Chronological Changes in Owen-Machine Made Bottles." Paper presented at the Society for Historical Archaeology Conference, Mobile, Alabama.
Millett, Florence. N.d. Tobey, Hillman. N.d. "Stewart Indian School Walking Trail. #8 Infirmary." Podcast. Stewart Indian School, Nevada Indian Commission. http://stewartindianschool.com/walking-trail/, accessed November 2, 2018.
Munsey, Cecil. 1972. *The Illustrated Guide to the Collectibles of Coca-Cola.* New York: Hawthorn Books.
Newman, Stell T. 1970. "A Dating Key for Post-Eighteenth Century Bottles." *Historical Archaeology* 4: 70–75.
Nicholas, George P. 2012. "Collaborative, Community-Based Heritage Research, and the IPinCH Project." *The SAA Archaeological Record* (September): 30–32.
Nicholas, George, and Julie Hollowell. 2008. "Ethical Challenges to Postcolonial Archaeology: The Legacy of Scientific Colonialism." In *Archaeology and Capitalism: From Ethics to Politics*, edited by Yannis Hamilakis and Philip Duke, 59–82. Walnut Creek, CA: Left Coast Press.
Olsen, Stanley J. 1963. "Dating Early Plain Buttons by the Forms." American Antiquity 28, no. 4: 551–54.
Panati, Charles. 1987. *Panati's Extraordinary Origins of Everyday Things.* New York: Harper and Row.
Patterson, Terry, and Elizabeth Post. N.d. "Inhalant Abuse: Huffing, Puffing, and Blowing Houses Down." West Virginia University, Extension Services.
Pease, Robert C. 1980. Genoa Quadrangle Geologic Map. Nevada Bureau of Mines and Geology, University of Nevada, Reno.
Pullin, Anne Geffken. 1986. *Glass Signatures, Trademarks, and Tradenames from the 17th to the 20th Century.* Radnor, PA: Wallace-Homestead Book Company.
Rivers, Sara. 1999. "An Analysis of the Buttons from Three Historic Homes in Western Kentucky." *Ohio Valley Historical Archaeology* 14: 29–35.
Robbins, Darryl. N.d. "Lifetime China, Prairie Gold." Robbins Nest. http://www.robbinsnest.com/homer-laughlin-china/other-hlc/prairiegold.html, accessed May 1, 2015.
Rock, James T. 1989. Tin Canisters: Their Identification. Manuscript on file at the U.S. Forest Service, Klamath National Forest, Yreka, California.

Scott, Tom. N.d. Nesbitt's Orange Bottles. 2013 Soda Bottles. http://www.nesbittsorange.com/Bottles/index.htm, accessed on May 1, 2015.
Silliman, Stephen W. 2009. "Change and Continuity, Practice and Memory: Native American Persistence in Colonial New England." *American Antiquity* 74, no. 2: 211–30.
———. 2014. "Archaeologies of Survivance and Residence: Reflections on the Historical Archaeology of Indigenous People." In *Rethinking Colonial Pasts through Archaeology*, edited by Neal Ferris, Rodney Harrison, and Michael Wilcox, 57–75. Oxford: Oxford University Press.
Smith, Linda Tuhiwai. 1999. *Decolonizing Methodologies: Research and Indigenous Peoples*. London: Zed Books Ltd.
South, Stanley. 1964. "Analysis of the Buttons from Brunswick Town and Fort Fisher." *Florida Anthropologist* 17, no. 2: 113–33.
———. 1977. *Method and Theory in Historical Archaeology*. New York: Academic Press.
Sprague, Roderick. 2002. "China or Prosser Button Identification and Dating." Historical Archaeology 36, no. 2: 111–27.
Springer, Ian. 2015. "Historical Archaeology at the Microscopic Scale: The Application of Geochemical and Macrobotanical Analyses." Master's thesis, University of Nevada, Reno.
Tarrago, Oscar, and Raymond Demers. 2010. "Case Studies in Environmental Medicine: Lead." Agency for Toxic Substances and Disease Registry. Original date, August 15, 2010. https://stacks.cdc.gov/view/cdc/5212/cdc_5212_DS1.pdf?.
Thompson, Bonnie. 2013. "The Student Body: A History of the Stewart Indian School, 1890–1940." PhD diss., Arizona State University.
Vogel, Ed. 2000. "Historic Indian School Falls under Scrutiny." *Elko Daily Free Press* 117, no. 78 (April).
Watkins, Joe E. 2000. *Indigenous Archaeology: American Indian Values and Scientific Practice*. Walnut Creek, CA: AltaMira Press.
World War II Impressions, Inc. N.d. Uniform, Work, Blue-Denim, M1937: American Made Uniforms That Fit and Last Like The Originals. http://www.wwiiimpressions.com/newusarmyM37denimworkuniform.html, accessed May 1, 2015.
Younie, Ashley. 2015. Faunal Analysis for the Stewart Indian School Project, Carson City, Nevada. Letter report submitted to the Stewart Indian School Project, Department of Anthropology, University of Nevada, Reno.

CHAPTER 7

Reflexive, Multivocal Interpretations of Stewart Indian School, and Best Practices in Heritage Management

Richard Arnold, Patrick Burtt, Sarah E. Cowie, Darrel Cruz, Eric DeSoto, Debra Harry, A.J. Johnson, Mark Johnson, Dania Jordan, Christopher C. LeBlanc, Ashley M. Long, Jo Ann Nevers, Sherry L. Rupert and Chris A. Gibbons, Diane L. Teeman, and Lonnie P. Teeman, Sr.

Introduction to the Essays

Inclusion of diverse voices is a central tenant of collaborative and Indigenous archaeologies. With that goal in mind, participants contributed essays that comment on any aspects of the project they chose, with the understanding that different stakeholders may have different insights and values, and thus could contribute in myriad ways. Some participants responded to a list of suggested questions based on conversations we had over the course of the field school. These included questions regarding Native/federal relations about heritage, archaeological terminology (e.g., "descendant community"), their roles in the project, and what they felt they learned/taught during the field school. Note that some authors shift in tense as they tell stories of place-based learning and memory anchoring at Stewart Indian School. Shifts from past to present and future collapse time in meaningful ways that phenomenologically link place and memory (see chapters 2 and 8). Other writers reflected on their prior experiences with heritage management and offered informed ideas for future best practices. Diverse, even critical, interpretations are central to advancing our goals for bettering heritage practices. As such, the following essays are as important to understanding Stewart Indian School as the more tangible archaeological results.

Essay 1. Richard Arnold

Chair of the Nevada Indian Commission; enrolled
member of the Pahrump Paiute Tribe

Stewart Indian School Collaborative Archaeology Project—A Living Legacy

The Stewart Indian School Collaborative Archaeology Project was an important undertaking in partnership with the Nevada Indian Commission (NIC), University of Nevada, Reno (UNR), and active involvement from other interested individuals. The basis for the project was to retrace the footsteps of the past through the science of archaeology that remains within the hallowed grounds of the former Stewart Indian School.

In order to talk about the project, one must recognize the past and the impact it had into the future. Since 1890 until its closure in 1980, Stewart Indian School touched the lives of many American Indian students, families, and faculty. Equally, countless others were affected directly or indirectly during this time of transition. While there, students with deep-rooted cultural beliefs, many of whom did not speak English from varied backgrounds, attended school to learn occupational trades with the ultimate goal of assimilation into mainstream society. Although the focus perpetuated systemic change, tribal students retained their culture and often integrated their beliefs into their daily lives at Stewart. Many times, students struggled with isolation or the notion of discounting their tribal culture to achieve vocational training that they were told would take them into the future. Conversely, American Indian students struggled and amazingly did not lose their sense of identity. During later years, the approach gradually changed, but it never broke their spirit or strong cultural bond that existed among classmates and the school.

Complexities of the past create opportunities for expanding knowledge, changing perceptions, and gaining a better understanding for the future. This fundamental concept became the inspiration for the Stewart Indian School Collaborative Archaeology Project. While considering what was thought to be a straightforward archaeology project, the undertaking became multifaceted, requiring an integrated and innovative approach of blending scientific methods, historical data, and the cultural insight of individuals connected to the area. Prior to project implementation, faculty from the Department of Anthropology at UNR initiated discussions with the NIC to formulate ideas to gain a glimpse into Stewart's past.

In turn, those ideas progressed into a formal presentation before the Commission, who provided further support with the understanding one key element was how best to embark upon a rigorous survey while maintaining sensitivity and respect. As with any study, the ability to acquire good data is essential while learning about the individuals who occupied the area and exploring the intriguing architectural resources that still remain.

In the case of Stewart, Indian students with strong cultural and historic ties to their homelands were uprooted and brought to Stewart, sometimes forcibly, to learn a trade to become assimilated into mainstream society. Most often students were challenged because of their removal from family members or other important social and cultural support mechanisms. Despite the intent of the federal government, those individuals who resided or were affected by the Stewart experience retained their strong cultural values reflected in their epistemological views and their lasting legacy.

Oftentimes a challenge for archaeologists is the focus on material culture and not living people's worldviews. Attempting to glean an understanding of inanimate items or past lifestyles is achieved by postulating a compartmentalized interpretation through educated conjecture. To the contrary, Indian people recognize the complexities of their culture, which become the basis for a broader understanding of the world that became interconnected with their school experience. Having the opportunity to view numerous archaeological projects over the years, archaeologists tend to discount diverging interpretations relating to artifact type. Often they boast about their "discovery" of a particular artifact or site. Conversely, in their retort, Indian people state, How can you discover something that was never lost! To some, archaeologists may merely examine an artifact without consideration to its voice or context and why it was located where it was found. To the contrary, tribal individuals often state you must listen to the voices and stories of the artifacts. To look at an artifact out of context or without knowing the rest of the story is analogous to reading one page from a book and trying to understand the author's message.

Admittedly, tribal views are gaining more notoriety using contemporary terms such as traditional or tribal ecological knowledge, or through the collective wisdom of key tribal knowledge holders. While these labels are important identifiers, tribal people know who they are, what they know, and who they will always be!

The Stewart Indian School Collaborative Archaeology Project was an important step to providing participants with guidance by trained archaeologists from the UNR. While apprehension from expectations was present, the project provided unique opportunities to expose participants to becoming better acquainted, while gaining a mutual appreciation and respect for each other.

As the project commenced, project participants integrated time to engage in listening sessions often with guest speakers to help understand the different perspectives that were present. This important aspect allowed tribal representatives the opportunity to share the importance of examining the world through Native eyes while archaeologists reinforced the necessity of working in partnership and learning from each other. These insightful discussions conveyed the role of material culture; however, if you look at things with limited vision, your world will remain narrow and be reflected in the conclusions you reach.

Another element that was reinforced was the limitation of focusing on things such as animal bones coupled with the narrow view of food yields that are derived. From the tribal perspective, animal bones and other artifacts are personified, each having feelings, voices, and eyes to tell a story of the social, cultural, and spiritual considerations that must be a central component to the discussion.

Throughout the project, different expectations were present leading to apprehensions, surprises, and sometimes disappointment. Never knowing what to expect, archaeologists identified resources while other times nothing was located. The absence of items was not being considered a failure, because the Stewart campus has a rich legacy that is embedded within the walls of the structures that were built with the assistance of student labor. Walking through the campus, the presence of the past remains and is expressed through the voices of the people and the land that watches over the school.

The partnership led to longstanding friendships and admiration thanks to each of the participants who shared a common vision based on commitment, dedication, and respect.

Essay 2. Patrick De?ileligi Burtt

Enrolled member of the Washoe Tribe of Nevada and California; current PhD student in history at the University of Nevada, Reno

When I wrote the following paragraphs, I was a freshman at Fort Lewis College working toward a Bachelor of Arts degree with a major in Native American and Indigenous Studies.

At the beginning of this project, my personal feelings towards archaeology and anthropology as academic disciplines were not positive. I have been exposed to issues regarding the Native American Graves Protection and Repatriation Act (NAGPRA) through a number of

FIGURE 7.1. Bernadine (Frank) James, enrolled member of the Washoe Tribe of Nevada and California, a graduate of Stewart Indian School in 1956 and grandmother of Patrick Burtt. Photo courtesy of the family of the late Bernadine James.

courses, literature, and workshops prior to the project. These experiences were mostly reflective of the way that many museums and institutions of higher education have neglected to abide by NAGPRA. Also, I am critical of many anthropological and archaeological claims of "heritage preservation"; I am weary of this process because it does not involve continuity or revitalization efforts in terms of tribal collaboration and utilization of project outcomes. Governmental agencies do not sway in mitigation efforts when there is an objective that is founded on monetary gain, and tribes and their interests have been both historically and contemporarily victimized by this process. The history of problematic research and development initiatives involving Indigenous Peoples by archaeologists and the federal government has been characterized by a lack of inclusion that has subsequently left Indigenous Peoples vulnerable to skewed interpretations and destructive development projects. This process has damaged the integrity of Native communities by allowing for bias narratives and urging economic expansion that is discriminatory.

I first heard of the project through the Washoe Tribal Newsletter and also through Dr. Debra Harry. I was the assistant oral histories coordinator for this project as well as a student. I was skeptical when I was first introduced to the public archaeology method, because it seemed that allowing the public to be introduced to the project would create a type of hype within the non-Native community in terms of people wanting to see some type of prehistoric Native objects. This was quickly refuted when our team explained that we were conducting a historic archaeology that would not include those types of objects.

The collaborative efforts between the Washoe Tribe's Preservation Office, the Nevada Indian Commission (NIC), and the University of Nevada, Reno (UNR) were undeniable. There were several efforts by both the Washoe Tribe Historic Preservation Office and the NIC to offer types of introductory seminars on Washoe Tribal culture as well as the history of Stewart Indian School to UNR's field school. These efforts had a lasting effect upon the students of the field school, which I witnessed personally through the efforts by the non-Native students to engage in a prayer every morning prior to starting work in order to offer an acknowledgment of tribal traditions as well as recognition of the history of Stewart Indian School. I, along with other Native individuals involved in the project, offered a prayer every morning where each member of the project (students, staff, faculty) had the decision and ability to use sage during the prayer. This is a cultural protocol for a project where we would engage in digging into the land which *Waśíw* people believe is an extension of ourselves. The prayer was also an effort to expose the group to an Indigenous paradigm. More specifically, a *Waśíw* epistemology, as we used spiritual medicines utilized by *Waśíw* people since time immemorial. As a group, we prayed every morning to offer respect and acknowledgment of the land and people that are still from that area, as well as to offer recognition of the ontological component of the *Waśíw* worldview, which informs the physical and cosmological spaces of *Waśíw* life.

Using the term, "descendant communities" versus "contemporary communities" is the basis of a discussion that I clearly remember having with Dr. Sarah Cowie and Diane L. Teeman. I brought up the fact that the term "descendant" when referring to contemporary Indigenous communities suggests that we are an extinct people, when in fact we are alive and thriving. The entire process I attempted to enter into by being the Oral Histories Coordinator was one that I felt was both ethical and respectful to the elders that offered the oral stories of their experiences at Stewart Indian School. As it was unclear on who would take ownership of the recorded materials from oral histories accumulated, I elected to protect the intellectual property of the interviewed attendees of the Stewart Indian School by accepting their stories as gifts and maintaining a method of mental archiving.

As I previously stated, this project was a historic archaeology field school where our focus was not in recovering prehistoric items. As a traditional *Waśíw*, those pieces of our history (material culture) carry their own stories and I know that is the primary reason that archeologists want to study them, but one thing that differs in my perspective is the spiritual aspect of where those objects came from and what they were actually intended to represent. The objects taken from the site have significant cultural ties being from the Stewart Indian School. We engaged in processes that made it possible to return the test units to their most natural state.

I was completely new to the whole process of archaeology but more importantly, I learned that there are people that are making real efforts to create an effective collaboration between archaeology and Native individuals and collectives. This project was focused on collaboration with Native entities where they actually had input, as opposed to just cosigning to the research. Any type of archaeological processes must include Native Nations when they are the entity being researched. This component is one that will benefit both sides of the spectrum and even create a bridge that has the ability to benefit concurrent agendas.

A free, prior, and informed consent from the tribe specific to that area is essential. One thing that I feel is extremely important in that relationship is not only the participation of tribal entities, but also the active engagement within all phases of the project. True collaboration involves all partners from start to finish of the project. With Native Peoples becoming more actively engaged in archaeological processes, I feel that there is hope for a general ethical process that archaeologists will be willing to engage in.

I wrote the previous paragraphs in 2013, and upon reflection in 2018, while having advanced in the academy past a master of arts and now in a PhD program, my ending optimism in archaeological methods and practice evolving to become more inclusive of Indigenous Peoples has become evidently legitimate. The collaborative archaeology model employed at the Stewart Indian School in the summer of 2013 has and will continue to be a framework available to future researchers working with Native Peoples.

Essay 3. Sarah E. Cowie

Associate professor of anthropology
at the University of Nevada, Reno

As a non-Native archaeologist, I learned more about archaeology on this project than any other of my career. As a social theorist and scientist, I found humanity in my work, and as an instructor, I learned a tremendous amount from students, volunteers, research partners, and consultants. I am so very grateful many of them agreed to contribute to this volume. This is the power of collaborative and Indigenous archaeologies, and it really only scratches the surface of what we experienced.

My interest in these approaches came from working, years ago, as an archaeologist with the Coronado National Forest in Arizona. I was a member of their newly formed Tribal Relations Team that sought a more holistic approach to heritage management (Cowie et al. 2009). Working with tribal members, both academic and nonacademic, federally employed and not, my eyes were opened to the fact that archaeology is less about things and more about living people. Like the tribal members I worked with, I also became frustrated with how little say tribal members have over their heritage and how much it matters. How could something so important to people be so out of their control? How could they be so removed from the process, despite the fact that consultation is intended to be inclusive?

In related research, I was studying Michel Foucault's postmodern concept of governmentality and began to see it as a partial explanation (see chapter 2). Likewise, I have been fascinated by "new" discoveries by Western science that resonate with longstanding Native observations of the world (e.g., the quantum mechanics of entangled particles across time-space continuums, which is remarkably similar to an Indigenous concept of *puha* or life-force; see chapter 1). I am still pondering what these things mean in light of Mark Johnson's brilliant observation that archaeological excavation is like "breaking through time" (see chapter 8). I wondered how often Western science and Native science speak past each other, but could eventually come to agreement. My professional interactions with Native heritage specialists led me to think of social capital as a possible bridge for competing discourses that are often silenced by governmentalized practices (see chapter 2). The Army Research Office had funding for projects involving high-level theory to deconstruct complicated problems on federally managed lands, and so the project began.

Among other things, collaborative archaeology at Stewart Indian School allows us to look further at the theme of removal, which ironically unites several components of this project and the problems that are at the heart of heritage consultation today. Here, I propose that governmentality can be used to explore two aspects of removal encountered during this project: historical removal of children from their traditional homelands and recent removal of artifacts from the site during archaeological fieldwork. We address these themes in greater depth in chapters 2 and 8, but here I will just mention the theoretical origin of the project, and how we collectively decided to work at Stewart Indian School.

This project was originally designed to study what appears to be an impasse in federal/tribal relations using the concept of governmentality to address discourses surrounding current cultural resource management (CRM) as a tool of the federal government, and to collaboratively work toward potential solutions by addressing the utility of building social capital (i.e., valued relations with others) as described in practice and agency theories. As described elsewhere in this volume, project archaeologists (Chris LeBlanc and myself) organized a series of formal and informal heritage discussions with tribal members in a collaborative, involved exchange of ideas. Through our extended social and professional networks (e.g., social capital—see chapter 2), a number of tribal consultants were identified to participate in the project, including members of several Great Basin tribes who are professional heritage specialists and students, as well as the Washoe Tribal Historic Preservation Office (THPO) and the Nevada Indian Commission (NIC).

We began a collaborative assessment of tribal needs and interests regarding heritage concerns in the local area. We discussed archaeological sites that could be considered for the focus of an archaeological field school. Only sites deemed suitable by tribal organizations were considered. Eventually, we decided together that the project would take place at the Stewart Indian School in Carson City, Nevada. Numerous tribal members asserted this would be the most appropriate site for a number of reasons, particularly to raise awareness of this important part of Native American history, to contribute to its preservation and interpretation, and to benefit numerous tribes whose members passed through Stewart during its ninety-year history.

I am so grateful that our research partners and other stakeholders trusted me to participate in this project and exchange ideas to such great effect. Admittedly, some of it wasn't easy, as we all actively sought to critique our own methods and perspectives, and—in giving up sole authority—invited others to critique us as well. But clearly it was worth the effort when I reflect on the stories and lessons in this volume.

Essay 4. Darrel Cruz

Cultural Resources Department Director, Tribal Historic Preservation Officer (THPO), and enrolled member of the Washoe Tribe of Nevada and California

I am the Cultural Resources Department Director and an enrolled member with the Washoe Tribe. My responsibilities working for the Washoe Tribe include the protection and preservation of Washoe heritage, promote education and outreach, and preserve and revitalize the Washoe language. The biggest problem with archaeology is the data recovery and collection policies; we prefer all artifacts and associated materials left in place rather than being removed and taken away to sit in a box somewhere. I think archaeological site eligibility standards should be revised to include and reflect tribal perspectives.

I became involved with the Collaborative Stewart Indian School Project when I was contacted by Chris LeBlanc and Sarah Cowie, project proponents. The project study area is within the ancestral lands of the Washoe Tribe and the Stewart Indian School was attended by Washoe children. I was a consultant for design criteria and during excavation of cultural resources to ensure our requests had been met.

One of the most notable experiences I observed during the project was the respectful treatment of tribal members and our cultural resources. The treatment of both people and artifacts is very important. A concern right off was the artifact collection; we do not want to see the removal of heritage resources. We wanted to be sure that any surveys or studies incorporated the prehistoric component and not be disregarded and minimized. Although the study area is owned by the State of Nevada, the prehistoric archaeological resources belong to the Washoe as our heritage. We asked that all prehistoric resources be studied and left in place. Our requests were honored by the project proponents and Nevada SHPO, who has the authority on cultural resources on state lands and that negotiation was successful.

I think the collaboration worked on this project because we were involved from the beginning, kept informed throughout the process, and communication with the tribe was consistent. I would like to think our response to collection policies made an impression. Having a tribal person contracted or employed on the project led to a better collaborative process.

The government contract archaeologists may be overstepping their roles in the consultation process sometimes. I think archaeologists should be open to new ideas and invite tribal opinions. It's going to improve quality and relations.

For example, analysis should be conducted on flake matter and not the artifact; that is our opinion and it is at the direction/discretion of the appointed delegate from the tribe to make the decision to bury or not to bury artifacts. The Washoe tribe has a cultural advisory council that provides advice to the appointed delegate to assist with decisions. As stated many times, we do not want to see our heritage resources erased. Always put things back the way it is found. We asked not to put artifacts in plastic bags before reburial because it was not found like that. There was no landscaping fabric when found, so we asked that it not be used when backfilling the test units.

Archaeologists and federal land managers in the future can work with other tribes and tribal members to figure out best practices for working on different tribes' ancestral homelands by making contact with the tribal cultural representative and work with him and his designated staff, advisory council, elders, and tribal members for a wider knowledge base. Most tribes are understaffed with limited funding and do not always have the time or resources to commit to the many projects. Start consultation early and don't overload with too many wordy sentences. Use a phone to call and make direct contact. Bring your project to the attention of the designated person, and try to meet at their location and invite them to the archaeological site for consultation and collaboration. You will get more out of the person on the ground than through email and letters.

Essay 5. Eric DeSoto

Enrolled member of the Fallon Paiute-Shoshone Tribe; experienced Archaeological Technician

I am a member of the Fallon Paiute-Shoshone Tribe from birth. I completed the University of Nevada, Reno (UNR) collaborative field school in summer 2013. I have plans to attend UNR to further my college education in archaeology. I was featured in Far Western Anthropological Research Group's latest documentary *Breaking New Ground: Native Americans in Archaeology*, which was released in 2014. I have worked for Far Western and ASM Affiliates for the last five field seasons from the coast of California to the lava fields near the Craters of the Moon in Idaho as an archaeological field technician, performing all phases of fieldwork from basic site identification and recording to complex data recovery. For Far Western my first project was the Ruby Pipeline in 2010- and 2011. The Ruby Pipeline spanned from Wyoming to Oregon. During this time I excavated over one hundred archaeological sites and performed data collection on all eligible sites. After excavation and data collection I worked as a tribal monitor for Power Engineers during the last phases of the pipeline construction. I also worked for Far Western on the Rim Fire postfire survey and in Bodega Bay for a highway rerouting project. For ASM my first project came after the completion of the UNR field school, in August 2013. This project was a very large (thirty thousand acres) rock art project that included verifying site locations, survey, site recording, and rerecording of previously discovered sites. I participate in traditional gatherings and gambling, such as pow wows and handgame. I also attend cry dances, when I have to.

I had a good idea of what archaeology and heritage preservation were because I had done it previously on the Ruby Pipeline and several other projects. I think that there was/is a lack of communication and understanding between tribal members and archaeologists. Many tribal members are under the impression that archaeologists are just there to take artifacts (aka "grave robbing"). Back in the day there weren't a lot of laws to protect Native heritage interests; therefore, early archaeologists often didn't understand about the disturbances and impacts that they were leaving at culturally sensitive areas. Today many tribal elders still believe archaeologists are out there without any regard to tribal interests or understanding in mind. I think that there are still a lot of problems with the government protocols. For example, there are still instances where tribal resources and artifacts are treated less delicately than white people's resources.

I was filming for the Far Western documentary, out of their Carson City office, when Terri McBride mentioned this project to me and told me that it was taking place at the historic and majorly controversial Stewart Indian School. I was a student on the field school. With my previous experience in archaeology I was giving helpful tips and hints to fellow classmates as well as project staff. Red [Patrick Burtt, this volume] and I also conducted morning and afternoon smudging and blessings for the crew.

I think the only time I had disagreements were with one of the field supervisors, nothing major, just technique and method disagreements, which are very common for the field of archaeology.

I believe collaboration happened. The students were eager and excited to learn about the traditional ways, as well as learn field procedures. It looked like Native Americans working together making sure that the scientific side of archaeology was being moral, as well as non-Natives working to make sure they treated artifacts and features with the most respect and understanding they could give.

One example is when every morning we used to smudge with sage, and anyone who wanted to participate would and did, not only, I believe, to be respectful, but also for their own safety as well. Also there were instances where we found possible flaked glass, which would be considered an artifact. We had a sit-down meeting with the class and discussed how to go about the flake or flakes, as far as should we rebury it where we found it or collect it for testing. Most agreed it was in the best interest of both parties to rebury the glass. Of course the different backgrounds of each student we had had different ideas of what was going on with certain artifacts, which I think is very important to hear everyone's point of view.

One thing I did learn from scratch was using the total station. It was interesting to learn how they worked as well as how much more precise they were for getting measurements and elevations. I felt all of us were teachers in a sense. This was a different kind of field school. We were learning, asking each other questions, and giving the best answers we could. It was nice the class was historic, as I have only worked on prehistoric projects previously. It was a very nice refresher class for all field assignments such as survey, excavation, and recovery.

I can't really say I felt like I taught anyone anything because we were all learning from each other. I really think we helped or did open each other's eyes at one point. I don't think anyone should take sole responsibility. We all were teachers as well as students.

In all aspects it was far different from any project I have ever worked on. Most methodology was discussed. We collaborated on the different philosophy by again talking about it with peers and taking in what we were taught by our guest speakers. The approach was actually pretty standard to most projects, as far as digging and collection of artifacts. The participants were great. It was good to have as much tribal input as well as the archaeological side. I believe we all enjoyed hearing the talks from all of the guest speakers.

A couple of things I've learned on this project are again, I agree with having much tribal input. It is so very important to be doing the ethical practice, as far as having the tribe or representing tribes being told about what is being discovered and recovered and how it should be handled. It was also great to have so many visitors stop and have an interest in what and why this particular excavation/project was going on. It was also exciting to know enough information to give great tours. I thought it was awesome to have knowledge from the elders and people who have been around the whole time, such as the groundskeeper and staff. It would be good if that could be implemented into every project, having more of a background of the people that experienced it, or even through oral histories through generations. Even though most, if not all, archaeologists know a great deal about Native people, some things definitely look different to a Native than to a non-Native person, or maybe they know something that you wouldn't or couldn't find in a book or have written down. With that being said, that is my main point about how important oral histories really are. That can also break down any kind of communication barrier that may come about down the road. Talking and sharing stories I think is a pastime that is fading away quickly.

Well, this particular question (about the history of problematic work by archaeologists and the federal government) I think is very self-explanatory. Most, if not all, older archaeologists (meaning when people started excavating and recovering artifacts) had no regard or interest in what the Native tribes had to say about digging and/or collecting in culturally sensitive areas. It seemed that the science and information were much more important than making sure you weren't digging up burials, sacred prayer sites, and collecting artifacts for personal collections of the Indigenous people. It's sad and disrespectful that it took so long for the federal government to implement any kind of law or restriction on what, where, and how the archaeologist's methodology was being conducted. But I do strongly believe archaeologists are becoming very aware of how things should be done in a manner that pleases the science as well as the tribal side of projects.

I believe this (archaeologists thinking about more than just subsistence, etc.) is an important part of collaborating on projects, as well as hearing oral histories. To me it seems the book side always comes first in an archaeologist's mind when in some cases it's not the case. When discussing the possibility, it's vital, I think, to have some Native input on the final analysis of some unknown artifacts. Although most artifacts are pretty obvious on what they are, there are cases where they are not what they seem and have much more importance than what meets the eye.

I haven't heard or had a lot of time to discuss this particular subject (Indigenous communities versus communities). So I cannot say which is proper, ethical, or offensive.

Most of the oral histories were handled by Mr. Patrick Burtt. Although he shared what he had learned, I feel if all of us were to get a person-to-person oral history people could understand how important the stories are and how badly they are fading into the past. The people telling the stories and the listeners own the stories. They should also pass the stories on. That's the best way to keep the stories alive.

I believe the reason for that (archaeologists not realizing diverse perspectives among tribal members) is because many archaeologists believe since they have the degree or paid so much time learning a particular skill set that they have a hard time hearing that they could possibly be wrong or unethical. After time though, most archaeologists start to have a more diverse sense of understanding differences and thought processes.

Most implications of removing artifacts from a site depend on the person(s) removing the artifact. Most Natives frown upon it while not knowing the intention of removal, while other most non-Native people would remove it not knowing the importance it may have to people from the area. We decided to recover some glass as possible "flaked" glass and treated it more cautiously and talked about how we should handle it as a class. We decided that it would be most ethical to treat them as possible flakes. It was very important for our class to discuss and understand all aspects of why we would treat it as a lithic instead of a broken bottle fragment. Also it was great that we all came to a mutual conclusion.

The best possible way to close a site is to return it back to its natural state before any disturbance had taken place. We decided that putting lithics back in the ground in a plastic bag was unethical and disturbing to the natural ground sediment. The same goes for the landscaping fabric, but that also would cause future "looters" to know the exact spot where lithics were discovered and reburied. I think all were great ideas (not using plastic bags or landscaping fabric) and answers to these problems.

One activity I thought was very good was the smudge every morning and after we were finished. Also how one of the field supervisors gave ochre to people who wanted it. I believe it was very important due to the place we were doing the field school. What I mean is the awful terrible things that occurred in Stewart's past. There is a lot of bad energy all over those places, as well as many other sites. Those things were done and given as forms of protection against bad spirits. As far as methodology we used, it was standard archaeological practice with a blend of Native insight, which meant doing all our measurements and paperwork correctly as well as keeping the highest ethical practices. We had multiple Native Americans working and taking the class, and we all shared our concerns and shared stories of why we should be taking those types of precautions. I think one of the most important things to keep these kinds of protocols in place is to push for tribal involvement in all aspects. Maybe even have guest speakers (elders, tribal members, or anyone with information on the subject) express their concerns before projects begin with anyone who is involved in the project.

I think archaeologists and federal land managers need to be honest and trustworthy with tribes and respect their needs, wants, and concerns. They need to have a good relationship or, of course, it will lead to some sort of turmoil in the future. Also having an open line of communication is vital. COLLABORATE respectfully.

Like I stated previously, the best way (that archaeologists and federal land managers can work with tribes better) I think is to have all sides in open discussion, stating what each party wants or needs to get done in order to pursue the goal. They need to make sure to try and have true collaboration on all levels; such as working with THPOs, even though most are very busy. Patience is key for sure. I know a lot of archaeology firms are always pushing for speed (as far as moving cubes), but I believe accuracy and moral standards stand much higher than any deadline. I think collaborative research before any project should and will eventually happen. Such as record searches for sites, there should be some kind of protocol on reaching out to contact any tribes in the area and let them know what is about to take place and have a plan to discuss disagreements and work toward progress. Even though some tribes very seldom care, realize, or understand what is happening in most cases; I feel it's most important to let them have a heads-up or plan for some sort of discussion about what is taking place in their lands. Again so I believe honest communication is vital.

I believe true collaboration is having the utmost understanding, respectfulness, and being able to communicate and express any concerns openly on a project. An example of this is if something is discovered, having a representative from the involved tribes, such as a monitor or even someone working in the field. I think it's so very important to get the problems that may arise addressed, understood, and verified as soon as possible. This way all parties involved may speak and respectfully discuss the issues and deal with them looking in from both ends of the spectrum. I think the more input the better. It looked much like our field school, but I do believe there is always room for improvement. There is always room to improve and grow. As long as archaeologists in schools and professionally continue to collaborate with Native people, to understand the intense relationships of different sites and different areas to the Native people of that land, there is a good chance of true collaboration in the future.

I think overall the field school was a huge success and everyone involved understood what was happening, and if we didn't, we talked about it. This field school should be the blueprint of what other field schools should be teaching and learning as well as taking these practices into the professional field. A great thing I learned is that most people do want to do what's moral or ethical; which made me very happy to work with people who had an open mind about other Native cultures and practices. The whole respect thing came into play when we would talk about what should be done to certain things; which made the class more than a class, it made it a whole learning experience, an experience I will bring with me into my future in archaeology.

I feel there will always be some kind of challenge to collaboration, as a lot of archaeologists simply do not understand the meaning of certain things. Certain things carry an aura or power with them that most average people will never understand, or choose not to. Until there is an open talk about what has happened through oral histories, data, and discussion, there will always be some clash of methodologies conducted by archaeologists. This also goes back to my thoughts on being respectful to the traditional things that an ordinary non-Native person would think is unimportant. Understanding is ultimately the best collaboration.

In my future, I see myself continuing down the archaeological path. I'm going to continue to tech in the field and cautiously pursue a higher degree in archaeology. As they say, the sky is the limit. This field school has made a huge impact in my fieldwork now and will forever.

Essay 6. Debra Harry

Enrolled member of the Pyramid Lake Paiute Tribe; Executive Director of the Indigenous Peoples Council on Biocolonialism (IPCB); founder of the Emerging Indigenous Leaders Institute; Lecturer in the Gender, Race and Identity Program at the University of Nevada, Reno

My role in the Stewart Indian School project was to provide an Indigenous perspective on research ethics for the student participants. This is a perspective many students perhaps have never had an opportunity to hear before, given the lack of Indigenous academic faculty in the region.

What is the history of problematic work by archaeologists and the federal government? Indigenous peoples typically approach any external research project with caution, and for good reason. Indigenous peoples have been on the receiving end of research carried out in insensitive, and sometimes, harmful ways. Research has historically been a top-down, outside-in process, with Indigenous peoples serving merely as research subjects without any meaningful participation or potential to benefit from outcomes of the research.

One problematic area is that the principle of informed consent is largely a subjective process. Although the principle of informed consent in human subjects research in Western ethics is centered on individual freedom of choice, the principle of free, prior, and informed consent (FPIC) for Indigenous peoples considers and respects the collective nature of Indigenous communities and collective rights as peoples first, and then individual consent, secondarily. In the collective process, specific procedures must be implemented in order to ensure true FPIC.

In the United States, current domestic laws do not sufficiently protect cultural property (Harjo 2002). Tribes should assert their sovereignty by developing and adopting tribal laws that will govern research and will protect their cultural property. Typically cultural property tends to be defined narrowly as historic objects and human remains. But Tribes have much more at stake as cultural property is both tangible and intangible, moveable and immoveable, whether it be songs, artifacts, sacred sites, the remains of the ancestors, traditional medicines, Indigenous knowledge about such medicines, or human and non-human genetic material. It is imperative that Indigenous peoples develop laws that protect the full range of our cultural heritage, and which assert our own principles and values in the governance of any research project that affects our peoples and/or our environments. Indigenous peoples can exercise self-determination by proactively protecting the legacy of our sacred cultural heritage not only for ourselves, but also for future generations (Riley 2005, 90–91).

Dr. Linda Tuhiwai Smith says, "*Coming to know the past* is part of the critical pedagogy of decolonization" (Smith 1999, 34). For the Indigenous peoples of Turtle Island, this critical pedagogy means re-centering the wisdom of our ancestors, as the primary position from which we think, act, speak, and transform our worlds. Central to the process of colonization is a deliberate effort to dehumanize the colonized. If an aspect of colonization is dehumanization, then decolonization necessarily requires an analysis and awareness about the process of dehumanization, and how we carry and perpetuate this learned behavior in our daily lives. Paulo Friere calls this process of awareness "concientization" (*conscientizacão* in the original); it refers to learning to perceive social, political, and economic contradictions, and to taking action against the oppressive elements of reality (Friere 1970). We must consciously act to re-humanize or decolonize our minds, hearts, and actions. Indeed, the process of decolonization has been a central theme in the Indigenous cultural and political movement for Indigenous rights.

Essay 7. A. J. Johnson

Enrolled member of the Reno-Sparks Indian Colony, of Washoe and Northern Paiute descent; experienced Archaeological Technician

I was sent to Stewart Indian Boarding School in 1973 as I wasn't doing very well in public school in Reno and my parents thought that the strictness of Stewart would straighten me up. My father and my older brother attended Stewart where they did well and my brother excelled in boxing.

To say the least boarding school in the seventies was a unique experience for me. We lived in dorms with other kids from different tribal reservations across the country. Everyone was assigned daily duties, lights were turned on and off, we were awakened daily by the residential aides, we were told when to eat and shower. If we didn't do what we were told, we got in trouble and our free hours or our passes taken away. It was opposite of the life I was used to.

One of the things I witnessed was the abuse of students by some teachers and the residential aides. Most of these aides were former students who stayed in the area and eventually got hired by Stewart. These former students may have experienced abuse of a more severe nature and they used what was done to them on the students they were in charge of. In today's world this would be abuse and these people would be locked up.

Many students loved Stewart boarding school and have good memories. My brother and sister who attended before and after my years have good memories of the place. I have memories too but some memories are marred by what happened to me and other students. I saw the good and the bad of Stewart boarding school.

A good memory is one of my teachers Mr. Hart, the math teacher who played music in his class. That was something that was unusual in any of my classes even when I was in public school. It was all classic country music and to this day when I hear a certain song it takes me back to Mr. Hart's classroom.

A sad memory is the overdose of a young girl that I had in my history class the semester before. This was really hard on the students at Stewart and it must have been devastating for her family. They sent their young daughter to school full of life and she came home in a box. I am sure this is how some families of children in boarding schools had their children come home. Some never got to go home as there is an old cemetery for the kids who never made it home at Stewart.

At Stewart I met a lot of nice people and had some good friends, but I preferred the freedom of living in Reno and being able to go to the convenience store without asking for permission. I knew that the confinement, restrictions, rules, brutal discipline, which I witnessed firsthand, went against my nature. I returned to public school, finished high school, and attended Haskell Indian Junior College in Lawrence, Kansas. Haskell was another boarding school but the atmosphere was a different educational and social experience for me. I liked it but I found that college wasn't for me. I returned to Reno and I worked several jobs and was out of work for about a year when the advertisement for the Ruby Pipeline Project came up in 2010 and my brother Mark and I applied.

Far Western Anthropological Research Group, a cultural resource management (CRM) company contracted by Ruby Pipeline, specifically recruited Native Americans to work as monitors and field technicians with on-the-job training. The project contract covered an area that covered Utah, Northern Nevada, and ended in Oregon.

We were hired after interviewing and we were excited to begin. We didn't know what to expect and as with many Native people we were hesitant to disturb the sites where our ancestors lived. We felt that if what was being done was disrespectful and it didn't feel right we would stop. We got a crash course on how to do the required work for the many phases of archaeology fieldwork. Each day we worked with experts in the field, each day was a hands-on learning experience for some of the phases of archaeological research. We were treated with respect and we learned as we worked. I have been working in this field since then and I hope to do this type of work for a long time as it is very rewarding, interesting, and with every assignment I learn something new. Every job whether it is historical or cultural has been educational for me and the people I work with are knowledgeable and know their job. Most of the people are very respectful, we share, listen, and we learn from each other.

Because of this job experience Mark and I both felt that more Natives have to be involved in the science of archaeology. We work with CRM companies who are very respectful and consult with the Native monitors from area tribes for artifact removal and storage. Collaboration is necessary for all involved: the construction company, the CRMs, and the local area tribes.

In 2013, Mark volunteered to do the Stewart field school for excavation along with other Native and non-Native people. He hoped to learn more about fieldwork, collecting, and categorizing artifacts found during the excavation of the various control units at Stewart Indian

School. His interest in Stewart was because of family: uncles, cousins, our dad, brother, and I are all alumni of Stewart boarding school. He is the youngest member of my family and Stewart was always talked about by my father in a good way.

Although Mark had five-years' experience as a field technician he wanted to learn more and that is another reason he attended the Stewart field school. The irony here is that he knew more than the other students and he was able to assist the teacher and instruct the students. This is something that made him very proud that as a Native, someone was listening to him and found his teaching valid. Being Native he was able to add the spiritual connection between the two worlds and the differing cultures. In our way we treat areas that we are working in with respect and use smudge, pray, and ask permission from the ancestors to be in the area. At the beginning and end of the day we offer prayers, water, or use sage and sweetgrass to cleanse ourselves and the area of negativity. Mark was never one to lead prayers as others were always there to take care of it for us in prior jobs. But at Stewart he stepped up to the plate to carry this Native tradition which makes me very proud. I am glad that he was strong and saw the need for this spiritual connection with the students and the respect it showed to them for the work they were and are going to be involved in.

My brother was not feeling well the week of the field school but he was committed to the project and he knew being at the school was important. His contribution along with his archaeology field techniques was from the Native perspective and he felt this was important in relaying this to the class. His health prevented him from returning to the work he loved. He passed in May of 2018.

Mark's thoughts, along with mine, other Native archaeology techs and Native monitors that I have met, all chose to be part of cultural resource management by being involved as workers and observers for other tribes with CRM projects on their lands. Sometimes tribes have limited resources and they don't send out monitors to observe. As Natives we help them by monitoring and observing in the field and leave the important decisions for the area tribe. Once tribes are involved they are more comfortable having us in their respective areas and that we will see that set protocols and procedures are followed during projects. In our time out on the Ruby Pipeline we encountered Native people who felt we were wrong to be working on the pipeline and we were selling out our people. I too felt like this before I started working as a technician. But I learned about the importance of Native involvement in CRM work, after all, what we find is part of the tribe. It belongs to them.

There has to be collaboration between tribes, CRM firms, construction companies, developers, and state and city entities especially when human remains are involved. Tribal monitoring is very important when this particular discovery is made. It's vital to preserve the dignity of the remains, tribal traditions, and honor the life as it is.

In this changing political climate, the current administration is all for opening up lands for oil/gas exploration and pipeline projects, sometimes showing little regard for cultural concerns that local tribes may have. The Dakota Access Pipeline is the perfect example of an administration that did not care about tribal concerns over water pollution, oil line leaks, and other environmental concerns in North Dakota. Any large project that is going to cause disturbance of the earth always has possibilities of human remains being discovered so involvement by local tribes should be mandatory. This is because they are most likely to be the descendants of the people who are uncovered.

Following protocol by the company, the tribe, or location site developers is very important. Having a local tribal person monitor the job and oversee all aspects is critical. Repatriation is very important as tribes have final say over the process. CRMs and tribes have to work together on this process with respect and care for the handling of remains found.

CRM by tribes is vital for recording their own history, and without it their past may be lost. The Native American Graves Protection and Repatriation Act (NAGPRA) is a federal law that is now more important than ever for all tribes. NAGPRA was passed to help tribes with concerns over looting of tribal remains at burial sites and the artifacts being sold on the black market to collectors. Unfortunately it was passed too late for some artifacts that were stolen years before and are in private collections.

In the different places I've worked I've seen firsthand the need for educated, trained Native people to work in the many fields of archaeology. At times while out at jobs I wished that I had more knowledge or could speak with another Native about the job. There are so many aspects of archaeology that I don't know. I wished that when I was younger I would have been exposed to this field so I could have gone to school and gotten into the work I enjoy earlier.

I would like to thank Sarah Cowie, associate professor of anthropology at the University of Nevada in Reno, for inviting me to participate in writing of this biography and essay for the Stewart Indian School excavation field school.

Essay 8. Mark Johnson

Enrolled member of the Reno-Sparks Indian Colony, of Washoe and Northern Paiute descent; experienced Archaeological Technician

[Editors' Note: A. J. Johnson provided the following paragraph to introduce the essay written by his late brother. "Mark Johnson is the youngest in a family of six of descendants of Northern Paiute and Washoe tribes. He was born to Vera Tobey and Brady Johnson, Sr. in Reno, Nevada. He grew up in Reno and he attended Orvis Ring Elementary School, Vaughn Middle School, and Wooster High School. He always worked throughout his life and found his most gratifying work as an archeological technician. He felt that his contribution to the field was important and necessary. He left this world in May of 2018."]

I am a member of the Washoe Tribe. I have lived there my whole life. I grew up there and I recently was hired by Far Western Anthropological Research Group to work on the Feather River Project. Before that I worked out on the Ruby Pipeline Project and that was my first experience with doing archaeology and excavation, so I really didn't know a whole lot. I work with heritage and things from the past by doing archaeological excavations and surveys.

Having had the experience working on the Ruby Pipeline kind of changed my ideas about what archaeologists actually do. Working on the Ruby Pipeline Project helped me to understand how and why we dig and how and why we record and document things. The problem

FIGURE 7.2. Mark Johnson teaching students at the field school how to lay out test units. Photo by Sarah Cowie, printed with permission from A.J. Johnson.

I see (how archaeology and preservation are conducted) is I really didn't understand too much about what was being done. I could see why an archaeological study needed to be done to help preserve whatever's there and it would ensure that the history there is properly documented. I found with the work we were doing at the school I was hoping that we didn't find any archaeological items or artifacts. It's good when there aren't any artifacts that have to be documented and written up. I just didn't want to see the project turn into a big thing, like if we found something significant down there. I think the problems (with how government agencies consult with tribes) are often with the tribes themselves, with the tribes not being interested enough to know that any artifacts or excavations are anywhere near their area. They should make it more their business by way of knowing whether there is any kind of work to be done and to make sure that there are monitors there and just to make sure that everything is being documented and taken care of the way it should be. I think that the tribes could be more informed by at least a presentation and even having the people that do the actual work to come out and just do a short presentation about any excavations or anything like that that needs to be done. That way it gives the tribes a heads-up on what is going to be done and they don't worry about everything being dug up and you don't disturb a lot, as some are really uptight about just digging in the ground itself and moving things.

I got involved in the (Stewart Indian School) project when I was invited by Terry McBride. She's been an anthropologist with the state and with the preservation society and we were working with her on a video for Far Western at that time and she was doing interviews with all the Native Americans that were working on the Ruby Pipeline Project to get their ideas of archaeology and how they felt about what they were working on and what they were going to do next. At that point, she knew about the field school, so she invited me to come down and suggested that I cut it up with the two of you. I had a couple days so I decided to come down and help. I have kind of a good background because I have family that actually attended Stewart Indian School and I'm a Washoe tribal member. So I thought maybe I would go down there and help them help out with the project. Then I actually wound up having the opportunity to teach the students down there about archaeological survey and survey techniques. I taught them how to use flagging tape, how to flag out an area, and how to make a map out of using a compass and direction. We also taught them how to excavate, too.

I had the experience of standing up and talking in front of a bunch of students and I'm giving them a little background information on how I tied into the field school and what I was doing there. The experience of teaching was pretty wonderful, as I have never had that experience before in my life or for any job. I can't recall any times where any of the methods or any of the policies that we went over were questionable or didn't sound right. Pretty much everything we did I found it sounded okay.

The experience that happened feels good being collaborative. We had members from the Stewart Indian School community come out and then we had people from the Washoe tribe along with everybody that was involved in the school and the project. So really I thought it was important for me to be there to be at the field school. I had family go there and that kind of gave me more incentive to show up at the field school and help out.

I got up to introduce myself and gave a little background of who I was and why I was there. I also told them about my family being in the school and I wanted to be there so that was one experience. But I thought it was important to say that there were especially a lot of local people that are familiar with the boarding school. Some of the stories that the old people came to tell about the history of the school really opened up the students' eyes. They didn't realize what the score was all about other than it being a good Indian school. A lot of the students really didn't know what actually happened to these kids and how they wound up there and what happened to the families while they were there. So, it opened some people's eyes and the students listened to what happened to all of these people and their spirits and how the school came to be.

This project was different because it wasn't actual work (for a proposed project) even though we went over the safety rules and all of the policies that we use in the field. That was a key difference. Other than the actual work we're doing, we are usually on a time schedule we are in a hurry to get things done. The field school was more laid-back and it wasn't like work at all. Also, contract work is a lot more pressure because they want to get it done and you're on their schedule. And you don't have a lot of time sometimes to get things you want done and there's always stuff that comes up that changes things.

Everybody (at the field school) was pretty organized and it was a really good experience there. I think we learned that having a collaborative project, and having all people come together does help a lot especially with the people in the Washoe tribe itself. I think they learned a lot by coming out and at least being interested shows that it erases all the stigma about archaeologists and what they really do and it sets people's minds at ease about the work that's being done so there's no negative feelings or anything about it. I also thought about how the project has been pretty open to the public. Whereas, when we are working on a contract project everything is pretty private. Collaboration made a big difference because everybody that was out there was on the same page with what we were doing and why the work was being done.

I don't really know too much about the history of problematic work by archaeologists and the federal government other than the government and the archaeologists oversee a lot of the work.

Descendant community sounds different than regular community. It's like there are other people in this community or the other half is Indian. For archaeologists it would be easier to just use the term *Numa* or find some other term to describe the people that are there because it makes them clearly sound different from a regular community. It's more sensitive politically and also it's more respectful and better to say the people and it really does help when you are working with people that have the respect to say so and know the difference.

The oral histories belong to the school itself and to the students that attended that school. And practically every student that's been there, or heard about the school, or has been invited to make presentations, or found a way to speak more about the experience they had at the school; that's where a lot of the oral histories come from. That way a lot of people would know the oral history and how important it is for that school.

I think people don't realize that because of that you know of other events too. They have their own opinions and ideas too, but when we collaborate everybody has an opinion about what's going on. And it's important to realize that by collaborating with tribes and helping them learn as much as possible about what they (archaeologists) are going to be doing, it helps with the whole process and it helps the relationships between archaeologists and tribes altogether.

There are always implications. Tribes want to remove artifacts from sites that are disturbed and want to document it and they want repatriation for the artifacts and stuff that we do find. I think it's important for everything to be documented. To feel that way whatever work is being done can be recorded and documented. Also, it's important for tribes to have everything put back into the ground where it was before. So, a lot of the work that we do when we're out there is keeping everything intact and trying not to scatter it.

I think the best way to return the site to as close to the way it was in the first place is to try to do as little archaeological studies as possible and trying not to disturb the ground too much or do any digging. I think it's important for all that you do on your survey and stuff to document as much as possible and elaborate on what kind of site it is and how to proceed or not.

It was important that the Native Americans respect digging into Mother Earth and that we pray and use sage to cleanse ourselves to make sure that we don't dig into anything that is harmful to us spiritually or in any other way. So, it was important for us to pray and cleanse ourselves everyday just so we protect everybody that was with us, that way we can all be together on the same thing. We had Diane and Lonnie, they were taking care of the prayers and the sage so we have that area covered. And I want to recommend that we could have that practice by having Native Americans right there with your work and when you're breaking ground or whenever you are doing any kind of digging. That could be a basic thing that goes on any time you work in the field.

I think the best way for archaeologists to improve their relations with the tribes is by actually hiring Native American technicians to come out and do the digging and monitors on each project. If you want a project in the area and there are Native Americans there, it always goes over better when you see that. The other part about archaeology is when they're working with tribes they can do more by presenting and making a bit better presentation of the project that they have in mind and what they plan on doing and then just basically having a meeting with all the tribes and everybody involved. The biggest and toughest part is that little bit of trust and they can work on that part by working with the tribes and making better presentations.

Essay 9. Dania Jordan

Graduate student in historical archaeology at the University of Massachusetts, Boston; museum technician at the Northeast Museum Services Center, National Park Service

My initial experience at the Stewart Indian School introduced me to the field of archaeology and provided me with the essential skills (i.e., excavations, mapping, GPS, etc.). I needed to know for practical archaeology. It was also the defining moment in me becoming an archaeologist and shaping the kind of archaeologist I am and would become. My experience at Stewart has taught me how to develop good relationships with the communities I am working alongside of, how to listen, and how to create a product that is beneficial and empowering to communities. Stewart has also taught me how to think long-term about the impacts a project may have on a community, and to think outside the academia limits or the limits we place on ourselves in academia when it comes creating products for communities.

In this field school, we worked directly alongside of the Washoe Tribal Historic Preservation Office (THPO) and the Nevada Indian Commission (NIC). This opportunity enlightened me about many things such as the importance of collaboration and heritage, what sovereignty is, how Natives feel about archaeology, how to choose a site relevant to communities, and how to be sensitive and respectful to the community I am working with. The objective of this field school was to preserve the history of the Stewart Indian School. This included locating the original schoolhouse. By finding this information out we were able to help the Stewart Indian School gain publicity and fundraising they needed in order to preserve the buildings on the campus site, as well as any other vision they may have for the school that will interest the public and continue the legacy of the Stewart Indian School for generations to come. Archaeology can aid in this process because archaeologists are able to help interpret artifacts and/or re-create a time period by making educated guesses about what an object is and how it was instrumental to humanity. However, in certain instances the communities in which archaeologists work can add to the archaeological record in that they have a better understanding of the material remains found on archaeological sites. This is why this project was enticing to me because the knowledge, the information uncovered from this site was given to us by elders that supported our archaeological findings. The term collaborative archaeology, as the name suggests, focuses on the collaboration with communities in the excavation, protection, and preservation of archaeological items. Additionally, this also includes sharing data with the community and including Native communities in the writing component of the project (Nicholas 2001, 37). Inclusivity is very pertinent to collaborative archaeology because collaboration within the archaeological discipline carries a multitude of meanings. Sometimes collaboration means simply consulting with a community—as a means of political correctness—and excluding them from any other component of the archaeological project. However, to have a mutually beneficial outcome for collaborative archaeology projects, sustaining and nurturing social relationships with tribal members is important.

During the field school I learned the impact that archaeology has on Native Americans. How archaeologists throughout the late eighteenth century and the nineteenth century invaded tribal and federal lands and extracted and removed artifacts and human remains from archaeological sites to be studied, interpreted, and curated in museums without tribal members, knowledge and consent (Silliman and Ferguson 2010, 53; McGhee 2008, 581). Thus, archaeologists granted themselves stewards of Native American culture, taking ownership for their research and not crediting Native Americans. In addition, archaeologists exploited Native Americans inappropriately, sometimes displaying them as savages, non-progressive, and barbaric. Archaeologists also revealed some of Native Americans' sacred practices and traditions. Therefore, performing collaborative archaeology essentially avoids archaeologists taking full ownership of archaeological findings as well as reduces the misinterpretation of Indigenous people. In doing so, I learned, when wanting to conduct research that includes Indigenous people, to engage tribal members in the early stages of research, have an open-mind, and set my cultural beliefs aside, do not limit tribes to only evaluating the options, work together to create an accurate depiction of Native Americans, and how to respect Natives.

In doing a project such as this, I learned the importance of heritage. Heritage is an inheritance of property or possessions. It defines who we are and it avoids people from having an identity crisis because it provides us with information that tells us where our ancestors are from, why we have certain traditions, why we celebrate certain holidays, why we eat certain foods, why we wear certain clothes, or even style our hair certain ways. All of these behaviors are an extension of the past and that is what heritage is, the link to our past and how we understand why we are the way we are. This is why heritage needs to be protected, preserved, and kept safe so traditions, treasures, buildings, and such can continuously be passed down from generation to generation in order for us to function appropriately as individuals, as members of a specific group, to distinguish ourselves from others, and to feel a sense of community and belonging. Knowing the importance of heritage and how it plays on a group's identity, I acknowledged that the role of the public in heritage preservation was to interpret the Indigenous people correctly and respect the Native peoples' culture. This includes allowing them to choose what is and what is not to be researched and publicized since many of their traditions are sacred. And if publicized or placed in mainstream society traditions may become unsacred and Natives may lose ownership over traditions. Therefore, managing heritage protects Indigenous people in that it protects sacred traditions. It also protects those traditions that are publicized because heritage management requires the appropriate interpretation of Indigenous people so that future generations can have access to them in order to keep traditions alive.

Learning about archaeology, Native American culture, and heritage during the Stewart Indian School archaeological project made me ponder on my status as an African American and how my background influences my attitude toward archaeology. Much like Native Americans, African Americans have been dehumanized and misinterpreted due to past representation of African Americans from an archaeologist's perspective. In other ways African Americans differ from Native Americans in that it is sometimes difficult to trace African-American heritage due to the loss of slavery records and forced assimilation. Therefore, much of African-American traditions are minimal and most that is known about African Americans is their enslavement. This is problematic in the African-American community because there is not much in a way of celebratory publications and exhibitions of African-American ancestry. Reflecting upon my status as an African American encouraged me to conduct further research to address the parallels of Indigenous archaeology and African-American archaeology and how past events affected the development of the two disciplines in archaeological practices. This also influenced the research I would conduct in my graduate studies at the University of Massachusetts, Boston. Two years after the

Stewart Indian Field School I went on to join the Eastern Pequot Field School session in Summer 2015, North Stonington, Connecticut. In doing so, I was able to develop an ongoing friendship with the Eastern Pequot Princess, Natasha Gambrell, and a few other tribal members who I keep in contact with. I do not believe I would have been able to develop and maintain these relationships if it were not for my experience at the Stewart Indian School. I ultimately entered graduate school wanting to study the benefits and challenges of collaborative archaeology and how it differed from other archaeology. As I delved deeper into graduate school my interest shifted, but I will never leave the tools, resources, and skills I learned at the Stewart Indian School too far behind me. I implement collaborative practices in all the research I conduct.

When working collaboratively with another group, communication is key; therefore, at the Stewart Indian School we spent a lot of time conversing among ourselves about how we should approach certain situations that had come about. For instance, the crew and I discussed intensively on what we should do with the flakes we found. The protocol says we should place them into a storage bag and place them back in the ground. Our Native crew members did not agree with the protocol so we discussed alternatives:

- Option 1—place the flakes back into the ground with organic material.
- Option 2—place the flakes back into the ground the same way they came out of the ground.

We all agreed on Option 2. Now, all our instructor had to do was get approval, which she did receive the "go" on placing the flakes back in the ground.

Throughout the field school we had many conversations and sat through many lectures, all of which were useful and informal. At the same time, it took away the time that we could be excavating. That is just one of many challenges of performing collaborative archaeology. Another challenge was that not many Native visitors agreed with what we were doing; therefore, we as archaeologists would receive unpleasant remarks like, "Have you found any dead bodies yet!" or "There's a spirit that snatches little kids up." These were scare tactics to discourage us from digging on the site of course. Some Native visitors were just forward and bluntly expressed their disapproval. And honestly I could understand their disposition. Historically, nothing good has ever come out of archaeologists excavating on Native land. At the same time, I do not believe many knew exactly what it was that we were doing and maybe that's where the misunderstanding came from.

The benefit of working alongside of Native Americans is that they can help us enhance the archaeological record. For instance, some animal bones were found and we quickly associated the animal bones with consumption until an elder came forward and corrected our understanding of animal bones. Simply put, not all animal bones are for consumption; some are used for spiritual rituals. Talking about ritualistic practices reminds me of the introduction we had in two spiritual rituals Native Americans performed—smudges and the carrying of ocher, which were both meant to protect us from bad spirits while on the field. Unfortunately, a Native volunteer was not so fortunate as he fell severely ill one day. After we received the news we did a smudge for him and took the day off. You almost can't help to feel guilty for his predicament because had we not been out there he probably wouldn't have been out there. He never did fully recover to come back out to the field but we kept him in our hearts throughout the field school. This exemplifies the building of relationships between archaeologists and Native Americans. That's what made this field school so meaningful. It wasn't just about "us"—the archaeologists but it was about "them"—the Native Americans. It was about giving back to a community. Empowering a community and informing the public that the Native Americans were here. This is their history. Their story to tell, not ours. We're just aiding in the process to help uncover the evidence and informing others how archaeology is not an isolate occupation.

Essay 10. Christopher LeBlanc

Heritage consultant, archaeological technician, and crew chief

I have worked in the field of archaeology and cultural resource management since 1994. I worked for the Coronado National Forest in southeastern Arizona as an archaeologist and member of the Tribal Relations Team from 2001 to 2010. During this time, I developed a deeper understanding of the importance of tribal relations and effective and mutually beneficial heritage consultation. The Forest Service is one of many government agencies that routinely consult with tribes using protocols designed to meet the governments' federal trust responsibility obligations to protect tribes' treaty rights, lands, assets, and resources. Whether consultation on a particular project is deemed a success or failure can often be attributed to how the protocols are interpreted and implemented. Projects that begin with consultation during the planning process, and provide numerous opportunities to engage in discussion in all stages of the project, are the ones that stand the best chance of being successful. Consultations that consist solely of sending letters and failing to incorporate Native perspectives into project planning and decision-making regarding the significance and treatment of heritage resources are far more likely to have problems than those conducted in collaboration with tribes.

My role as heritage consultant on the current project began by meeting and developing relationships with local tribal representatives and heritage professionals, identifying potential collaborators and consultants, and beginning to assess tribal needs and priorities. The Stewart Indian School Collaborative Archaeology Project was the result of relationships developed with many local and regional partners, including the Washoe Tribal Historic Preservation Office (THPO), the Nevada Indian Commission (NIC) and their Stewart Advisory Council, and the Nevada State Museum. Working together as partners we determined that the Stewart Indian School would be the location based on tribal needs, scheduling, feasibility, and access. The next step in making the Stewart project successful was collaboration in the development of an archaeological testing plan that identified specific survey and excavation areas that would benefit the ongoing preservation efforts at Stewart. The plan was approved by the Nevada State Historic Preservation Office, and the Stewart Indian School Collaborative Archaeology Field School was offered as a six-credit course through the Department of Anthropology at the University of Nevada, Reno.

The Stewart Indian School Collaborative Archaeology Project often looked like a traditional archaeological field school. Field school is typically the first hands-on experience students have with archaeology, and many skills and techniques must be learned. Students in the field school learned a variety of important technical skills including: survey and excavation methods, artifact identification, site map and excavation unit plan view and profile drawing, compass use, surface collection and excavation unit setup, identifying unit locations within larger ground penetrating radar grids, trowel and shovel use, identifying changes in soil color and texture, and completing field forms. This field school offered several notable exceptions. Students met with former Stewart attendees, listened to guest speakers at the NIC, and took field trips to the Nevada State Museum and Dat So La Lee's house. Most days on this field school began and ended with a smudging/blessing. Many people also carried small bits of ocher in their packs or with them. These methods were appropriate to our project because we were excavating in a very emotionally charged place, and these practices are a reminder to be mindful and respectful.

Additional time was built into the daily schedule to make sure everyone had the opportunity to ask general project or site-specific questions and provide comments. This included questioning archaeological methodology, which does not often happen in a field school or professional setting. We learned that removing artifacts from a site has the potential to lessen tribal claims and ties to their land. Based on student concerns raised during a group discussion, we requested and received authorization from the State Historic Preservation Office to rebury artifacts and excavation units without using either plastic bags or landscaping fabric. Through discussions and listening to tribal priorities, we were able to determine that the removal of historical artifacts from the site would be permitted while the removal of earlier artifacts would not. In archaeology it is often taken for granted that all artifacts are to be collected, analyzed, boxed, and curated in an approved curation facility. This project changed that paradigm by questioning normal procedures, and whenever possible, tribal wishes were deferred to. The goal was to make a good faith effort at collaboration and stretching to find new and creative ways to build relationships. In this particular case, following standard archaeological procedures and protocols had the potential to create distrust in working relationships. Scheduling time to have these open discussions provided the opportunity to avoid these unwanted consequences.

Archaeology and higher education could be improved by widely expanding this collaborative model, resulting in the training of a new generation of archaeologists who will influence and benefit the profession and scholarship by incorporating more Native perspectives. Knowing that Native people have diverse perspectives is obvious for many, but not all. Archaeologists and land managers may "get it right" sometimes, but other times may have serious issues. Therefore, it is important that archaeologists and land managers who make decisions regarding heritage resources have appropriate sensitivity training, either in school or in collaboration with local tribal groups. Having training and knowledge of diverse perspectives will give archaeologists and land managers additional skills to make better decisions.

Archaeology would also be improved by including different types of analysis. The last several decades of archaeological research have been heavily biased toward questions regarding subsistence strategies. Subsistence is only one component of a larger picture. Archaeologists often ask the same questions out of habit. Through improved consultation and relationship building, archaeologists can begin to ask different types of questions. The field of archaeology stands to be in a position to tell a much richer story of human history. Public archaeology would also benefit from shifting emphasis from objects toward a more anthropological and culturally sensitive view of the people and the significance of their relationship with place and the importance these heritage resources have to living relations.

Having more Native people involved with archaeology projects adds an element of openness and furthers relationship building after a long history of distrust. It is not surprising that the more archaeologists and the federal government show respect for Native people and their views, the more the levels of distrust are reduced. My hope for the future of archaeology and archaeological research is that there will continue to be more and more opportunities for Native people who can bring new depths of knowledge and sensitivity to the field.

Essay 11. Ashley M. Long

Archaeologist, Bureau of Land Management,
Shoshone, Idaho Field Office

Many people ask the question, "What makes archaeology collaborative?" The answer to this question is as complex as it is simple. A truly collaborative project is one that involves Indigenous communities throughout the entire research process, from project conceptualization to writing and publishing. While this seems very straightforward, the actual process of collaborating requires constant flexibility and communication to maintain the open relationships that are needed.

I was first introduced to collaborative methods when I participated in an ethnographic field school in Ancash, Peru. The purpose of that field school was to introduce students to participatory action research and to the importance of working with communities and involving them in anthropological research. After participating in that field school I began to look for more opportunities to use collaborative methods in research. Fortunately, I was introduced to Dr. Sarah Cowie and jumped at the opportunity to be a part of the collaborative archaeology project at Stewart Indian School. The project at Stewart is an excellent model for implementing collaborative methods, and I will discuss a few events that occurred during the project that I believe epitomize what collaborative archaeology should be.

During the excavations, I found the most influential result of collaboration to be the daily smudging rituals that all field school staff participated in, including students, faculty, and volunteers. While this particular component was not associated with the archaeology, for me it stood out as a prime example of what collaboration can do for communities and how it can have grand effects far beyond its initial scope. This was a primarily Native ceremony that each of us participated in out of respect for the beliefs of those who were working with us, and also the people in the Native communities who view the campus as a very important place. It was a chance for many of the younger students to learn firsthand about anthropological methods such as participant observation, but it was also a chance for all of us to see the world from a new perspective, a Native perspective, even for just a short time every day.

Another occurrence that demonstrates the effectiveness of collaboration involves the archaeological procedures involving artifacts and the backfilling of test units. During the excavations we learned that several Native and non-Native participants felt that the backfilling process was inappropriate since artifacts were to be placed in plastic bags and the excavation units lined with landscaping fabric before the units were refilled. We therefore halted our excavations and discussed why and how we could remedy the backfilling issue. These were incredibly significant moments in the collaborative process, because we would stop our work and take the time to consider every perspective and reach a unanimous solution before we moved forward. As far as creating a model for future collaborative projects, this would be one of the most important aspects. Collaborative projects must remain fluid and flexible throughout the entire project for it be truly collaborative from start to finish.

However, all of this is not to say that collaboration is a simple task. In fact, there are many hurdles to be jumped in these types of projects that require honest and open communication by all participants. During the field school there were several moments where I felt out of my element somehow, or just generally uncomfortable. I struggled to understand the concern over the use of plastic bags and landscaping fabric. However, I realized that by staying open-minded, asking consistent and respectful questions, and reflecting on all our perspectives, I was able to better understand my colleagues' concerns. So, there is a learning curve for all of us when we participate in collaborative projects. In the end, the point is to reach the goals of the community as best as possible and this may or may not require mitigation such as removing the use of plastic bags and landscaping fabric from the project design.

Since the conclusion of our project, I have found the skills I acquired to be invaluable. My experience during this project instilled a strong sense of respect for Native communities, their customs, and beliefs. Now, as I help to manage cultural resources for a public lands agency, I am more prepared to conduct thoughtful and productive collaborative consultation with numerous tribes. I hope to continue to incorporate these collaborative methods into my everyday responsibilities as an archaeologist.

Essay 12. Jo Ann Nevers

Enrolled member of the Washoe Tribe of Nevada and California, and respected Washoe historian

I served as one of the tribal consultants to work on the project entitled Collaborative Historical Archaeology and Preservation at Stewart Indian School for the year 2013. I am a member of the Washoe Cultural Resource Advisory Council with Darrel Cruz, Tribal Historic Preservation Office for the Washoe Tribe of Nevada and California.

The goals of the Washoe Cultural Resource Advisory Council are to protect, preserve, and promote Washoe heritage through direct management, and promote Washoe heritage through education/outreach and language revitalization. We work with internal and external organizations to protect cultural resources. Our Council has five members representing the different Washoe communities located at Reno-Sparks Indian Colony, Carson Indian Colony, Stewart Colony, Dresslerville, Woodsfords Colony, and off-reservation Washoe not living on these colonies. We have a Tribal Historical Preservation Office (THPO), who works closely with local, state, private, and Federal entities and advises the WCRAC as to the latest developments occurring on or affecting the Washoe tribal cultural heritage.

I have worked as an archaeological technician for the Nevada Department of Transportation and have monitored many archaeological projects for the Washoe Tribe for over thirty years and have written about Washoe history, places, and culture (Nevers 1976, 2011, 2015). I am familiar with most aspects of archaeological excavations and I am dedicated to the preservation of our culture, heritage, and lands. I have worked recently monitoring the work being done on the Legacy

Trail, Truckee, California in 2014 for the Far Western Anthropological Group, Davis, California. In 1979–1980 I was an undergraduate at the University of Nevada, Reno (UNR) studying anthropology.

Funding for the Stewart Indian School project was provided for by a grant to UNR from the Army Research Office's Younger Investigator Program. Dr. Cowie was awarded the three-year Young Investor Grant from the Army to outline a strategy for humanizing the process of respectful consultation between tribes and the federal government. The project was approved in partnership with the Washoe Tribe, Nevada Indian Commission (NIC), and the Stewart School Advisory Committee. For the record, this land that encompasses the Stewart Indian School is held in trust for the Washoe Tribe of Nevada and California.

My job was to observe the project making sure that the objectives of the project were being met. I attended the research design meeting with Darrel Cruz, Tribal Historic Preservation Office; Sherry Rupert, NIC; Diane Teeman, Burns Paiute Archaeologist; Chris Gibbons, NIC; Sarah Cowie, UNR; and Chris LeBlanc, UNR heritage specialist. Ms. Cowie gave an update on the project objectives and components such as excavation methods, areas of interest, and treatment of artifacts. The Washoe Tribe requested that all artifacts that were found on the Washoe tribal lands, along the area which had been pointed out as an old Washoe prehistoric site, be reburied at the site. This would be especially true with regard to human remains as we have tribal customs regarding these matters.

Because of involvement of all interested parties this project was successful from the very beginning. Discussions must be held between all interested parties as was the case here with the Washoe Tribe and others who have a stake in what is occurring and the repercussions if someone is left out from the start.

Essay 13. Sherry L. Rupert and Chris A. Gibbons

Executive Director of the Nevada Indian Commission; enrolled tribal member of Washoe and Paiute heritage

Curator, Stewart Indian School Cultural Center & Museum, Nevada Indian Commission

In the summer of 2013 the State of Nevada Indian Commission (NIC) worked with the University of Nevada, Reno (UNR)'s Department of Anthropology, and the Washoe Tribal Historic Preservation Office (THPO) on a collaborative archaeological excavation and field school at the historic Stewart Indian School in Carson City, Nevada. The NIC is located at the 110-acre State-owned property that is home to over sixty historic buildings from the Stewart Indian School. The school was the only nonreservation Indian boarding school in Nevada and operated from 1890 to 1980 with a federal mandate to educate American Indian children, initially from the Great Basin Tribes (Washoe, Northern and Southern Paiute, and Western Shoshone), but eventually this led to the acceptance of children from tribal nations throughout the West. Today, the NIC is working to develop the Stewart Indian School into a cultural heritage destination, which includes the establishment of the Stewart Indian School Cultural Center & Museum and corresponding Welcome Center, as well as utilizing many of the school buildings for historical interpretation. The learning opportunities at the Stewart Indian School are numerous and this field school was a key example of how the campus can still be used as an educational facility.

The initial role of the NIC during this project was to identify potential individuals within local tribes, its Stewart Advisory Committee, as well as, the state of Nevada for involvement in the field school. During the field school, the commission office hosted various presentations, which included a presentation by Sherry L. Rupert, the Executive Director of the NIC on the history of the Stewart Indian School. Also, the Commission's Stewart Advisory Committee, made up of state agency representatives, Stewart alumni and former employees, tribal representatives and scholars helped identify potential locations for excavation that would aid in future historical interpretation of the school. In addition, Chris Ann Gibbons of the NIC aided in gathering research on the school which included numerous historic photographs.

The NIC was extremely pleased that UNR chose the site of the historic Stewart Indian School for their field school. It was refreshing to see a change in the way archaeological methods are being taught, while at the same time respecting the American Indian culture and listening and learning from Native people. It was also important that both Native and non-Native UNR students worked together during the field school and learned about the Stewart Indian School and its importance to Nevada's history and its future. The staff from UNR, Sarah E. Cowie and Christopher C. LeBlanc, took the time to make sure all stakeholders were invested in the project. With the completion of this field school it is the commission's hope that it will be a model for future collaborative archaeological projects and that tribes continue to have a voice, as collaboration in theory should be multiple individuals, many voices working together to reach an agreeable outcome.

Essay 14. Diane L. Teeman

Enrolled member, tribal councilperson, and Cultural & Heritage Department Director of the Burns Paiute Tribe, and PhD student in anthropology at the University of Nevada, Reno

I am a Northern Paiute woman with an advanced degree in anthropology (archaeology specialization). My journey in this field has been long and sometimes weary as I have worked with many to increase collaboration between Indigenous North Americans and archaeologists. I have heard of collaborative work occurring in places for limited duration, but nothing that has been sustained. At times I have questioned the efficacy of our efforts to achieve truly collaborative working relationships between Natives and archaeologists. During the summer of 2013 I had the good fortune of being a part of the Stewart Indian School Historic Archaeology Collaborative Field School, an experience that gave me renewed hope in the future potential of collaborative archaeology. The field school was an instance where something magical happened. We as participants and collaborators, each opened ourselves to greater understanding, and in doing so also cleared new paths for the future.

I first became involved in cultural resource management (CRM) in 1988 when a training opportunity became available through my tribe, the Burns Paiute Tribe. I had no idea what an "archaeological technician" did, but the position paid for by the Organization for Forgotten Americans (OFA) paid almost twice per hour what the current minimum wage was, so I jumped at the chance.

It was during my training and work experiences that first year working on the Malheur National Forest, a forest which is largely comprised of my tribe's former (and illegally taken away) Malheur Reservation, that I learned of the Numic Expansion Hypothesis (NEH). In short, the hypothesis claims that by using linguistic models developed in the study of European language diversification, it is possible to track the diversification of Native languages within the Uto-Aztecan language subphylum. In applying this linguistic model, it has been hypothesized that "Numic" cultures, including Northern Paiute's, may have "expanded" into the Great Basin as late as one thousand years ago. For my people in the northernmost reaches of our culture area, some have hypothesized my ancestors have been here as little as five hundred years. This, in spite of the archaeological evidence in the Great Basin of Oregon which spans at least fifteen thousand years. My tribe's knowledge of ourselves is that our people have been here since time immemorial. Our ancestors watched and handed down the stories of experiencing the formation of the Cascade Mountain range. This NEH hit me like a bullet and seared into my mind like a hot poker! How could anyone dare to say such things? I went to elders in my community to ask if they had heard of this story being spread about our people, they had not. Determined to learn more, I continued to look for anything and everything written about us. I quickly learned that the NEH was the interpretive lens through which much archaeological study in the Great Basin was evaluated. I also learned that unbeknownst to my community, with our many tribal elders, the archaeologists (many of whom had never even come to our community), were considered the experts on our people's history.

I realized some of the potential ramifications of this system; primarily that others held our tribe's future in their hands. With a peer-reviewed publication, "they" could make or break any number of sociopolitical claims my tribe may hold or seek in the future. My outrage grew, and I vocalized my opposition to this system at every opportunity. My eyes were open, I was aware, and I was determined to make a difference. I was told that if I didn't like the system, or the way we were being represented in academic circles, that I could go back to school and change it. From that moment my life's work was set. I tried to keep an open mind by telling myself, perhaps I am so ignorant and simple that once I achieve a Western education, I may find that all or at least some of what has been written is factually based; some wizard behind the curtain that we, as tribal members have never yet met. But, I was unwilling to accept anything that had been "hypothesized," until I was satisfied it was factually supported. I later came to understand my natural sense of logical technique went by at least one title, critical theory.

Over the last thirty years, I have worked to learn and unpack all that is the NEH and believe me it has a lot of baggage. Perhaps more importantly, I have come to understand that the NEH, although highly offensive to some, is not the greatest enemy to my tribe's past, present, and future. The NEH is a symptom of a far more endemic illness. I now understand that our society's ability to most fully capture the deepest and most sincere forms of knowledge and understanding are being stymied by a system that has its roots deeply grounded in colonialism and the residual unequal power dynamics that result from knowledge creation. Our contemporary mainstream society has accepted, often unquestionably, the knowledge creation machine that is Western academia, and through the unquestioning acceptance of it helped perpetuate a system that produces incomplete truths as knowledge.

The issue of access in these knowledge and power dynamics is one that has been at the forefront of discussion in many arenas since at least the 1960s. Many advances have been achieved in sociopolitical realms to level the playing field and increase equality of access for all. Women, racial minorities, people with disabilities, people whose sexual/gender identities aren't those of mainstream society, have each had their trials and triumphs toward greater equality. But still lingering to a great degree is the commonly held assumption that the knowledge derived from Western society's tradition is the only knowledge that should be taken seriously or given due consideration. While some knowledge has been given a stamp of approval after scrutiny via the scientific method, the fact remains that without the "nod" of Western society's knowledge-generating machine, Indigenous cultures' ways of knowing don't stand a chance of being considered valid. During my sojourn into archaeological inquiry, I have met some very enlightened people, but also have encountered many who for various reasons have chosen not to participate in the decolonization of our discipline. Questioning and challenging the status quo is a daunting if not dangerous task from the standpoint of anyone who wants to maintain a position in a given career track. But the time is at hand for growth of both representation of Indigenous scholars in archaeology, as well as increased representation of Indigenous ideological realities.

When I learned of the Stewart Indian School Historic Archaeology Collaborative Field School, I thought about the irony of it all. Here we are to be in a place where our Native children were brought to be assimilated from their way of being into another culture's reality. Our efforts in this same space were to broaden the opportunities for acceptance of numerous different ways of seeing the world into a process and reality that could be accepted by multiple worldviews.

Another issue that seems to hinder the decolonization of archaeology is the desire, albeit sometimes unconscious, to maintain the status quo. Or perhaps in some instances, the problem is that researchers are not open to considering changing well-established ways of doing things because it would be outside their comfort zone.

In at least two instances during the Stewart Indian School Collaborative Historic Field School, the status quo was examined, and the methods modified to meet the challenge. The first instance concerned whether the lithic materials that were excavated during the field school exercises could be reburied, and if so, what manner (if any) of demarcation the items should have when placed back in the excavated units. The second instance occurred during documentation of lithics prior to reburial, and the question of the appropriateness of photographing the cultural items was raised.

As professional archaeologists, we have been taught to meticulously excavate while taking copious notes so that the one chance of capturing all that we can from the archaeological record is not wasted. We do this because archaeology is destructive in nature. Once the soil is moved by our trowels and shovels the ability to effectively apply Western science to the study of the past in that space is gone forever. We also document everything because as we are told, yet in my experiences rarely happens, someone else may come along to study the curated artifacts to either test our results, or to ask new questions of the artifact assemblage.

The question of *whether* excavated artifacts should be curated in a repository is not frequently asked. In fact, when I have spoken about this issue with other people in my discipline they are usually taken aback by the mention of artifact reburial. The exceptions to this status quo being the reburial of human remains, associated funerary items, unassociated funerary items, and artifacts excavated from private property. In instances of excavated materials from private property, the owner of the property simply has to request that the property be returned at the conclusion of the archaeological research, and in such instances, the final disposition of the excavated items is uncertain. In cases of human remains and funerary items, archaeologists are infrequently involved in the reburials but understand that reburial is increasing in frequency as tribal peoples move to reclaim their ancestors.

In my work I have sought the advice and direction of tribal elders and traditional people in the Northern Great Basin to reduce my own spiritual liability, but to also advocate for a more culturally inclusive way of practicing archaeology. Of my many inquiries I can assertively affirm that there is overwhelming agreement within our Great Basin cultures that artifacts are to be left where they were found, and if for some reason, the artifacts are taken for further analysis to another location, the appropriate measure upon completion of study is to return the artifacts to their home. The reasoning behind this position is that each item left on the landscape by our ancestors has *Puha*. The item has its own *Puha*, but also the *Puha* left on it of the person who it originally belonged to, and that *Puha* can be harmful if it is brought to another place or rubs off on an unsuspecting person. Additionally, the *Puha* and the individual artifact are part of a community of items and essences that have been incorporated into the environment of a place, and they "live" there and have a role in the landscape community. To remove items is to change the landscape and the cultural item community that was created by our ancestors. Finally, although many archaeologists believe they are "protecting" artifacts by digging them up and taking them to a repository, traditional Northern Paiute people believe the act of taking items from our ancestors' important places to be a socially and legally acceptable form of looting, which will eventually lead to the total annihilation of the physical record of our people in our lands, as well as a disruption of the symbiosis of our important landscapes. Some tribal governments, including my community, have allowed limited destructive analysis of lithic materials for the purposes of sourcing materials and performing relative dating testing, but the goal is always to have the "body" of the lithic materials remain.

Having said that, it has rarely been an option of consideration that artifacts be reburied at the conclusion of an excavation, but the Stewart Field School Plan listened to the tribes' concerns and assertions, and through footwork and discussion, Dr. Cowie was able to find a mutually acceptable path forward, and the lithic materials recovered during the excavation process were reburied at the conclusion of the field school. Another opportunity for consideration of the status quo arrived when it was time to prepare the units for the reburial of the lithics. One of the tribal students vocalized his opposition to the placement of geotextile fabric in the units and challenged the necessity of it. This was an "aha" moment for me and I believe for many of the others who participated in the conversation that day. Unlike the hustle and bustle of many excavations focused specifically on excavation of cubic meters of soil, we were able to stop, stand back, and evaluate the issue when a concern was raised about our practices. We together, as a group, assessed the pros and cons of the geotextile, and as a group decided it was unnecessary. One person said (paraphrasing) that if there was a question in the future, any archaeologist worth their weight should be able to easily identify the previously excavated unit via the soil matrix versus the intact subsurface component surrounding it.

Another "aha" moment for me personally came about when I was given the task of documenting the lithic materials prior to reburial. I was asked to measure and photograph each item, something I have done hundreds of times before in my day-to-day work in the field and lab. One of the field school participants came up to me as I was preparing to photograph the artifacts that would eventually be reburied. He asked if it was necessary to photograph the artifacts and were there other potential ways to effectively document the items without photography. The question hit me like a brick! I asked myself, "well, is photography necessary?" While photographing some types of features is inappropriate from my worldview, the question of the appropriateness of photographing lithics had never crossed my mind. My own tribe had never discussed it as a problem and in fact often requests it for documentation. Just then, Dr. Cowie came to the workstation and asked if we needed help. We relayed the question and discussed how we could still document the items affectively without using photography. At the conclusion of our discussion, it was determined by consensus of those participating in the discussion that flakes would be photographed, and the formed tools would be drawn and measured.

Many of the issues of concern about appropriate treatment of an important cultural landscape that arose during the Stewart Indian School Historic Collaborative Archaeological Field School were not unusual. What I found so remarkable about the experiences of this field school was that an atmosphere of trust and mutual respect was enjoyed, and because of it we were able to have open conversations about issues that under different circumstances could have created an atmosphere of mistrust and discontent. Through those conversations we are able to find consensus in how we would move forward together, instead of majority vote deciding how we would proceed, or the Principle Investigator making executive decisions without group consensus.

One of the problems I have seen play out over and over again is the idea among some researchers that the tribes who are willing to work along with the established methods of archaeological practice are enlightened or cooperative, and those who aren't are backwards or agitators. Since the beginning of Indigenous-non-Indigenous interactions, a dichotomy has been in play that portrays those Natives who are more accommodating to Western Society's values and practices as "good," and labels those who have cultural systems far different from Western society as "bad." This undercurrent is felt to this day in many areas, but is often very apparent in archaeological circles. The tribes who are able to meet the expectations and needs of the researcher because the research does not severely clash with that particular tribe's ideological needs are considered more congenial, while tribes who because of their own ideological assertions are often pitted against the interests of archaeological research endeavors, are labeled as backwards, ignorant, or obstinate. I once had a supervisor who momentarily forgot I was Native American, and proceeded to talk about those "damn Indians" that wouldn't agree to destructive analysis of ancestral human remains. Such value judgments are hurtful and unproductive. It has always struck me as being anti-anthropological to assign value judgments to other cultures based on the researcher's ability to have free reign with the material cultural remains (including ancestral human remains) of those cultures. I believe it is residual institutionalized colonialism that is transferred intergenerationally from professors to students in our discipline that perpetuates such attitudes. It is my hope we can begin to consciously recognize when the "Good Indian–Bad Indian" scenario rears its ugly head, so that we may work to extinguish it.

As anthropologists, we archaeologists need to think more holistically. Even though archaeologists often create and perpetuate the existence of "cultures" based solely on the archaeological record, we need to consider that some if not all of our hypotheses may be very inaccurate. The very limited material record that we attempt to understand is only an infinitesimal fraction of the entire story. Perhaps we should humble ourselves, and quiet our minds and imaginations long enough to listen to and cooperate with those who inarguably have a closer link to the material culture and the landscape upon which we impose our ideas and practices.

This was the primary difference I experienced repeatedly during the Stewart Indian School Historic Collaborative Field School that has never been present to the same degree within other archaeological projects in which I have participated. Learning to listen, attempting to understand, and accepting at face value the assertions of "the other" has the potential of broadening our understanding of the past far more so than disregarding or misinterpreting the knowledge Indigenous cultures hold. Including everyone's voices and considering all voices as valid can only lead to greater cross-cultural understanding and improve our understanding of the past.

Essay 15. Lonnie P. Teeman, Sr.

Enrolled member of the Burns Paiute Tribe and Lead Tribal Archaeological Technician in the Culture & Heritage Department of the Burns Paiute Tribe

I have worked off and on as an archaeological technician since I was in high school. My other work experiences include welding, wildland firefighting, and construction labor. I am a member of the Burns Paiute Tribe in Oregon. I currently work for my tribe as a tribal archaeological technician. I enjoy doing this kind of work and I've had mostly good experiences while working in archaeology. I've also had some not-so-great experiences, but the good has outweighed the bad.

Doing archaeological technician work allows me to work outdoors and I also enjoy being able to see the things my ancestors left behind on the countryside. Some of my best experiences include: finding things during pedestrian survey and helping teach the other people on the crews how to survey in our area. I also like to travel to other places to work, and experience those places. I like meeting people from other areas and learning from their experiences. I have worked with quite a few other tribal members over the years but none of the archaeologists in charge of the work have been tribal people except for when I worked for my wife. I like when my lack of a college degree in archaeology isn't held against me. I always try to learn and do the very best job I can when I am given responsibility, but when I am treated like I don't know anything, it is disrespectful to me and also Native Americans. One of my recent negative experiences involved my supervisor belittling me by telling me out of nowhere that "she is above me" and what I do on the job means nothing. The funny thing is that she is so inexperienced and unorganized that she didn't even bring a map with us of the place we were supposed to survey, and then she failed to take pictures and had to drive back (a ten-hour round trip), just to get pictures of the area we surveyed. I guess what bothers me is that having a degree seems to hold so much weight, but I would trust someone with field experience over someone with a degree any day. I think it's best to have both schooling and experience.

I like working with people who respect the tribal people of the place where they are doing archaeology, and I like having the ability to practice my beliefs without having to hide them. I also like being able to practice my beliefs without having to worry that someone is working to interview me and record my ways without me knowing it. I think most, but not all of the people I have worked with the last five years or so, have been respectful of tribal ways, even if they didn't understand them. Sometimes it gets tiresome having to be the person to explain tribal practices, but with more Natives working in this field it is getting easier. Plus, I think someone has to be the voice for our Ancestors, and if I need to help them I don't mind. One thing that is sad to me is when cultural items are removed to be locked away from their origin. Before, a lot of the tribal people said archaeology was nothing and called the people involved in it bone diggers and other names. Now, it seems like some people support the tribes getting involved in archaeology projects to help protect our cultures.

I came to the Stewart Field School to get more college credit for archaeological field school and learn more about historic archaeology, the school, and Carson City, Nevada. I heard it was a collaborative project between the tribes and the archaeologists and I wanted to see how things worked out. So far, I am enjoying my time and learning a lot. It will be good to get back to work though. My tribe has told me they are proud I am working to continue my education and that my job will be waiting for me when I get back. So I am thankful for this opportunity. I wish they could help with living expenses, but maybe in the future they can help people when they go to field school. I hope there will be many more collaborative projects like this for tribal people to get involved with archaeology. It's hard to take the time away from making a living, but it is worth it and I hope others will see it that way eventually.

Works Cited

Cowie, Sarah E., Christopher C. LeBlanc, Mary M. Farrell, and Nicholas C. Laluk. 2009. "Multivocality in the Forest: A New Approach to Tribal Relations on the Coronado National Forest, Arizona." *Arizona Anthropologist* 19: 1–16.

Friere, Paulo. 1970. *Pedagogy of the Oppressed*. New York: The Seabury Press.

Harjo, Suzan Shown. 2002. "An Approach to New Law to Protect Cultural Property Rights." *Indian Country Today*, January, 20.

McGhee, Robert. 2008. "Aboriginalism and the Problems of Indigenous Archaeology." *American Antiquity* 73, no. 4: 579–97.

Nevers, Jo Ann. 2015. 1976. *Wa She Shu: A Washo Tribal History*. Reno, NV: Inter-Tribal Council of Nevada.

———. 2011. "'Under Watchful Eyes': Washoe Narratives of the Donner Party." In *An Archaeology of Desperation: Exploring the Donner Party's Alder Creek Camp*, edited by Kelly J. Dixon, Shannon A. Novak, and Julie M. Schablitsky. Norman, OK: University of Oklahoma Press, 2011.

———. 2015. "*Da?aw?aga*: At the Edge of the Lake." In *Tahoe: A Visual History*, edited by Ann M. Wolfe. New York: Skira Rizzoli Publications.

Nicholas, George P. 2001. "The Past and Future of Indigenous Archaeology: Global Challenges, North American Perspectives, Australian Prospects." *Australian Archaeology* 52: 29–40.

Riley, Angela R. 2005. "'Straight Stealing:' Towards an Indigenous System of Cultural Property Protection." *Washington Law Review* 80, no. 69: 69–164.

Silliman, Stephen, and T. J. Ferguson. 2010. "Consultations and Collaboration with Descendant Communities." In *Voices in American Archaeology*, edited by Wendy Ashmore, Dorothy Lippert, and Barbara J. Mills, 48–72. Washington, DC: Society for American Archaeology.

Smith, Linda Tuhiwai. 1999. *Decolonizing Methodologies: Research and Indigenous Peoples*. London: Zed Books, Ltd.

CHAPTER 8

Concluding Lessons from Stewart Indian School: Governmentality and Social Capital in Best Practices

Diane L. Teeman, Sarah E. Cowie, Terri McBride,
Ashley M. Long, and Christopher C. LeBlanc

Artifacts from life at Stewart Indian School could be used to construct a misleadingly simple story in which students dutifully wore their uniforms, played with toy trucks and porcelain dolls, went to their academic classes, and worked hard at their vocational duties. In reality, there was much more going on, and the implications of these seemingly innocent artifacts illustrate the lengths taken to assimilate Native children into Euro-American culture.

As an institution of Western culture, the Stewart Indian School's landscape helped to inculcate the students with those values espoused by the administration. The green lawns and blooming flowers veiled the underlying implications of the design, which influenced students by placing certain structures in their constant view (see chapter 6). However, taking a perspective informed by the theoretical concepts from the archaeology of childhood, consider the many other avenues taken by residents of Indian boarding schools. Children were not completely autonomous, but they were not completely dependent or controlled either; there is plenty of evidence to suggest that students acted outside of the strict guidelines imposed on them by the administration and continued to practice their customs, perhaps intentionally away from adults' eyes.

Although the archaeological data provided a glimpse of life at Stewart Indian School, the goal of this project has always been to demonstrate the effectiveness of collaborative archaeology and the benefits it provides to all those involved. It was through collaboration that we were able to explore new alternatives for analyzing artifacts and to positively identify the past location of a historic school building. Collaboration allowed us to create a fruitful and mutually beneficial relationships among Native and non-Native stakeholders, scientists, and the public. And through collaboration we were able to create opportunities that will hopefully result in further preservation and interpretation efforts, as well as the eventual designation of Stewart Indian School as a National Historic Landmark. In other words, the partnerships sustained throughout this project provided for its success in reaching initial research goals and in acquiring invaluable information that may have been impossible to obtain otherwise. Finally, this project can be viewed as one example of the growing necessity for a more collaborative archaeology that pays due respect to both Indigenous rights and Western scientific standards. Efforts to decolonize methods and practice Indigenous archaeology show that doing so is highly productive in terms of performing research, successfully balancing science and ethics, and ultimately humanizing archaeological practice (e.g., Atalay 2006, 2012; Colwell 2016; Smith and Wobst 2005; Smith, L.T. 1999; Watkins 2000).

Consultation

This project originated for the specific purpose of addressing the apparent impasse in communication that occurs regularly around heritage issues on Indigenous ancestral homelands that are now under the legal jurisdiction of public entities. The only way these miscommunications will change is through growing numbers of American Indians working in archaeology and discussing their work in a culturally appropriate way in their tribal communities. This suggests, too, that the field of archaeology itself needs to be more receptive, and non-Native practitioners have a great deal to learn from Native colleagues in order to better advocate for resources at the state and federal levels. Native colleagues have advocated for years for an all-inclusive archaeology, one in which diverse world perspectives are presented, debated, (at times) merged, and applied. The field of archaeology will improve through this pragmatic approach. Multiple viewpoints will make estimations of the past more refined.

Resource management plans are a much better way to gain understanding of the tribal knowledge of areas, since the plans are not project-driven. One downfall of obtaining tribal knowledge of an area prior to an impending construction project is that in reality, tribal consultation and ethnography is very time consuming (Brooks 1997, 214). Resource management plans are medium-range planning documents that are not fit into a construction project. Further, eliciting information from tribal members for resource management planning benefits land management practice as it allows tribal members to choose what they want to share, and to choose which sites they want to visit. In effect, knowledgeable tribal members take the wheel and drive the bus toward a view of their past they want agencies to see. The agency benefits by having a readily available baseline study of traditional sites and areas already documented for projects that require Section 106 consultation (see chapter 1). Indeed, these types of studies are more collaborative than Section 106-driven ones, and agencies should secure funding to develop and update resource management plans.

Although a management plan was not part of this project, it was an example of sincere attempts at collaboration between non-Natives and American Indian students and stakeholders. Everyone had a voice in decisions regarding where to locate excavation units and the final disposition of unearthed artifacts. Once students became familiar with resources at the Stewart Indian School campus, they were encouraged to share opinions on culturally appropriate ways of conducting archaeological data recovery. At the time of publication, this could not have happened on a Section 106 project, limited by project boundaries, project timelines, and project-specific data needs, but perhaps various forms of such collaboration may be attained in Section 106 processes in the future.

American archaeology has become more diverse over the last twenty years and is moving toward a culturally appropriate methodology, especially in the Western United States. More American Indians working in the field and more Tribal Historic Preservation Officers (THPOs) and tribal review and compliance staff are reviewing undertaking notices and compliance reports. These shifts drive more dialogue about archaeology involving various American Indian perspectives.

Archaeological Practice

The theory and methods employed by collaborative archaeology and Indigenous studies are very similar. The two fields share the common goal of incorporating Native voices into research. However, Indigenous researchers take it a step further by ultimately developing a field based on the cultural and epistemological beliefs of Indigenous communities that attempts to decolonize archaeology through critique of the disciplines, ontological and epistemological assumptions.

Collaborative archaeology requires the full involvement of Indigenous communities throughout the entire research process; therefore, standard collaboration methods are diverse and every individual project follows its own unique strategy (see Colwell-Chanthaphonh and Ferguson 2008). There are several common themes found throughout all collaborative work—inclusion, reflexivity, fluidity, and respect. All of these components are apparent in the application of every aspect of research design, but certain areas preclude others in terms of significance. Respect is a meaningful theme in this methodology because it is essential to developing a collaborative relationship. As Nicholas (2008b, 241) puts it, "what lies at the heart of working with Indigenous communities are four essentials: respect, trust, patience, and common sense." The same is true for Indigenous research, where showing respect to ancestors and traditional customs is of upmost importance. Collaborative and Indigenous methodologies emphasize high ethical standards and respectful behavior at every level. They decenter the frame of reference, are reflexive in design, demonstrate a concern for community participation, and remain flexible as to all conditions of the Indigenous community (Nicholas 2008a, 1666).

The contiguous inclusion of Indigenous communities stands as the backbone of collaborative archaeology. Researchers and Indigenous communities work together throughout the project as a unified team, not as two parties working toward separate goals. The process normally begins with the archaeologists approaching members of an Indigenous community and initiating discussion about an interest in participating in archaeological research (Nicholas 2012, 30). This entails the researcher approaching the community about the potential for a research study that is appropriate and potentially beneficial for the people. George Nicholas (2012) describes a similar process from his work on the Intellectual Property Issues in Cultural Heritage (IPinCH) Project that is in collaboration with Indigenous groups in Canada, the United States, Australia, New Zealand, and Kyrgzstan. During this project, individual studies begin with a member of the community identifying important issues and then codeveloping a research design with a IPinCH team member (Nicholas 2012, 30). This first step is very significant in that it demonstrates respect and subsequently sets the stage for a truly collaborative project. If the community accepts the project then the next step is to develop the research design.

Collaborative research designs require the archaeologist to frame research questions around the questions and concerns of the Indigenous community. Rather than enter the process with a thoroughly developed proposal, it is important that the research design is a collection of ideas presented from both the archaeologist and the various stakeholders. For the design to be most effective, it needs to be created with fluidity in mind so that alterations can be made efficiently. Fluidity is important because many collaborative projects will evolve as new topics for discussion arise during fieldwork. As Lightfoot (2008, 216–17) suggests, "rather than viewing the writing of a research design as a finished, binding product, we may want appreciate it as a work in progress that will continue to grow and change as collaboration flourishes and intensifies over time."

The fieldwork will be unique according to the relative project designs, but there are going to be similar aspects practiced across collaborative projects. It is imperative that participants in the project remain reflexive and respectful during fieldwork, especially when conducting excavations and handling artifacts. There is extensive history and scrutiny of the mistreatment of Indigenous material culture and skeletal remains by archaeologists. In the United States, much of this is due to the epistemological discrepancies between many Native American cultures and most archaeologists. Many Indigenous groups view objects as sentient and not necessarily removed from the present. Many Native American cultures traditionally believe that the past is a living part of the present and cannot be separate. Thus, artifacts are seen as incredibly sensitive materials that should be handled with the utmost respect since they are a direct connection to ancestors (Zimmerman 2001, 173). Additionally, in many Native American communities, oral tradition takes precedence over any Euro-American historical or archaeological technique. This sentiment will be expressed continuously in projects that work cooperatively with Indigenous peoples (Nicholas 2008b).

Nicholas (2008a) explains how collaborative projects can have multifactorial scales of investigation that range from landscape analysis to artifact analysis, and from tangible to intangible cultural heritage. Issues may arise concerning typical survey techniques and site sampling methods, but generally, field methods will include standard site survey and excavation procedures. There is often less focus on empirical methods of Western science, with emphasis placed on tribal empiricism rooted in oral traditions, traditional epistemologies, and spiritual phenomenon and practice. Some ethnographic methods may be employed as well, including focus groups and interviews (Nicholas 2008a, 1666).

Indigenous archaeology projects may also require the use of low-impact field methods and may require a specific artifact reburial program after analysis. According to Nicholas (2008a), the practice of ceremonial activities is another widespread occurrence of collaborative field methods. Indigenous and non-Indigenous members of the field crew conduct certain rituals before, during, or immediately after finishing fieldwork. Some instances include smudging of artifacts or the smudging of participants before and after fieldwork to protect them from different spiritual elements (Nicholas 2008a, 1667). The practice of ceremonial rituals during fieldwork is typically not seen in standard archaeological projects and is seen as a unique function of collaborative archaeology.

Just as the research design development and fieldwork, artifact analysis is conducted in collaboration with stakeholders. Similar to the limits that may be placed on artifact collection, some boundaries may be placed on the level of analysis allowed on particular materials. Some examination methods, such as isotopic analysis or radiocarbon dating, are destructive and may not be acceptable under the terms of a collaborative research design. What is acceptable varies from project to project, but usually involves analysis that does little to alter the artifact's original state (Nicholas 2008b).

This methodology highlights the importance for the continued inclusion of the stakeholders alongside the archaeologists during all aspects of the project to promote reflexivity and respect during the final stages of research, including the writing process. According to Watkins (2006), many Indigenous communities have argued that words carry an implicit judgment with them. Archaeologists, through word choice, have the responsibility of accurately representing the reality of the past with respect to the beliefs of various stakeholders, especially Indigenous groups. Therefore, researchers must be hyper-aware of the underlying meanings behind their words and how various cultures may interpret them differently (Watkins 2006, 105). Collaborative methods remove this bias because Indigenous communities are involved throughout the writing process, making it easier to avoid inappropriate language that may negatively affect the relationship.

Even though the field of collaborative archaeology has grown exponentially over the past few decades with hundreds of archaeologists actively changing their methods, there is still a necessity for more significant cooperation between archaeologists and Indigenous communities. This is largely due to issues of control and ownership of the past—many archaeologists still cringe at the idea of losing control over research design (Nicholas 2008a). It is therefore important for researchers who practice collaborative archaeology to publish materials that explain how the process "may lead to greater enrichment and sharing both in terms of what and how we know about the past and . . . of dealing with it in the present" (Nicholas 2008a, 1668).

Research Ethics

Philosophical ethics discusses what *ought to be* in the abstract, whereas applied ethics is the process of adhering to a guiding set of ethical principles while performing academic research. Of all the academic disciplines, ethical standards are perhaps the most developed within those disciplines that require a great degree of interaction with nonacademics. In the twentieth century, the developing ethical standards for research focused primarily on medical research, especially the disparities in the treatment of research subjects based on class and race (e.g., the Tuskegee syphilis experiment). The most critical turning point in academic research ethics came with the Vermillion Accord. The following discussion by Swazey and Bird (1997, 1) of the importance of ethics training in academia among the natural and physical sciences and engineering is easily applicable to all academic disciplines:

> There are many differences, as well as similarities, within and between the cultures and conventions of the disciplines and subdisciplines in science and engineering that affect the content of what is being taught, as well as how and by whom it may be taught most effectively. Further, although we are dealing with research ethics only in the context of higher education in the United States, even here there is a great amount of socio-cultural diversity among the students and postdoctoral fellows, faculty, administrators, and others involved in many fields of academic research.

It is important to be aware of this diversity, and not to assume that everyone approaches the subject from a common social and cultural framework. People from different societies and cultural traditions have a range of attitudes, beliefs, and values that affect how they define ethically "acceptable" standards and practices, what they define as "ethical" issues, and how they perceive and respond to those issues.

One of the most common misconceptions within academia is that, because Western science is employed to conduct research in the physical and social sciences, that not only is the process objective, but that all researchers employing the scientific method are in agreement of the accuracy of those methods as a tool for acquiring knowledge. It has not been until the diversification of the student population within academia that the question of the role of personal subjectivity in all aspects of the scientific research process has been approached. There are at least two considerations that need to come into question when asking what role ethics plays in academic research: (1) what ethical considerations have been discussed in the development of a research project as it relates to academic concerns, and (2) what ethical considerations are to be employed when academics conduct research in nonacademic settings such as those directly and/or indirectly involving Indigenous communities.

While questions related to how academics devise their research to consider the potential effects of their research conclusions is still in its infancy, there has been increased development in the degree to which researchers seek out interaction with communities to make sure the research methodologies are in keeping with sometimes diverse cross-cultural ethical considerations.

Ethics in Archaeology

Cultural anthropologists and biological anthropologists working with living subjects have long discussed ethical practices when working with research populations. However, it has only been within the last couple of decades that Indigenous communities have been given much consideration with regard to how archaeological research affects those communities.

In cases where the academic researcher is performing research that has not traditionally required the direct engagement of nonacademics, there are few specific requirements the researcher must complete in order to complete that research. The findings of such research are publishable, and the potential impacts of such research on nonacademics are rarely a consideration. Currently, archaeologists associated with research universities are rarely required to complete any review of their research proposal by their university's human subjects' compliance review board as archaeological research by definition has been deemed to deal with "past cultures." Of course, there is a recognition that archaeology can and does affect Indigenous communities, but the academic research protocols currently employed by many research universities have yet to catch up to this realization. To change this protocol, archaeological efforts at such research universities will need to "self-identify" the potential impacts of their work to their respective human subjects compliance review boards. The Harvard Project on American Indian Economic Development, State of Native Nations (2008, 291) commented on the changing relationship between Western scientific researchers and Native tribes in the following:

> Indigenous cultures are rich knowledge systems that reflect vast generational experience with the land, animals, plants, natural processes, healing, and history. For years, these knowledge systems were effectively dismissed by non-Indian institutions. Native peoples valued them, but non-Natives generally did not.

> That is starting to change. Some of that change is encouraging to Native peoples, some is more than a little troubling to them, and the process overall involves difficult intellectual property issues for everyone concerned.
>
> On the positive side, historians, archaeologists, and paleontologists (among others) are paying closer attention to Indigenous knowledge and Native oral histories. The "combined approach" that melds oral history and mythology with physical science and fieldwork can provide all scientists working in these fields with deeper insights into research methodologies and perspectives.

The combined approach they allude to in this passage for archaeology concerns a variety of new approaches to inclusion of Indigenous communities in various facets of archaeological research. Such approaches are given different names such as: community archaeology, Indigenous archaeology, and collaborative archaeology.

While community and collaborative archaeological approaches have been applied to work conducted between archaeologists and both Indigenous and non-Indigenous communities, Indigenous archaeologies focus specifically upon both the methods and methodologies of archaeology with the specific goal of inclusion of Indigenous perspectives. Each of these approaches are beneficial in varying degrees to the needs of Indigenous communities as they each increase the degree of inclusivity of nonarchaeologists in the research process.

Archaeology and Indigenous Communities

Archaeology is by definition the study of past cultures. It has often been viewed by its practitioners as a separate and distinct approach to knowing humanity from other sub-disciplines of anthropology that deal firsthand with living peoples. The realization that Indigenous communities whose heritage is intertwined with the material record Westerners call the "archaeological record" first became a widespread sociopolitical issue in the 1960s, when Indigenous people began having a greater voice.

Issues of land and cultural landscapes are central to many traditional Native American/First Nations. Often, the existence of a particular culture is strongly intertwined with the landscape, as are moral codes, subsistence, and spirituality. These aspects of culture are difficult if not impossible for archaeologists to identify and gain nuanced knowledge of without firsthand interaction with members of Indigenous communities.

The ethical treatment of Indigenous cultural remains is also sometimes a difficult topic to reach agreement upon between Indigenous communities, archaeologists, and museum/repository curators. For instance, some items may need to be nourished or fed while located within a repository. Bringing food into a curatorial facility to remain with artifacts is often frowned upon by museum staff. How to determine how the ethics of museum management can mesh with Indigenous ethical concerns is something that will continue to need to be worked out.

Inclusion of Indigenous Peoples' Voices

In the United States, federal cultural resource law has developed primarily in consideration of Western archaeological interests. Likewise, the traditional methods and methodology of archaeology have developed from the epistemological assertions of the dominant culture. Cultural resource management (CRM) laws, such as the National Historic Preservation Act (NHPA), require consultation with Native Americans. Such "consultation" however does not require the concurrence of the affected tribe(s) (King 1998, 155). Because of this, some tribal cultural resource personnel (Dongoske and Anyon 1997; Howard 2002), and archaeologists (Tsosie 1997; Brooks 1997) have voiced dissatisfaction with the current CRM process in the United States.

One reason for some Indigenous people's resistance to archaeology has been that archaeological research does not effectively engage the epistemological systems of "the other" beyond perhaps making ethnographic note that non-Western cultures have differing worldviews. Archaeologists who assert that archaeology can help Native Americans learn about their own culture only tend to exacerbate animosity. While some tribes find archaeology to serve as a sociopolitical tool, others find such ideas of archaeology as holding the key to tribal history to be presumptuous. Some scholars have argued that anthropology/archaeology only tells a Western narrative of "the Indian" (Youngblood 2000, 65; Battiste and Henderson 2000, 32). Many of the Indigenous peoples who have entered the field of archaeology have primarily done so, not because of what they believe archaeology can do for their people, but because of what it *has done* to them.

Inclusion of Indigenous Peoples' Epistemologies

Akin to the lack of Indigenous peoples working in archaeology and the scarcity of Indigenous voices currently represented in archaeological method and theory is the silencing of Indigenous peoples' epistemologies in archaeology. Indigenous people's ways of knowing the world have historically been discounted. Indigenous scholars face daily assaults on their epistemological beliefs by the institutionalized social Darwinism still at work within archaeological texts, curriculum, and theory. Indigenous cultural narratives are treated by many as fiction and our cultural practices are sorted into categories with value-laden terms such as: simple, primitive, and uncivilized. Although social Darwinism was invalidated by anthropologists long ago, Western ethnocentrism still permeates the nomenclature of our discipline. The uninitiated continue to assume that today's Western society is the most "advanced" culture that has ever existed, when in fact, "advancement" is a relative term.

The scarcity of inclusion of Indigenous epistemologies in mainstream archaeological theory impedes earnest efforts toward cross-cultural reconciliation. Linda Tuhiwai Smith (1999, 33) discusses the domination of Indigenous worldviews by Western theory in the following passage:

> Indigenous people have been, in many ways, oppressed by theory. Any consideration of the ways our origins have been examined, our histories recounted, our arts analyzed, our cultures dissected, measured, torn apart, and distorted back to us will suggest that theories have not looked sympathetically or ethically at us.

Western archaeological theory has served, in at least some cases, to distort Indigenous histories until they become foreign to the very people they subject. The accepted narratives of Indigenous peoples have become the majority culture's narrative of Indigenous people's histories. Deloria (1969) asks why Indians should continue to allow themselves to be the private zoos of anthropologists? Given archaeology's poor historic relationship with Indigenous peoples, it is no wonder that many Indigenous peoples are repulsed by the thought of actually studying and practicing within the discipline.

Most archaeologists appear to prize the Western scientific epistemological system over all others. But can we really say that one culture has a more "valid" epistemological system? If you are an absolutist, you might try. But history tells us that the dominant epistemological system accepted and/or imposed upon a given population at any given time usually belongs to the culture with the greatest sociopolitical control at that particular moment (Henderson 2000, 65). We are moving beyond the era of following with blind faith the ontological and epistemological assertions of Western science. Within the critique of Western science, why not also consider that Indigenous communities, with their various ontological, epistemological, and ethical standards, might have something substantive to contribute to the discussion.

Ethics and the Future of Archaeology

As mentioned earlier, an apparent and major problem in attempting to come to an answer for how ethics in archaeology can be inclusive of Indigenous peoples' perspectives and concerns is that there is no overarching set of ethical ideals for archaeologists that concerns the effects of archaeology upon Indigenous communities. While the lack of such overarching ideals is problematic for the interests of some Indigenous communities, there is no reason why individual archaeologists can't work toward making Indigenous community focused ethics a part of their research methodologies. The ethical statement of the World Archaeological Congress (WAC) approaches an ethical stance, which focuses on Indigenous community equally to the archaeological record. Bringing about change within the other state, regional, national, and international archaeological organizations will take continued and persistent efforts by Indigenous scholars, Indigenous communities, and archaeologists who support those communities.

Change in the form of inclusion of Indigenous voice in archaeology is happening. The inclusion of Indigenous peoples in archaeological research once primarily meant that archaeologists hired laborers from Indigenous communities to assist in the menial labor aspects of archaeological field research. But through greater collaborative efforts Indigenous people are participating in ever more meaningful ways in research efforts.

Present and Future Ethical Considerations in CRM and Tribal CRM

Current CRM practices are guided by the federal and state legislation which delineates the appropriate protocols for conducting various types of assessments of the existence of places and things of cultural importance.

Many Indigenous tribal communities are either establishing THPOs or creating departments within their tribal administration specialized in practicing both "Indigecentric" CRM and heritage protection and management.

At the time of this writing, and for some time, innovators in collaborative and/or community archaeological research have been leading the way toward more cross-culturally inclusive forms of research. The word "collaboration" is becoming more and more popular in academic archaeological circles as a positive aspect of doing ethically sound archaeological research. Many believe they have a common understanding of what collaborative efforts entail. While those who have successfully participated in one or more collaborative archaeological projects understand how collaboration worked in those particular instances, collaboration is always a unique experience. So, what *is* collaborative archaeology? Collaborative archaeology is akin to community archaeology in many aspects, while it differs in others.

According to Marshall (2002, 211), *community* archaeology's greatest contribution to broadening perspectives within archaeology, involves "relinquishing of at least partial control of a project to the local community." Furthermore, Moser et al. (2002) propose a seven-step criteria of a successful community archaeology program which includes: communication and collaboration, employment and training, public presentation, interviews and oral history, educational resources, photographic and video archiving, and community-controlled merchandising. While collaborative archaeology may potentially incorporate any to all of Moser et al.'s seven-step criteria, the primary component collaborative archaeology shares with community archaeology is a partial relinquishment of control. Relinquishment of partial control is necessary to allow community members and/or community representatives to participate in the research as colleagues. While relinquishment of partial control may seem an intimidating proposition for some researchers, the benefits, some of which we discuss, far outweigh any potential risks.

Like community archaeology, collaborative archaeology involves bringing communities affected by archaeological research into the project as full partners in all aspects of the archaeological research project. Collaborative archaeology, however, as it concerns Indigenous communities, varies from standard community archaeology pursuits, because Indigenous communities frequently hold differing sociopolitical and epistemological concerns for cultural locations; which is less frequently the case in community archaeology projects.

Archaeological pursuits have been occurring without collaboration with Indigenous communities for many decades; those who have not yet participated in a collaborative project might ask, why change now? Those archaeologists who have either experienced successful collaboration with Indigenous communities, or support such efforts, have a multitude of responses to this question.

Archaeological research has and will always affect the sociopolitics of Indigenous peoples; their voices should be in concert with archaeological researchers as a means of making the research more holistic and more scientifically robust. Furthermore, working together as colleagues creates relationships between archaeologists and Indigenous peoples that assists in building empathy and understanding for one another.

Those intrepid and innovative researchers who have ventured beyond the norms of archaeological practice to work toward collaboration have done so for a variety of reasons, but their work has served to blaze a trail for what is the inevitable future of archaeology. Of this Ferguson (1996, 63) states:

> Archaeologists are in the midst of restructuring their relationship with Native Americans. . . . Much of the impetus for this change resulted from the criticism of archaeology by Native

> Americans, which led to passage of the Native American Graves Protection and Repatriation Act of 1990 (NAGPRA). NAGPRA has indelibly changed how archaeologists will work in the United States. The issues raised by Native Americans about why and how archaeological research is conducted, however, go beyond NAGPRA to the paradigmatic basis of archaeology. Archaeologists will have new opportunities available to them if they work in partnership with Native Americans in studying the rich archaeological record in the Americas.

Although Ferguson doesn't use the term "collaboration," the work he discusses is collaborative, as archaeologists strike "partnerships" with Indigenous communities in research that affects those communities and/or their traditional lands (1996, 64).

Collaborative archaeology brings Indigenous communities into various projects as fully involved researchers, instead of their previous role as *the researched.* Furthermore, as some archaeologists have pointed out, working with Indigenous communities makes archaeological research more accessible to the public, which is a goal we think we all share.

From various conversations we have had with archaeologists, we have identified two primary perceived risks hindering some from engaging in collaborative archaeological efforts. The first perceived risk for some researchers is the danger that other archaeologists might think you have "gone Native" because you collaborate with Indigenous communities. As more archaeologists "come around" and new archaeologists enter the discipline willing to work collaboratively with Indigenous communities, this perceived risk of ridicule will diminish. This is evidenced by the fact that other innovative changes that initially met with ridicule have eventually gained broad acceptance.

Furthermore, some who currently reject collaborative efforts might argue that collaborative research is not "objective" or "scientific" because of the relationship collaboration between Indigenous communities and archaeologists entails. This perception, however, is a logical falsehood, as "objectivity" as it was first introduced by analytic philosophers and later adopted by other disciplines is an unattainable goal under any conditions. Great efforts should be made to identify biases of all kinds including those of the archaeologists, prior to the initiation of any research activity. Collaborating with Indigenous communities as "colleagues" simply requires the identification of any additional biases potentially affecting the research project. Both of the perceived risks aforementioned are created and perpetuated by peer opinion. Further works in collaboration between archaeologists and Indigenous communities will ultimately quell those concerns.

The risk of collaborative efforts failing is a real possibility. At least in some cases, this occurs because participants' initial conceptions of what should be happening as a part of collaboration don't materialize. Such failures oftentimes are the result of misunderstandings among collaborators of what is needed for a successful collaborative project. Greater "front end" communication, along with frequent "checking in" between all colleagues, can and will reduce and/or alleviate this risk. The benefits or gains collaborative research brings not only to the individual archaeologist performing the research, but the archaeological community as a whole, far outweigh the risks.

Where We've Been, Where We're Going

Even though some archaeologists have been actively collaborating with Indigenous communities for some time, collaborative works are still far from the norm. While many of those engaging in collaborative projects agree that Indigenous communities involved in the project must be full partners in the research, there is no model that will work for every research project. Each Indigenous community is as unique as the particular archaeological research proposed, and the particulars of successful collaboration for a project will only be identified through the actual process of collaborating throughout the project from beginning to fruition. Because of this, the most reasonable way to study or to find potential models of successful collaboration is to see what has worked in the past for others, and adopt and/or amend those past strategies to fit the particular community and project, but also to be ready to invent or initiate new strategies. Collaboration really needs to begin with the collaborative model being created by the community and the researcher so that it is comprehensive and represents the interests and needs of all colleagues within the project.

Open communication prior to research design, along with a mindset that community and/or community representatives are peers and full colleagues, is integral to successful collaboration. Collaborative partnerships between Indigenous communities and archaeologists are the key to improving working relationships between these groups. A comprehensive discussion of what has been accomplished thus far by archaeologists and Indigenous communities is needed; both to assess how far we have come, and to determine where we need to go to further such efforts. Incorporation of discussion of collaboration with Indigenous communities in archaeological field methods classes is needed, as well as within archaeological theory seminars.

Within the current policies, there is only so much that can be done; recent federal instruments have been progressive. The biggest, most immediate opportunity for positive change is in the attitudes of land managers and archaeologists. This is why, on this project, we lost an opportunity to involve administrative Army personnel, who did not make time to participate. We need more involvement from nonheritage specialists. These relationships cannot be improved from behind a desk, and it will take more than just heritage specialists to make this shift. It needs to happen at all levels and among all areas of land management. People need to meet with tribal members face to face, regularly, and maintain those relationships, especially when there is no project immediately on the horizon. Land managers and archaeologists need to respect input from tribal members, meet with them in the places that are federally managed, directly at sites that are important so memories and wisdom can be drawn from those landscapes. They need to ask for input at all stages of projects, before and during decision making. Land managers and archaeologists need to see and personally experience the fact that Native peoples care deeply about heritage in their ancestral homelands.

It is our hope that this project offers some strategies for humanizing the process of respectful consultation between tribes and the federal government, and that archaeologists can contribute to that process. There are a number of decision-making situations and protocols that could benefit by the implementation of this federal/tribal consultation model, including most fundamentally:

- More fully meeting federal trust responsibility obligations
- Demonstrating the pride, responsibility, and honor associated with the profound duty of caring for and conserving heritage resources on lands currently managed by the federal government (see Franklin 2011, 7)
- Redefining what constitutes effective consultation through open dialog with tribes and reference to tribal heritage documents (e.g., NATHPO 2005, White Mountain Apache Tribe 2004)
- Expediting federal undertakings, mitigating fewer heritage-related lawsuits, and generating better public relations
- Building a network of relationships and generating social capital for all parties.
- Considering revisions or additions to current federal heritage legislation to more adequately address tribal sovereignty.
- Respectful communication and collaboration with tribes is aligned with the federal trust responsibility, provided the discourses are such that meaningful communication is possible. It may not be possible to avoid conflict altogether, but disagreements can be learning opportunities in long-term relationships, if federal employees, archaeologists, and representatives and tribal members continue to communicate, especially when they are not required to do so.

Conclusion: Governmentality, Social Capital, and Humanizing Research

Archaeologists and land managers doing daily work with heritage resources are usually so busy and underfunded that it seems impossible to envision large-scale restructures of our heritage system. The concept of governmentality begins to illuminate the complex technologies of power in place within a system that has tremendous momentum, driven by legislation, academic training, and policies created decades ago and without much input from Indigenous peoples. Governmentality has only recently been applied to critiques of CRM and heritage legislation in the United States (e.g., NAGPRA), but the beginnings of such research show the potential for using this concept to deconstruct conflicting discourses around heritage (Palus et al. 2006; Smith, L. 2000, 2001, 2004; Smith and Campbell 1998).

Many heritage specialists, Native and non-Native alike, are dissatisfied with current practices and their ability to affect positive change. Perhaps Stewart Indian School reminds us of the big changes we would like to see, inspires us to make extra efforts, and reminds us why we care. How we address the past does affect present relationships among people, things, and landscapes, and we must remember this in the context of colonial and (post)colonialist processes.

Like other, similar schools in the United States, Stewart Indian School was mandated by the Bureau of Indian Affairs (BIA) and established through federal policies designed to force assimilation (see chapters 2, 4, and 5). Some biopolitical goals were made visible in the early years, in forcing boys to cut their hair short and subjecting children to Western health and hygiene procedures; archaeological evidence for this elaborates the documentary and oral histories. Also in this early period, children were required to march in lines and wear military uniforms; this bodily discipline is further evidenced in embossed Army buttons excavated at Stewart. Other biopolitical goals were less visible. Stewart, like many of these schools, was designed to teach children skilled trades, training their bodies and minds to make them into productive members of the American workforce. The federal government recognized some of the implications of removing children from their homelands. Their removal was not just a physical one, but also a process that removed them from their tribes' political economies and placed them into the American capitalist economy, teaching them to be both producers and consumers. For example, many graduates from Stewart recall earning small amounts of money and then buying treats at the school store. Furthermore, the removal of children from their homelands had widespread repercussions that created disconnects between the landscape and the cultural and spiritual knowledge embedded within specific places, a process famously articulated in Keith Basso's *Wisdom Sits in Places*. Losing access to their homelands made it harder to access cultural memories and prescriptive, ethical stories from the ancestors that give guidance to future generations.

The removal of children from their traditional homelands to this school has been addressed throughout this volume, and has traumatic repercussions for communities that have been felt for generations. As mentioned in chapter 1, the use of archaeology in addressing and perhaps even helping to heal trauma is an area of future research. At this point we are better positioned to discuss the implications of removing artifacts from archaeological sites, and the fundamental miscommunication that often occurs around this issue.

On this collaborative archaeology project, we developed the research design with input from our research partners and other tribal members who participated in various ways, as students, staff, and interested public. From the beginning, the Washoe THPO stated that they would generally rather see artifacts left in place, but agreed that because the artifacts were technically state property and could be used for future site interpretation, UNR archaeologists could collect most of them to analyze in the laboratory and curate in perpetuity. This is part of standard data collection procedures in archaeology. However, the Washoe THPO requested that we not keep the lithic artifacts or flaked glass, and that we instead do minimal field recording of these items and rebury them in the TUs at the end of the project (see Darrel Cruz essay, chapter 7). There was some discussion of alternatives among tribal members; some suggested that we might learn more from additional research into lithic sourcing. However, after further discussion, consensus emerged indicating that it would be best to leave certain items, especially ancient ones, at the site as a way of maintaining their connection to the land. A second round of discussions took place with the Nevada State Historic Preservation Office (SHPO), State Lands Office, and Nevada State Museum to make sure we were within the legal and ethical parameters of archeological practice; the SHPO indicated that this practice was increasingly common in the Western United States and approved the plan (Rebecca Palmer and Ron James, personal communication).

This shift in practice has important implications. On the one hand, archaeologists have long advocated for the indefinite curation of artifacts removed from archaeological sites, citing the need to curate data that future scientists can revisit. The expense of permanent curation that has driven some archaeologists to catch-and-release or no-collections methods (where all artifacts are analyzed in the field and returned to the site immediately) has been critiqued by some archaeologists (e.g., Heilen and Altschul 2013; see chapter 3). Numerous legal instruments outline the rationale and procedures for preserving sites for future research and collecting data from sites that are impacted by various activities. For example, the 1966 NHPA requires agencies to protect sites and "encourage owners who are undertaking archaeological excavations to . . . allow access to artifacts for research purposes" (NHPA 1966). Clearly, in this instrument and others, the government requires agencies and the archaeologists who work for them to make artifacts available for future research. But the law is subject to interpretation. Do artifacts need to be in a museum to be available? Or could archaeologists re-excavate them if left at the site? It is written to protect heritage resources, but from whom and from what threats? Might it be more important to protect people than resources? And who wrote this legislation in the first place? Authoring of governmentalized discourse produces knowledge about what is legal and ethical (see chapter 2). Comparatively few Native scholars were part of this knowledge production in the mid-1960s. If more had been, it might have reflected very different values and ethics that emphasized tribal sovereignty regarding objects of cultural patrimony.

In contrast to how the federal legislation was written, one of our research partners, the Washoe THPO (Darrel Cruz essay, chapter 7), explained the importance of leaving certain artifacts in place:

> If all the artifacts are removed from the landscape, then we have nothing to show that we were ever there. That is why it is so important to leave archaeological materials, lithics etc; in place. It is our story and we want to maintain that connection to the landscape. Nobody should have the right to erase history by the removal of material evidence.
>
> We strongly advocate that all archaeological materials be left in place and only agree to removal if the archaeological materials are threatened from destruction, theft or some other adverse effect, but that doesn't mean adverse effects are acceptable." (Darrel Cruz, THPO, Washoe Tribe of Nevada and California, personal communication, March 31, 2014.)

His comments reflect knowledge and values that are not present in the governmentalized discourse discussed above. For instance, many American Indian tribes respect power that is tied to specific places and objects, power that should not be casually disrupted (for additional discussion, see Diane L. Teeman essay, chapter 7). As an example, among Numic-speaking tribes, this power is known as *puha* which, according to cultural anthropologist Alex Carroll Ruuska and her colleagues, "pervades all manifestations of the physical world and concentrates in certain people, places, and objects to higher degrees than in others" (Carroll et al. 2004, 129). Intentional disposal of objects on the landscape is sometimes an effort to both "harness" the power of that place and "lend" power to that place (Carroll et al. 2004, 131). Citing work by Jay Miller (1983, 79–80), they further describe *puha* "as a cosmic force that, together with the life force, forms the fabric of the universe; . . . it constantly flows through a web-like structure that connects all things and beings, human or otherwise, that make up the universe" (Carroll et al. 2004, 129). As such, ordinary places become charged with repeated use, prayers, depositing artifacts, storytelling, linguistic inscription, and memory-anchoring (Carroll et al. 2004, 132–33; Basso 1996).

So, in essence, *an archaeological project that disturbs the earth may adhere to federal and state regulations, but still risk disrupting the very fabric of the universe.* A quick story from the Stewart Indian school project illustrates this possibility. On the day we first broke ground on the excavation in 2013, Mark Johnson, the eldest member of our crew who was an archaeological technician and also a tribal member, gave a prayer and led us in smudging with burning sage (see Mark Johnson essay, chapter 7; sadly he passed away in 2018). He explained the seriousness of what we were about to do: disturbing the earth, displacing things from where ancestors had left them, literally "breaking through time" (Mark Johnson, personal communication). The concept he described is similar to Shannon Lee Dawdy's (2010, 762) hope for archaeologists to explore "alternative temporalities" and "new possibilities that come from willfully collapsing archaeological and ethnographic time." It is also similar to discussions of *puha* or life-force, throughout this volume. Mark's opening prayer and our ground disturbance at once converged with this place's dark past, its contested present, and uncertain future. The next day when we arrived at the site, we found the largest owl we have ever seen, and it had died of unknown causes. This owl had been seen on-site regularly, at least since the first day of the field school. Owls are often considered messengers warning people of potential future trouble, often about issues surrounding death. We learned later that day that Mark had a stroke and was recovering in a nearby hospital. We don't know if these remarkable events are connected, but it was a startling experience for all of us to say the least. We have never seen a group of undergraduates suddenly take their studies so seriously, and it clearly became a spiritual experience for many. Upon advice from other tribal members, we sent medicine and prayers to Mark for his recovery, and followed expanded protocols to protect the crew as we proceeded to disturb the earth in our research. We shared tobacco, we smudged every day, we carried ocher in our field packs, and we left small offerings to the spirits of the children who lived, died, and remain in that place.

In conclusion, we express gratitude that Mark and other participants are contributing authors for this multivocal volume to explore these complex ideas and their implications for archaeological practice. It is clear that the acts of removing children from their traditional homelands and removing artifacts from sites are connected. Past and present legislative processes regarding education and heritage management have been entangled with biopolitics and knowledge production, and have similarly acted upon landscapes, human bodies, and objects of cultural patrimony. They both are driven by similar processes of governmentality that create power imbalances between those who control legislation and those who do not, but exclude consideration of other kinds of power that are important not only to tribal sovereignty and inalienable rights, but perhaps also to the very fabric of the universe that connects us all.

Works Cited

Atalay, Sonya. 2006. "Indigenous Archaeology as Decolonizing Practice." *The American Indian Quarterly* 30, nos. 3 and 4: 280–310.

———. 2012. *Community-Based Archaeology: Research with, by and for Indigenous and Local Communities.* Berkeley, CA: University of California Press.

Basso, Keith. 1996. *Wisdom Sits in Places: Landscape and Language among the Western Apache.* Albuquerque, NM: University of New Mexico Press.

Battiste, Marie, and James Youngblood Henderson. 2000. *Protecting Indigenous Knowledge and Heritage; A Global Challenge.* Saskatoon, SK: Purich Publishing Ltd.

Brooks, Robert L. 1997. "Compliance, Preservation, and Native American Rights:

Resource Management and Cooperative Venture." In *Native Americans and Archaeologists: Stepping Stones to Common Ground*, edited by Nina Swidler, Kurt E. Dongoske, Roger Anyon, and Alan S. Downer, 207–16. Walnut Creek, CA: AltaMira.

Carroll, Alex K., M. Nieves Zedeño, and Richard W. Stoffle. 2004. "Landscapes of the Ghost Dance: A Cartography of Numic Ritual." *Journal of Archaeological Method and Theory* 11, no. 2: 127–56.

Colwell, Chip. 2016. "Collaborative Archaeologies and Descendant Communities." *Annual Review of Anthropology* 45: 113–27.

Colwell-Chanthaphonh, Chip, and T. J. Ferguson, eds. 2008. *Collaboration in Archaeological Practice: Engaging Descendant Communities*. Walnut Creek, CA: AltaMira Press.

Dawdy, Shannon Lee. 2010. "Clockpunk Anthropology and the Ruins of Modernity." *Current Anthropology* 51, no. 6: 761–93.

Deloria, Vine, Jr. 1969. "Anthropologists and Other Friends." In *Custer Died for Your Sins: An Indian Manifesto*, 78–100. Norman, OK: University of Oklahoma Press.

Dongoske, Kurt, and Roger Anyon. 1997. "Federal Archaeology." In *Native Americans and Archaeologists: Stepping Stones to Common Ground*, edited by Nina Swidler, Kurt E. Dongoske, Roger Anyon, and Alan S. Downer, 188–96. Walnut Creek, CA: Alta Mira Press.

Ferguson, T. J. 1996. "Native Americans and the Practice of Archaeology." *Annual Review of Anthropology* 25: 63–79.

Harvard Project on American Indian Economic Development, State of Native Nations. 2008. Conditions Under U.S. Policies of Self-Determination. Oxford: Oxford University Press.

Heilen, Michael, and Jeffrey H. Altschul. 2013. "The Accuracy and Adequacy of In-Field Artifact Analysis: An Experimental Test at Two Archaeological Sites in the Western United States." *Advances in Archaeological Practice: A Journal of the Society for American Archaeology* 1, no. 2 (November): 121–38.

Henderson, James Youngblood. 2000. "Postcolonial Ghost Dancing." In *Reclaiming Indigenous Voice and Vision*, edited by Marie Battiste, 57–76. Vancouver, BC: University of British Columbia Press.

Howard, Ted. 2002. Unpublished paper given at the Desambaatu: People Working with People Session, 28th Great Basin Anthropological Conference, Oct. 9–12, Elko, NV.

King, Thomas F. 1998. *Cultural Resource Laws and Practice: An Introductory Guide*. Walnut Creek, CA: AltaMira Press.

Lightfoot, Kent G. 2008. "Collaborative Research Programs: Implications for the Practice of North American Archaeology." In *Collaborating at the Trowel's Edge: Teaching and Learning in Indigenous Archaeology*, edited by Stephen W. Silliman, 211–27. Tucson, AZ: University of Arizona Press.

Marlow, Jim. 2002. "Governmentality, Ontological Security and Ideational Stability: Preliminary Observations on the Manner, Ritual, and Logic of a Particular Art of Government." *Journal of Political Ideologies* 7, no. 2: 241–59.

Miller, Jay. 1983. "Basin Religion and Theology: A Comparative Study of Power (*Puha*)." *Journal of California and Great Basin Anthropology* 5: 66–86.

Moser, S. 1995. "The Aboriginalization of Australian Archaeology." In *Theory in Archaeology: A World Perspective*, edited by Peter J. Ucko, 150–77. London: Routledge.

NATHPO (National Association of Tribal Historic Preservation Officers). 2005. "Tribal Consultation: Best Practices in Historic Preservation." Washington, DC: NATHPO.

NHPA (National Historic Preservation Act). 1966. As amended through 1992. http://www.nps.gov/history/local-law/nhpa1966.htm, accessed November 17, 2014.

Nicholas, George P. 2008a. "Native Peoples and Archaeology." *Encyclopedia of Archaeology* 3: 1660–69.

———. 2008b. "Melding Science and Community Values: Indigenous Archaeology Programs and the Negotiation of Cultural Differences." In *Collaborating at the Trowel's Edge: Teaching and Learning in Indigenous Archaeology*, edited by Stephen W. Silliman, 228–48. Tucson, AZ: University of Arizona Press.

———. 2012. "Collaborative, Community-Based Heritage Research, and the IPinCH Project." *The SAA Archaeological Record* (September): 30–32.

Palus, Matthew M., Mark P. Leone, and Matthew D. Cochran. 2006. "Critical Archaeology: Politics Past and Present." In *Historical Archaeology*, edited by Martin Hall and Stephen W. Silliman, 84–104. Malden, MA: Blackwell Publishing.

Smith, Claire, and H. Martin Wobst. 2005. *Indigenous Archaeologies: Decolonising Theory and Practice.* One World Archaeology, no. 47. London: Routledge.

Smith, Laurajane. 2000. "'Doing Archaeology': Cultural Heritage Management and Its Role in Identifying the Link between Archaeological Practice and Theory." *International Journal of Heritage Studies* 6, no. 4: 309–16.

———. 2001. "Archaeology and the Governance of Material Culture: A Case Study from Southeastern Australia." *Norwegian Archaeological Review* 34, no. 2: 97–105.

———. 2004. *Archaeological Theory and the Politics of Cultural Heritage.* London: Routledge.

Smith, Laurajane, and Gary Campbell. 1998. "Governing Material Culture." In *Governing Australia: Studies in Contemporary Rationalities of Government*, edited by Mitchell Dean and Barry Hindess, 173–91. Cambridge: Cambridge University Press.

Smith, Linda Tuhiwai. 1999. *Decolonizing Methodologies: Research and Indigenous Peoples.* London: Zed Books Ltd.

Swazey, Judith P., and Judy E. Stern. 1997. "Teaching and Learning Research Ethics." In *Research Ethics: A Reader*, edited by Deni Elliot and Judy E. Stern, 1–19. Lebanon, NH: University Press of New England.

Tsosie, Rebecca. 1997. "Indigenous Rights and Archaeology." In *Native Americans and Archaeologists: Stepping Stones to Common Ground*, edited by Nina Swidler, Kurt E. Dongoske, Roger Anyon, and Alan S. Downer, 64–76. Walnut Creek, CA: AltaMira Press.

Watkins, Joe E. 2000. *Indigenous Archaeology: American Indian Values and Scientific Practice.* Walnut Creek, CA: AltaMira Press.

White Mountain Apache Tribe. 2004. *Cultural Heritage Resources Best Management Practices. Version 9.13.2004.* Whiteriver, AZ: White Mountain Apache Tribe Heritage Program, Historic Preservation Office.

Zimmerman, Larry J. 2001. "Usurping Native American Voice." In *The Future of the Past: Archaeologists, Native Americans, and Repatriation*, edited by Tamara L. Bray, 169–84. London: Garland Publishing, Inc.

Acknowledgments

First and foremost, the editors, authors, and everyone associated with this project acknowledge and give thanks and respect to the children of the Stewart Indian School. It is an honor to dedicate this volume to them. Special thanks to all the alumni and community members who visited the excavation and shared their stories of this important place. The editors would also like to thank everyone at the Nevada Indian Commission and its Stewart Advisory Committee, especially Sherry L. Rupert and Chris A. Gibbons, for their partnership in the project, assisting in all of the developmental procedures, and, of course, for providing the opportunity to collaborate with tribal members on an archaeological field school. Also, we are grateful to the Washoe Tribal Historic Preservation Office, especially Darrel Cruz, the Washoe Tribal Historic Preservation Officer, for his significant contribution to the project as a research partner and stakeholder. Richard Arnold, Chair of the Nevada Indian Commission, gave an influential talk at the field school and provided considerable advice on the interpretations of faunal remains, which became a significant component to the interpretations discussed in this volume. We would also like to extend heartfelt thanks to the late Albert Phoenix, tribal elder from the Pyramid Lake Paiute Tribe, for his blessing of the participants during the field school. Thanks also to the late William Oliver who shared his knowledge of the Stewart Indian School's history. Thanks to Terri McBride for volunteering on the project, helping us connect with each other, and sharing her extensive knowledge of collaborative archaeology and the Stewart Indian School.

We are also grateful to Dr. Debra Harry, member of the Pyramid Lake Paiute Tribe, for her excellent presentation on informed consent and research involving Indigenous peoples during the field school. Her discussion of decolonizing methodologies inspired us to research those issues more thoroughly and to eventually focus this volume on such methods in archaeology. The authors would also like to express gratitude to Jo Ann Nevers, Washoe tribal elder and historian, and alumnus of Stewart Indian School, for a talk on her personal experiences living at the school, and what life was like for Washoe tribal members before and after contact with Europeans. Thanks also to Larry Hale, tribal member and retired Stewart Facility Supervisor, and to Ron Bodnar, current Stewart Facility Supervisor, for providing the rare, original campus maps that provided invaluable information on the location of historic buildings on campus.

Ron James, former State Historic Preservation Officer, and Rebecca L. Palmer, current State Historic Preservation Officer, provided advice and guidance in obtaining permissions for the site. Thanks also to Ron James for his visit to the field school and presentation on the archaeological history of the site. Thanks to Gene Hattori of the Nevada State Museum for giving guidance on the excavation, and on working with regional tribes.

Additionally, we thank all of the wonderful students and volunteers who participated in the 2013 field school: Amy Balagna; Patrick Burtt, a Washoe tribal member; Delaney Childs; Eric DeSoto, a Fallon Paiute-Shoshone tribal member; Callie Greenhaw; Charles Hutcheson; Dania Jordan; Jessica Leonard; Lonnie Teeman, a Burns Paiute tribal member; and Nick Teipner.

Thanks also to the many volunteers who aided in the cleaning, cataloging, and analysis of artifacts after the field school: Ashley Atwood, Amy Balagna, Lisa Ena, Robert Furlong, James LeFleur, Leona Novio, Austin Offenbacher, Samantha Redman, and Cavin VanGeem. Special thanks must go to Robert Leavitt and Lisa Machado, who both provided vital assistance during this process. Also, Dania Jordan and Rose Matschke worked many hours during all of the cleaning, cataloging, and analysis of artifacts. Callie Greenhaw and Eric Terzich helped create figures for the volume. Ashley Younie and Evan Pellegrini conducted the faunal analysis, and Ian Springer analyzed wood and soil samples.

Special thanks go to the late Mark Johnson, a Washoe and Paiute tribal member of the Reno-Sparks Indian Colony, who volunteered on the project, shared his experiences as an archaeological technician, and gave us some of our most important lessons on spirituality and respectful protocols. We are also grateful to A.J. Johnson, who joined this project in 2018, for his kindness and support of our efforts to honor the memory of his late brother Mark Johnson, as well as sharing his own important stories of attending Stewart as a student and later working as an archaeological technician. Thanks also to Amanda Hartman for introducing us to A.J. Johnson; we appreciate the many good things that come from collegial heritage networks. The editors are also grateful for the many participants in this project who thoughtfully contributed their knowledge and experiences in writing essays for this volume, making possible our shared goals for multivocality.

We are also grateful to Justin Race for his encouragement and support of publishing our multivocal approach. Two anonymous peer-reviewers provided excellent feedback that much improved the manuscript and offered welcome encouragement. Patrick Burtt, Ashley Long, and Daniel Montero provided editorial assistance in finalizing the manuscript, contributors' essays, and figures. Luke Torn and Cindy Coan of University of Nevada Press provided copyediting and indexing that was much appreciated. We appreciate Alrica Goldstein, the Editorial, Design, and Production Manager at the University of Nevada Press, for moving the manuscript toward completion.

The research reported here was funded under grant awards entitled "Governmentality and Social Capital in Tribal/Federal Relations Regarding Heritage Consultation" (#W911NF1210205 and #W911NF1610150) from the U.S. Army Research Office/Army Research Laboratory (ARO/ARL), Young Investigator Program (YIP), and Presidential Early Career Award for Scientists and Engineers (PECASE). The views expressed are those of the authors and should not be attributed to the ARO/ARL. We are grateful to Dr. Lisa Troyer and Dr. Stephen Lee at ARO for supporting high-risk research in social science, and for recognizing archaeology's potential to help modern societies.

Any errors or oversights are the responsibility of the editors. We are grateful to everyone for contributing their insights and knowledge to this project, and we hope to do right by them in this volume.

About the Contributors

Richard Arnold is Chair of the Nevada Indian Commission and an enrolled member of the Pahrump Paiute Tribe. He has been a strong advocate for encouraging communication between archaeological and Native communities for many years, and has also been a long-term advocate for preservation efforts at Stewart Indian School.

Patrick DeʔIleligi Burtt is an enrolled member of the Washoe Tribe of Nevada and California (Wašiw) and a direct descendent of the Tule River Tribe (Yokut). Burtt completed his bachelor of arts in Native American and Indigenous Studies from Fort Lewis College in 2016 and earned a master of arts in American Indian Studies from the University of California, Los Angeles in 2018. Burtt has a heritage of family members that attended Stewart Indian School, including his maternal grandmother, the late Bernadine James. Currently, Burtt is pursuing a Doctor of Philosophy in history with focuses in Native American history, Nevada and the West, and United States History at the University of Nevada, Reno.

Sarah E. Cowie is an associate professor of anthropology at the University of Nevada, Reno. She holds a doctorate in anthropology from the University of Arizona, and has worked in heritage management throughout the United States. Her earlier work emphasized the archaeology of power relationships in industrial capitalism, and has more recently turned toward collaborative and Indigenous archaeologies. Her research in archaeology has received recognitions from the Society for Historical Archaeology, the National Academy of Sciences, and the White House. In upcoming research, she is grateful to join Diane L. Teeman and Lonnie Teeman (see below) and descendants from at least a dozen Native communities in studying the 1879 forced march of *Neme* (Paiute/Shoshone) people from Oregon to Washington (see below for Diane L. Teeman's project description of "Our Ancestors' Walk of Sorrow").

Darrel Cruz is an enrolled member of the Washoe Tribe of Nevada and California. Cruz has been the Director of the Washoe Cultural Resources Department/Language Program from 2010 to 2014 and served on the Washoe Tribal Council from 2010 to 2014. Cruz was the Director of the Washoe Cultural Resources Department/Language Program from 2010 to 2014 and served on the Washoe Tribal Council from 2010 to 2014. Currently, Cruz is the Director of the Washoe Tribe Historic Preservation Office, a position he has held since 2008.

Eric DeSoto is an enrolled member of the Fallon Paiute-Shoshone Tribe. He was a student on UNR's archaeological field school in summer 2013, and he plans to attend UNR to pursue further education in archaeology. DeSoto has worked for several cultural resource management firms in the Great Basin, such as Far Western Anthropological Research Group and ASM Affiliates. He participated in the Ruby Pipeline Project and was featured in Far Western's documentary *Breaking New Ground: Native Americans in Archaeology.*

Chris A. Gibbons began with the Nevada Indian Commission in 2005 and is currently the Curator for the Stewart Indian School Cultural Center & Museum. As Curator, Chris primarily works on organizing and preserving the archival documents, photographs, and artifacts that tell Stewart's history and feels very fortunate to be part of the team responsible for opening the Cultural Center and Museum. Chris is a graduate of Southern Oregon University with a degree in history and minors in both Native American studies and art history. Currently, she is working on obtaining a master of arts in museum studies from the University of Oklahoma. Before coming to the commission, Chris worked in educational outreach and programming for the Southern Oregon Historical Society.

Dr. Debra Harry is a Numu-Kooyoee Dukaddo woman from Pyramid Lake, Nevada. Dr. Harry serves as a Lecturer for the Gender, Race, and Identity Program at the University of Nevada, Reno. Dr. Harry has authored numerous articles related to the protection of Indigenous Peoples' biodiversity and traditional knowledge, including "Biocolonialism and Indigenous Knowledge in United Nations Discourse" (2011), and "Indigenous Peoples and Gene Disputes" (2009). She also contributed a chapter titled, "Acts of Self-Determination and Self-Defense: Indigenous Peoples Responses to Biocolonialism," as a contribution to the book *Rights and Liberties in the Biotech Age*, edited by Sheldon Krimsky and Peter Shorett (2005). In 1994, Dr. Harry received a three-year national Kellogg Foundation Leadership Fellowship and studied the field of human genetic research and its implications for Indigenous peoples. Dr. Harry earned her Doctor of Philosophy degree in the Faculty of Education at the University of Auckland under the supervision of renowned Maori scholar, Dr. Linda Tuhiwai Smith. Dr. Harry's dissertation, titled "Indigenous Wisdom in the Biotech Age: The Development of New Knowledge in the Context of Biocolonialism," was recognized on the Dean's list for academic excellence. In 2012, Dr. Harry was honored with the Seventh Generation Fund's Be A Good Ancestor Award. And in 2013, Dr. Harry received the Nevada Indian Commission's "American Indian Achievement Award for American Indian Youth Services and Role Model of the Year" in recognition of her exemplary Emerging Indigenous Leaders Institute.

A. J. Johnson is an enrolled member of the Reno-Sparks Indian Colony, of Washoe and Northern Paiute heritage. He is an experienced archaeological technician. He writes, "My name is A. J. Johnson and I am an enrolled member of the Reno-Sparks Indian Colony of Washoe and Northern Paiute descent. My father is from the Walker

River Paiute Tribe from Schurz and my mother is from the Washoe Tribe of Nevada and California. I am currently working as a Phase II field technician for several cultural resource management (CRM) companies in Nevada and California. My involvement with the Stewart archaeological field school comes because I was invited by Sarah Cowie to write an essay on having done this type work along with my youngest brother Mark Johnson. We both worked on the Ruby Pipeline and we both worked with the same companies sometimes together or at times with other crews at different sites."

Mark Johnson was an enrolled member of the Reno-Sparks Indian Colony, as the youngest in a family of six descendants of Northern Paiute and Washoe tribes. He was born to Vera Tobey and Brady Johnson Sr. in Reno, Nevada. He grew up in Reno and he attended Orvis Ring Elementary School, Vaughn Middle School, and Wooster High School. He always worked throughout his life and found his most gratifying work as an archaeological technician. He felt that his contribution to the field was important and necessary. He left this world in May of 2018.

Dania Jordan earned her bachelor of arts in anthropology from University of Nevada, Reno. Currently, she is a graduate student in historical archaeology at the University of Massachusetts, Boston, and is a museum technician at the Northeast Museum Services Center, National Park Service. She writes, "During my undergraduate studies at the University of Nevada, Reno, in summer 2013, I participated in the Collaborative Archaeology field school at the Stewart Indian School in Carson City, Nevada. Since the field school I have been enrolled in the University of Massachusetts, Boston historical archaeology graduate program. I've participated in the Eastern Pequot Field School in North Stonington, Connecticut and I have also been a project instructor for the Mary M. B. Wakefield Charitable Trust excavation at the Wakefield Estate in Milton, Massachusetts. Additionally, I have held many internships within the National Park Service, including developing an archaeology curriculum for the National Park Service's Urban Archaeology Corp program in Lawrence, Massachusetts. Now, I hold a seasonal museum technician position at the Northeast Museum Services Center, National Park Service, where I primarily work on the archaeological collections from the Abiel Smith School (a historically all-black primary school from the nineteenth century), which is one of the sites included in Boston African American National Historic Site. The site also serves as my thesis topic; it will address how black institutions had dual roles within the black community. As a result, the Abiel Smith School may have not been only functioning as an educational institution, but also as health center since African Americans would have not been part of mainstream medicinal practices."

Christopher C. LeBlanc is a heritage consultant at the University of Nevada, Reno. He received his bachelor of arts from the University of Southern Maine in 1994 and has over twenty years of experience in the fields of cultural and heritage resource management. Since 2015, he has also worked as a crew chief and archaeological technician for Kautz Environmental Consultants, in Reno, Nevada.

Ashley M. Long is a professional archaeologist with experience across the Southern United States, Northern California, Great Basin, and American Southwest regions. Ashley was born in the Mississippi Delta, where she first became interested in anthropology after learning of her family's diverse heritage. She studied anthropology and human rights at the University of Southern Mississippi before traveling west to continue her education at the University of Nevada, Reno, where she received her master's degree in anthropology with an emphasis on collaborative archaeological methods, writing her master's thesis on the Stewart Indian School project. Ashley continually strives to develop collaborative relationships with Native communities through her work as an archaeologist for public lands agencies. She currently serves as the archaeologist for the Bureau of Land Management, Shoshone Field Office, in southeastern Idaho.

Terri McBride has expertise in documenting American Indian traditional areas and sites. She has volunteered in preservation efforts at the Stewart Indian School for over ten years, and recently completed an oral history project with Stewart alumni and a planning document for future interpretation of the historic school site.

Jo Ann Nevers is an enrolled member of the Washoe Tribe of Nevada and California. She attended Stewart Indian School as a youth, as did her parents and also has experience working as an archaeological monitor. She has served the Washoe Tribe as a member of a number of boards and committees and as the Secretary-Treasurer to the Washoe Tribal Council from 1982 until 1987. She is recognized by the Washoe Tribe as the leading historian on Washoe history, and has authored chapters in *Tahoe: A Visual History* and *An Archaeology of Desperation: Exploring the Donner Party's Alder Creek Camp*. She also wrote a highly respected history of the Washoe Tribe, entitled *Wa She Shu: A Washo Tribal History*. She visited the Stewart Indian School archaeological field school in 2013, gave a public talk about the school's history, and shared her insights into archaeological practice.

Sherry L. Rupert was appointed as the Executive Director of the American Indian Alaska Native Tourism Association, Inc. in 2019. During the Stewart Indian School Project, she was the Executive Director of the State of Nevada Indian Commission. In 2013, she was sworn in by Governor Brian Sandoval as the first American Indian woman to be appointed a member of his cabinet. Mrs. Rupert is a graduate of the University of Nevada, Reno with a bachelor of science degree in business administration. Currently, she is the Chairwoman of Nevada's Indian Territory, a marketing arm of the Nevada Commission on Tourism, and was awarded several Excellence in Tourism Awards from the Nevada Commission on Tourism for her success in promoting and advancing tourism in Indian Country. She was also awarded the 2009 Human and Civil Rights Award from the Nevada State Education Association for her work in the advancement of Indian education in the state. Mrs. Rupert was also elected President of the Board of Directors for the American Indian Alaska Native

Tourism Association (AIANTA) in 2014, and since 2013, she has served on the prestigious U.S. Department of Commerce Travel and Tourism Advisory Board (US TTAB), which is the advisory body to the secretary of commerce and the White House on matters relating to the travel and tourism industry in the United States. Mrs. Rupert is an American Indian of Paiute and Washoe heritage. She is also a proud Native Nevadan, born in Carson City and raised on the Washoe Reservation in Gardnerville, Nevada.

Alex K. Ruuska is an associate professor of anthropology at Northern Michigan University in Marquette, Michigan. She has a master of arts and doctor of philosophy in anthropology, and a master of arts in existential-phenomenological psychology. She served as the University Indian Ruins Residential Scholar at the University of Arizona during her 2016–2017 sabbatical.

Ian Springer received his master of arts degree in anthropology from the University of Nevada, Reno in 2015. He specializes in historical and industrial archaeology, with a primary focus on mining and logging in the American West. He currently works for the California Department of Transportation as an archaeologist in Northern California.

Diane L. Teeman is a member of the Burns Paiute Tribe, and Director of the Burns Paiute Tribe's Culture & Heritage Department. She has served several terms as an elected and appointed Burns Paiute Tribal Council member. Diane completed undergraduate and graduate studies at the University of Oregon in the departments of anthropology and philosophy and is currently a doctoral candidate at the University of Nevada, Reno, in anthropology. Her dissertation research topic focuses on identifying the prisoner of war removal corridor that was used in January, 1879 to march well over five hundred *Neme* (Paiute/Shoshone) men, women, and children from Oregon to Washington. This project, "Our Ancestors' Walk of Sorrow," is being completed through the lenses of Indigenous and collaborative archaeological methods, and theory and includes numerous researchers and consultants. Diane has also served as a member of the Society for American Archaeology's Committee on Native American Relations and was an early member of a North American tribal archaeological network known as the "Closet Chickens." Diane has spent the past thirty years working toward tribal culture and heritage protection and revitalization. Her greatest joy is being the grandmother of four handsome boys who she hopes will carry on this work.

Lonnie P. Teeman Sr. is a member of the Burns Paiute Tribe and the Lead Tribal Archaeological Technician in the Culture & Heritage Department of the Burns Paiute Tribe. Lonnie has completed undergraduate coursework at Lane Community College, the University of Oregon, and the University of Nevada, Reno, in anthropology focusing on archaeology. In his work with the Burns Paiute Tribe, Lonnie leads field repatriation and reinterment activities in addition to standard cultural resource management efforts. Lonnie also assists the tribal elders in the community to participate in heritage field trips and language revitalization activities. Lonnie is also a collaborator and descendant member of the "Our Ancestors' Walk of Sorrow" research project team.

BONNIE THOMPSON-HARDIN is a historian of American Indian and women's histories. Her dissertation is a history of the Stewart Indian School from 1890 to 1940, which explores the different ways the federal government tried to transform students' bodies through their physical appearance, the built environment, health education, vocational training, and extracurricular activities such as band and sports.

JOE WATKINS is President, Society for American Archaeology (2019–2021). He holds a doctor of philosophy in anthropology from Southern Methodist University and currently works as a Senior Consultant at Archaeological and Cultural Education Consultants. He is a Choctaw Indian from Oklahoma and is a leading scholar of Indigenous archaeology and ethical heritage practices.

Index

Page numbers in italics indicate illustrations.
The letter "t" after a page number indicates table data.

H